LETHAL GLORY
DRAMATIC DEFEATS OF
THE CIVIL WAR

LETHAL GLORY
DRAMATIC DEFEATS OF THE CIVIL WAR

PHILIP KATCHER

ARMS AND
ARMOUR

This book is dedicated to the memories of
SERGEANT BYRON KEAR,
Co. D, 144th Ohio National Guard, and
REV. GEORGE MINGINS,
US Christian Commission

Arms and Armour Press
A Cassell Imprint
Wellington House, 125 Strand, London WC2R 0BB.

Distributed in the USA by Sterling Publishing Co. Inc.,
387 Park Avenue South, New York, NY 10016-8810.

Distributed in Australia by Capricorn Link (Australia)
Pty. Ltd, 2/13 Carrington Road, Castle Hill,
NSW 2154.

British Library Cataloguing-in-Publication Data:
a catalogue record for this book is available
from the British Library

ISBN 1-85409-239-1

Designed and edited by DAG Publications Ltd.
Designed by David Gibbons; layout by Anthony A.
Evans; edited by Michael Boxall.
**Printed and bound in Great Britain by
Hartnolls Limited, Bodmin, Cornwall**

Contents

Acknowledgements

Many people helped in putting this book together. Those involved with the 130th Anniversary re-enactment of Pickett's Charge, especially the Army of Northern Virginia's Charles Clark, Don Johnson, P. West LaVan, John Ogle, Don Patterson and Jim Williams, provided a great deal of insight into that 'dramatic defeat'. Individuals, especially Howard Mitchell, of the living history 54th Massachusetts Infantry Regiment, was quite helpful. Charlie Jernigan was kind enough to share his knowledge on the New Mexico campaign. Thomas Boaz has been very helpful in a number of ways. Thanks go, too, to Sue Kerkgyarto for the additional material she found for the book. John Wirebach read parts of the draft and offered some thoughtful suggestions as to its improvement. Special thanks are due to Rod Dymott for his encouragement and the chance to produce this book.

The illustrations in this book
consist entirely of drawings, either period wood-cuts
or sketches executed by eyewitnesses and subsequently printed.
The idea was to avoid static studio shots of participants such as
generals, or calm photographs of pieces of terrain that are often
difficult to understand in terms of the action that took place there.
Instead it was decided to attempt to capture the immediacy of
the action by reproducing – given the relatively primitive
state of photographic technology during the
Civil War – contemporary engravings.

Introduction

The American Civil War commander, no matter on which side or in which theatre, had one aim always in mind – the total destruction of the enemy in battle, reducing his forces to a panic-stricken mob that fled or surrendered. It was rare however for an army to be totally defeated in battle. Even at Chancellorsville, where the Army of Northern Virginia under General Robert E. Lee, thoroughly trounced its opponent, the Army of the Potomac under Major General Joseph Hooker, the losing army wasn't crushed. True, it suffered casualties in large numbers, and its morale drooped visibly. Its general was thoroughly discredited both in the public and the military eye, but within two months, at Gettysburg, the defeated army was able to turn the tables and hand Lee's victorious troops the worst beating they had ever taken.

If there were a single reason for this, it was that the only way that an army could be destroyed or dispersed was by attacking it again and again until its lines no longer existed and further resistance was futile. So the emphasis in all battles of the period was on the attack.

But between forces of anything like the same size, the attack was generally doomed. The 0.58 calibre Springfield/Richmond or 0.577 calibre Enfield rifled musket, the standard infantry longarm, had made the attack almost impossible to succeed unless the odds were overwhelmingly in the attackers' favour. An infantryman so armed could fire a heavy bullet, almost an ounce of soft, tissue-destroying lead, accurately to some 900 yards. At that distance, the bullet could penetrate six inches of soft pine.

Furthermore, the ignition system of firearms had been greatly improved since the Napoleonic Wars, whose battles tended to shape most military thinking of the time. The flintlock musket which had been the main infantry longarm required separate careful movements to prime the piece and cover the pan containing the loose powder. The caplock musket had

made that system obsolete. The caplock used a copper cap containing ful-
minate of mercury which could be rapidly placed on the cone, and was
impervious to wet weather, unlike the flintlock.

It would be a sloppy, ill-trained infantryman indeed who could not fire
some five decently aimed shots every minute using a caplock rifled musket.
As the charging infantryman on level, unbroken ground could cover only
109 yards a minute at a dead run, a defender could get off five rounds while
his attacker was coming on. If only half of them actually hit an attacker, that
would still be more than enough to stop an attack by at least 100 per cent
more attackers than defenders. Since most charges started at a distance of
some 200 yards, the distance most close actions began, the average defender
could fire at least eight shots before attacker and defender crossed bayonets.
At that rate, the defence had a very large advantage.

The average field cannon of the Civil War fired a ten- or twelve-pound
shot, compared to the average six-pounder of the Napoleonic Wars, and
more rapidly thanks to the use of friction primers instead of the older match
and linstock method of firing. Cannoneers were able to get off eleven
rounds of canister at infantry attacking them from some 350 yards before
they could close.

Most defenders had artillery, so their advantage was almost impossible
to overcome and attacks were usually dead before they started. Even the
best of generals such as Lee continued to employ Napoleonic-style frontal
assaults that usually failed totally. Pickett's Charge at Gettysburg in July
1863 and Fredericksburg in December 1862 were attacks of this type.

But some attacks did succeed. An attack had several things going for it:
usually overwhelming numbers – odds of at least five to one if there were to
be any chance of success; the attackers were usually enthusiastic, inspired to
victory, and most attacks that succeeded were by men who were fighting on
their home ground. The introduction of Afro-Americans into the Union
ranks often gave southerners added reason, if not desperation, to overwhelm
a defending or attacking group of Afro-American Union soldiers, and there
was too the element of desperation that stemmed from the prospect of
defeat. Some Confederate attacks in 1864 seem to have been more desperate than in 1862 when victory seemed not only possible but even likely. The
defenders might be exhausted from days of constant attack or shell and
smallarms fire.

The commander of the losing side usually made some serious mistakes.
Stupidity at high command level, on both sides, was a definitive factor dur-

ing the Civil War. Commanders sometimes believed their own propaganda that they were invincible or that the positions they had selected and the available personnel could not be defeated. Initially many Confederate leaders at all command levels suffered from an arrogance that led them seriously to believe that they could defeat many times their own numbers of northern labourers and immigrants. Later, some Union commanders became sloppy, especially in areas long under their domination such as in the western border states and along the Atlantic seaboard. Sometimes commanders far from the battle site were unable to appreciate the realities of the position they asked their soldiers to defend; they failed to visit and determine the facts for themselves. Why else would Confederate troops have maintained any defence of Forts Henry and Donelson or Union commanders declined to reinforce posts along the North Carolina inlets in 1864?

Attacks that were unexpected often succeeded. Commanders and garrison troops who had been in one place for a considerable time often became complacent. Union sailors generally had freedom of the South's rivers because of the much smaller number of Confederate naval vessels and sailors to man them. This induced a certain laziness that sometimes was their downfall.

Naval power played somewhat surprisingly a large part in battles deep in the interior of the country. The United States features wide, deep rivers and the side that controlled them often controlled the land around them. Indeed one land battle – Fort Henry – was won by naval power alone.

The north had a tremendous advantage in any engagement where naval power would play a part simply because of its industrialization. It was more able to design, manufacture, and man all sorts of craft from deep sea men-of-war to river gunboats. Yet Confederate naval designers and manufacturers did an astonishing job in their creation of the novel iron-clad, and had they been able to build and man more of them they might have changed the face of the war; but getting able-bodied seamen from an agricultural society was a difficult proposition. As it was, the results achieved by the handful of iron-clads that were produced were well worth their cost; the *Albemarle* decided the battle of Plymouth, North Carolina.

Often the outcome of a battle such as Fredericksburg was obvious to the rank and file, if not to their generals, before it had begun. The men at the front end knew whether they had a chance of taking a position or not. The fact remains, however, that they still made desperate but pointless charges such as at Fredericksburg although knowing that wounds, death and defeat would be the result. Why did they do this?

After years of study most experts in military psychology agree that soldiers fight not for causes or glory or pay, but for their fellow soldiers. Their immediate fellows are their cause and must not be let down. This was especially the case in the Civil War when units were mostly recruited in small towns and friends and relatives joined up together. It was not uncommon to find several brothers in the same company. Each soldier's mate was the most important person in his life at the moment of battle crisis, and he would not let his 'pard' down. Were one to shirk one's duty, even a completely foolish duty such as charging up a bare slope at men behind a stone wall firing back, one would be disgraced in the eyes of one's neighbours.

Added to this, the Victorian code of ethics called for stoic behaviour in the face of the enemy. Men were praised for not showing fear. Wounded men were lauded for not crying out in agony. The dashing soldier charging forward in the face of certain death was considered not only exemplary, but to be the norm. There was no place for cowards. But after some years of fighting, these sentiments were largely abandoned. The soldiers realized that it was smarter to dig in than to remain in the open, and they learned that everyone felt fear, that this was not only normal but intelligent.

Civilians, however, maintained their heroic view of warfare to the very end, and treated with contempt returning soldiers who had not behaved in a manner they considered to be 'heroic'. Many Confederate veterans after the final defeat found more understanding from Union veterans than among fellow southerners who had never seen battle. Since the soldiers hoped to return and live back among these people, they were sometimes driven to attempt more than was reasonable.

Afro-American soldiers, of course, had several additional motives. They had to prove themselves true 'men' in this same Victorian mode, both to themselves and to the whites. Years of slavery had reinforced a belief among most whites that most blacks were lazy, stupid and cowardly. After all, who but a lazy, stupid coward would remain a slave? Therefore black leaders such as Frederick Douglass called for especially heroic behaviour on the part of their people so that they could enter a post-war society as something closer to equals among the whites.

Then too, the black soldier fought from a tremendous sense of fear of what would happen to him in battle. From the very beginning Southern whites gave every indication that they would treat black and white soldiers differently. They would be loath to take them as prisoners of war, since it offended their perverted Victorian sense of honour in war to fight against people who were obviously their social inferiors. Any blacks taken prisoner were sure to be put into slavery, even if they had been born and lived free all their lives. So there was a special desperation on their part. Generally, however, the losers became prisoners of war. After all, both sides considered themselves to be Christians who would not harm a helpless person, and both honoured the international law that governed the treatment of prisoners after battle. They gave medical aid to wounded men and not always after their own wounded troops had been tended. They fed and clothed prisoners, at least to a minimum. This was often very minimal in southern prisons where production was as feeble as the infrastructure. Indeed, an interesting aspect of the Civil War was that once the fighting was over there was a tremendous empathy between soldiers from both sides, who willingly shared what food and water they had. In the end, they were all Americans.

In some instances, where keeping prisoners was impracticable for one reason or another, the captives were paroled, the prisoner swearing an oath not to take up arms again until notified that he had been properly exchanged. In theory paroled prisoners were to report to a camp on their own side where they could be kept in military discipline while awaiting exchange. This was usually the case with paroled Union soldiers, but many paroled Confederates simply went home, often to fight no more.

Most civil wars are marked by brutality, but this was not usually the case in the American Civil War. Only in a handful of instances did the winning side get out of hand and kill men who had already surrendered or who could no longer fight. This happened at Ball's Bluff, Virginia, apparently because both sides were so raw in the ways of warfare that the Union troops didn't think of surrendering when their cause was lost. It happened to the Confederates there not because they were keen on shooting Yankees, but because the Union troops didn't surrender. The victorious Confederates apparently didn't think of ceasing fire in order to ask them to do so. Later, however, as passions rose in the heat of the war, such killings were carried out intentionally.

Obviously, the thought of Afro-Americans bearing arms inflamed many southern white soldiers. The killings at Fort Pillow, Tennessee, and the Crater at Petersburg, Virginia, were really not surprising. Perhaps more surprising – and proof of an overall American moral code that frowned on such barbarity – is the fact that these instances were infrequent.

Killings after surrender also took place among neighbours who had taken opposite sides, especially in the western theatre where frontier rules still predominated. These rules were quite tolerant to those who killed transgressors, even for reasons that would be considered fairly trivial back in the more civilized and effete east.

So when Forrest's Tennessee Confederates met fellow Tennesseans who wore Union blue, they were more apt to kill them out of hand than to take them prisoner, as happened at Fort Pillow. Even farther west, in Missouri, which for years before the war had been a hotbed of killings between those who favoured slavery and those who didn't, these killings were commonplace. In fact, victors often mutilated, Indian-style, the bodies of their victims. The killings at Centralia were especially horrifying, but not out of the ordinary for that place and time.

And the victors? How did their victory end? Usually, after the fighting had stopped, they took pause to see how their unit had fared. Who was dead? Who wounded? Who was missing? Who had survived? They often walked about the battlefield like modern souvenir hunters, sometimes rummaging through the pockets and haversacks of the dead and wounded for items of value or food and water. Often they searched for the bodies of friends or relatives. For most the mental strain of battle was very exhausting and many promptly fell asleep. Others found themselves astonishingly hungry and had to find something to eat. Some prayed; others wrote home.

Usually even victorious units became badly disorganized in the course of the action. Commanders had to spend much time calling rolls and getting their units organized before they could even think of following up to pursue a retreating enemy or moving on to another enemy post for yet another attack.

In most cases, therefore, the victory was the end in itself. There was no follow-up. As a result, many Civil War battles counted for little. Lee could win Chancellorsville magnificently, but the Union army could return to win Gettysburg and then go on to win the war. While commanders looked to each defeat as perhaps bringing a dramatic end to the war, none of them was ever that. It was all rather like the US Army officer who, in talking to a Vietnamese officer after that war, remarked, 'You know, you never did defeat us in battle.' 'Ah,' the Vietnamese replied, 'but that is irrelevant.'

So most Civil War victories were in reality irrelevant.

1
The Surrender of Fort Sumter
12–14 April 1861

Threats to the security of the United States during the first seventy-five years of its existence were largely external. British troops in two separate wars were able to land their troops on American coasts and capture the country's cities with relative ease. Only strong, permanent fortifications outside Baltimore prevented that city's capture, while New Orleans was saved by temporary fortifications outside the city.

Seeing this, the young American government spent much of its small military budget on setting up a school, the US Military Academy at West Point, New York, to train military engineers to build the type of masonry fortifications outside port cities which were so favoured in military thinking. The US Army embarked on a massive fortification building project around the major American ports which continued throughout the 19th century.

Charleston, South Carolina, was blessed with a lovely harbour whose entrance could be fortified fairly easily. It had been captured by British troops in the Revolutionary War, but since then, the US Army had spent a great deal on its defence. By 1860 there were four forts, but none of them was in very good shape.

Fort Johnson on James Island dated from the Revolutionary War. Built on a point that jutted into the harbour, it had been abandoned some years earlier and by 1860 was essentially a deserted ruin.

Castle Pinckney was located on Shute's Folly Island, in the harbour, some three-quarters of a mile from the city's docks. The small semicircular fortress, facing the water, had several heavy guns mounted in it, but its garrison consisted of a single ordnance sergeant whose job it was to keep the guns clean and ready for use.

Fort Moultrie, named after a Revolutionary War South Carolina general, was the city's most important defensive position, but years of peace and general neglect had taken their toll. Its ageing commander, Lieutenant Colonel John L. Gardner, who had been commissioned in the War of 1812, had a garrison of only eight officers, 61 enlisted men organized into two companies, and thirteen musicians in the 1st Artillery Regiment's band. More interested in the pleasant social life of Charleston, where he lived, than in military preparedness, he had allowed sand to drift up unchecked against the 16-foot tall brick walls to the extent that by now an attacker would have little more than an easy stroll from the base of the walls to the top. Indeed, troops inside the fort were sometimes bothered by cows ambling up and over the fort's walls. The walls were overlooked by two high sand hillocks from where sharpshooters could easily fire. In 1829 the Army began work on a fourth fort, Fort Sumter, also named after a South Carolina Revolutionary War hero. It was built at the mouth of the harbour on an artificial island made of granite leavings brought south from New England quarries. The all-brick walled fort, built in the shape of a pentagon, was designed to mount 146 guns. Its maximum complement was a garrison of 650 men. Low military budgets meant that work proceeded slowly at best, so that by 1860 although the outer walls were up, none of the guns had been mounted, nor was the interior ready for occupation.

In 1860 the city these forts were designed to defend was the centre of much political controversy. That year was an election year and, for the first time, it appeared as if a new political party, one hostile to slavery, had a good chance of winning the presidential election. Slave owners feared that if that happened the extension of slavery to new territories would be threatened. Laws that stipulated that slaves who had fled to northern and western free states be returned could be ignored or, even more frighteningly, overturned.

Most South Carolinians felt that this could not be allowed, but this was not the first crisis in which their state had been pitted against northern and western states. In 1828 Congress had passed a Tariff Act to protect manufacturers, most of whom were in the north-east. South Carolinians, whose society was essentially agricultural, objected to having to pay more money to support those outside their state. Their politicians devised a doctrine of nullification which held that any state could reject a Federal law that went against that state's interests. In 1832, following the passage of yet another tariff, the South Carolina legislature passed a sweeping ordinance of nullification that declared all tariff laws null and void, and authorized the state to resist the Federal government's attempts to enforce them.

President Andrew Jackson, himself a southerner from Tennessee, took a strong pro-Federal government stand. He got the US Congress to pass a Force Bill to allow him to use troops to execute all Federal laws. War appeared very possible.

The crisis was averted, however, when Kentucky Senator Henry Clay prepared a compromise tariff, which Congress quickly passed, that was acceptable to the south. South Carolina's legislature formally rescinded its nullification act, but declared the Force Bill null and void in that state.

The symptoms of crisis having been smoothed over, nothing further happened, but the basic problem, whose legislature would have final authority in each state, the state's or the Federal government's, remained. And the issue that would test that basic debate, slavery, grew hotter over the thirty years before 1860. An increasing number of people, mostly in the north and free-labour west, were against the practice. Indeed, a whole new political party, the Republican Party, had grown up with an anti-slavery stance as one of its basic attractions. By the time of the 1860 elections the slavery question had so divided the country that no party seemed likely to win a clear majority. This could give the northern states, whose voting populations were growing at much faster rates than southern states, the decisive voice as to who should be president. Republican Party candidate Abraham Lincoln had a very good chance of winning the election. South Carolina's political leaders vowed that the state would leave the Union if that were to happen.

In the face of an impending political crisis, US Army officials quietly began beefing up the defences of their forts in southern territories. In September they sent Captain John G. Foster, Corps of Engineers, to Charleston to oversee the cleaning up of Fort Moultrie and the completion of Fort Sumter. Foster opened an office in Charleston to hire stonemasons and mechanics to do the job. Not finding enough local talent, he sent to Maryland for men who had worked for him on an earlier project. Soon they were at work removing the sand from Moultrie's walls and renovating the fort's interior. At the same time, Gardner asked, unsuccessfully, for two companies of reinforcements together with enough men to bring his two companies at Moultrie up to regulation strength.

On 15 November Gardner received, not more men, but orders relieving him of command and sending him to San Antonio, Texas. Kentucky native Major Robert Anderson, 1st Artillery Regiment, replaced him. The 55-year-old Anderson was a class of 1825 West Point graduate who had

seen combat as an aide to Major General Winfield Scott in Mexico where
he had been wounded. His invalid wife Eliza, whom he left in New York
when he went to Charleston, had been born in Georgia. He also owned
slaves, at least until 1860, so Anderson might have been thought to be able
to communicate easily with local state leaders. At the same time, his loyalty
to the Federal government was unquestioned.

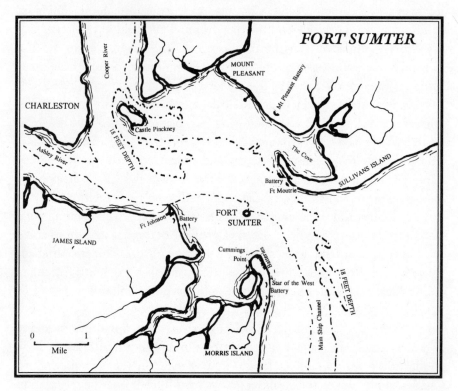

Anderson's orders declared that he was to be careful to avoid anything
that could provoke the South Carolina forces to react against the forts, as
for example adopting any stance that could be construed as hostile. 'But you
are to hold possession of the forts in this harbor, and if attacked you are to
defend yourself to the last extremity. The smallness of your force will not
permit you perhaps to occupy more than one of the three forts, but an attack
on or an attempt to take possession of any of them will be regarded as an
act of hostility, and you may then put your command into either of them
which you may deem most proper to increase its power of resistance. You
are also authorized to take similar steps whenever you have tangible evidence of a design to proceed to an hostile act.'[1]

Anderson had been aghast at what he found at Moultrie. He quickly realized that it was impossible for his small force to defend it against a determined aggressor. None the less, he pressed on with the fort's repairs, at the same time sending 34 workmen to Castle Pinckney to clean up that post as well. He selected known Union men for this task and had them given some rudimental arms training so that they could defend themselves if the post were attacked. Pinckney, Anderson thought, could be defended easily enough, but in the event the workmen refused to fight, saying that they were not there as warriors.

Anderson's officers agreed that Moultrie could not be easily defended from an in-land assault and the only chance for the garrison would be to quit the post and go to the as yet unfinished Fort Sumter. Anderson did not believe that war would come, but his officers disagreed. Moreover, since the Democratic Party in the north had been against Lincoln, the officers feared that if war broke out it would totally divide the country beyond state borders; they thought that at least 20,000 Democrats in New York alone would take arms on the side of the south.

Anderson was loath to leave, saying that his orders stated that Moultrie was to be his post. But as local citizens became more and more vociferous about taking the fort, he began to change his mind. Clearly the hostile intent of the local militia and civilians, many of whom wore blue cockades on their breasts to indicate their pro-South Carolina loyalties, indicated such a threat as would allow him to concentrate his force in one of the four forts in accordance with his orders.

Anderson, too, wanted more men, but the 16,000-strong US Army, mostly stationed in the west to deal with problems between Indians and whites, could not release anything like the number of reinforcements needed to prevent forts in southern states from being captured if those states were to secede, even if the government were agreeable. The Army did send Anderson enough food to maintain the garrison for six months.

On 6 November Lincoln won the election; according to law his inauguration would not be until March. On 12 November a group of state militiamen surrounded and mounted a guard on the Federal arsenal in Charleston, ostensibly in case of a 'slave insurrection'. The US Secretary of War made no move to forbid this, and this encouraged South Carolinians to believe that there would be no problems with Washington about their secession. In an effort to keep the lid on the situation, lame-duck President James Buchanan promised several South Carolina congressmen on 10

December that he would not send reinforcements to Charleston's harbour forts after they had assured him that South Carolina would not attack the forts. Even so, some hot-heads in South Carolina began acting as if they were at war with the United States.

South Carolina's political leaders called a special convention in Charleston and on 20 December 1860 they voted to take the state out of the United States of America. South Carolina's lead was followed by a number of other southern states, although the important states of Virginia and North Carolina did not immediately leap after them. Together the six southern states sent representatives to Montgomery, Alabama, where they formed a new Confederate States of America. The US Senator from Mississippi, Jefferson Davis, was elected the new country's president.

The acts of secessions of the various southern states and the formation of a new country left, of course, a number of questions to be answered. Would the Federal government respond as it had under Andrew Jackson? Buchanan, an indecisive individual at best, made no move to act as forcefully as had Jackson. Indeed, he indicated that he felt secession of a state was illegal, but, on the other hand, the Federal government had no legal authority to stop it.

If South Carolina were no longer a part of the United States, what was the status of US government property in the state? After all, there was a large number of items, ranging from stamps in post offices to guns in forts, that were the property of the national government, not state property. The state's feeling was that everything that had belonged to the national government in the state had now become the property of the state, since the state was its people's sovereign political body. The governor of the 'Republic' of South Carolina sent a team of three commissioners to discuss turning over the forts within state limits to their own government. They felt that these negotiations would be easy, and that the Federal government would accede to their demands quickly. Southern leaders did not want or expect any bloodshed. They believed that the US government would, in the end, surrender them peaceably.

Buchanan acted unexpectedly. He refused to hand over the forts or anything else that had not yet been taken over by state troops.

While talk was going on in Washington, the government organized its volunteer militia bodies into a South Carolina army. They took over such US government buildings as were not defended, but none where there was a possibility of bloodshed. Anderson and his officers watched these goings on with great alarm. They were highly vulnerable, waiting for the attack on their fort which they felt must come soon. They had proof. Late at night on 20 December a guard at Fort Sumter aroused the fort's officer of the day to point out an unlighted steamer slowly working its way around the fort's walls. It looked as if the crew were taking soundings. A few days later the same boat was seen near Castle Pinckney. When challenged, a man aboard yelled back, 'You will know in a week'.[2]

Finally, on 23 December, Anderson received further instructions from the War Department, telling him to 'hold possession of the forts in the harbor of Charleston, and, if attacked to defend yourself to the last extremity,' although not to sacrifice his command on 'a mere point of honor'.[3] These orders were ambiguous, but made up his mind as to what he would do, and his plans involved Fort Sumter, whose occupation would cut off access to Charleston's harbour.

As early as 9 December, he reported to the US Army's Adjutant General, Colonel Samuel Cooper, who would soon join the Confederate army: 'I hear the attention of the South Carolinans appears to be turned more toward Fort Sumter than it was, and it is deemed probably that their first act will be to take possession of that work.'[4] If he were to save the garrison at all, he would have to save Fort Sumter.

He sent for the post quartermaster. After swearing him to secrecy, he told him to take three schooners and some barges and embark the post's wives and children and rations. If local patrols asked him what was going on, he was to say he was taking everything north, out of the way of danger. In fact, he was to anchor off the ruins of Fort Johnson and hide there until he received a signal telling him that the garrison had indeed moved to Fort Sumter. Then he was to bring everything to that post.

On the day after Christmas Anderson summoned his officers to the parapet of Fort Moultrie. When Captain Abner Doubleday arrived, Anderson left the group already assembled there and walked over to him. 'Captain,' he said, 'in twenty minutes you will leave this fort with your company for Fort Sumter.'

Doubleday was shocked. For all their talk of moving to Sumter, he had somehow not really expected it to happen. 'I rushed over to my company quarters and informed my men, so that they might put on their knapsacks and have everything in readiness. This took about ten minutes. Then I went to my house, told my wife that there might be fighting, and that she must get out of the fort as soon as she could and take refuge behind the sand-hills.

I put her trunks out of the sally-port, and she followed them. Then I started my company to join Captain [Truman] Seymour and his men.'[5]

Doubleday's men left about sunset and the local militia seem to have been elsewhere – he thought they were taking a siesta. The US Army men were unchallenged. After going about three-quarters of a mile through Moultrieville they reached a low line of sea-wall where they found several boats that had been previously hidden there. The awkward landsmen got into them and slowly rowed out into the harbour towards Fort Sumter.

'Soon I saw the lights of the secession guard-boat [the *Nina*] coming down on us,' Doubleday wrote. 'I told the men to take off their coats and cover up their muskets, and I threw my own coat open to conceal my buttons. I wished to give the impression that it was an officer in charge of laborers. The guard-ship stopped its paddles and inspected us in the gathering darkness, but concluded we were all right and passed on. My party was the first to reach Fort Sumter.'[6]

Anderson left a surgeon, four non-commissioned officers, and seven privates back at Moultrie with orders to be ready to fire the fort's guns if the troops in the boats going out to Sumter were attacked by southern guard-boats that patrolled the harbour. As soon as they received the signal that the main body had reached Sumter they were to spike Moultrie's guns and destroy the gun carriages and the ammunition. They also cut down the fort's flagstaff before leaving for Sumter. 'The step which I have taken was, in my opinion, necessary to prevent the effusion of blood,' Anderson reported to army headquarters in Washington.[7]

Southern workmen, some of them holding pistols, met Anderson's troops at the gateway into the fort. A couple of pro-Union men cheered, but the rest were clearly upset about the events. 'What are these soldiers doing here?' one of them angrily asked Doubleday. 'What is the meaning of this?'[8]

Doubleday had his men fix bayonets and assemble the workmen on the parade ground in the centre of the fort. In the meantime the rest of Anderson's men had arrived. Once all the troops were in place, he had a small cannon fired from the top of the fort's walls. This was the signal to his quartermaster officer to bring his boat-loads of women, children and supplies from just off Fort Jackson to Sumter. When these had been disembarked, the pro-southern workmen took their places in the boats to be returned to Charleston.

The next morning, when they found out about Anderson's move, Charleston's residents were furious. South Carolina's governor sent some of his aides out to Sumter to demand that Anderson return his men to Moultrie. Anderson refused, saying that while he was a southern man, he was also responsible for defending Charleston harbour, and that is exactly what he would do. In the meantime, South Carolina's militia occupied Fort Moultrie and Castle Pinckney where they found some of the armed workmen who had chosen not to be warriors hiding under their beds. The militia took over the engineer construction office in Charleston where they found detailed maps of Sumter, and all the records of its construction.

'Why did that green goose Anderson go into Fort Sumter?' wrote diarist Mary B. Chestnut, wife of one of South Carolina's senators, on 7 April. 'Then everything began to go wrong.'[9]

She was wrong. Everything began to go wrong for the secessionists when the southern-leaning members of Buchanan's cabinet left, to be replaced by hard-line northerners like Attorney General Edwin M. Stanton, who would later be Secretary of War in Lincoln's cabinet. Stanton and the new Secretary of War, Kentuckian Joseph Holt, stiffened Buchanan's resolve. They drafted a message for him to give South Carolina's commissioners, flatly rejecting any chance of pulling Anderson out of Sumter. Moreover, they talked Buchanan into reinforcing Anderson's meagre garrison.

Meanwhile Anderson put his men, including the loyal civilian workmen still in the fort, to work putting it into good, defensible shape. At first they could only work in the daylight hours, since they had not brought any lights with them. Later, several of the wives managed to get passage to the fort and smuggled in a box of candles and a bandbox full of matches. Fearing trouble, Anderson, after thanking them for the lighting equipment, had them returned to Charleston from where, after staying a couple of days in a hotel, they managed to book passage north.

As it turned out, the fort needed more than one box of candles. When searching through the stores the ingenious light keeper found several barrels of oil. He quickly rigged up tin tubes, each a wick thick, which he fitted into cork discs wide enough to float on the top of coffee cups filled with whale oil. The resulting lights soon appeared in every casemate.

Anderson's immediate concern was a potential landing under cover of darkness by South Carolina militiamen who could easily overwhelm the fort's 65 defenders, and a number of embrasures were bricked up to deny a landing party entrance to the fort.

Figuring that the wharf by the main entrance would be the best place for such a landing, two five-gallon demijohns filled with gunpowder were laid under the wharf pavement. The friction primers in these 'mines' were linked by lanyards that passed into the fort so that the devices could be detonated from within, and the lanyards would be a tripwire for the unwary. Another mine was laid on the esplanade, a broad granite sidewalk that extended the length of the gorge wall where the fort's entrance and wharf were on the outside. Bullet-proof shooting boxes were built to overlook the walls, and hand-grenades were fashioned from shells fitted with lanyards and friction primers to explode when thrown. These grenades were stacked along staircases where they could be easily reached by the defenders in the upper levels.

Flagstones intended for building were piled up in two tiers in front of the casemates, partially covering them and making them splinter-proof.

While Anderson's men were so engaged, the chief of the US Army, Major General Winfield Scott, arranged for some 200 soldiers and additional supplies to be embarked in a plain, unarmed merchant ship, the *Star of the West*, in the hope that she could get to Charleston clandestinely.

Anderson wasn't informed that these were on the way. On 9 January, Captain Doubleday saw through his telescope the ship flying its large US flag just outside the harbour entrance. But the ship's mission had been reported in the press across the country, and Anderson and his men were virtually the only people in the dark. It had been rumoured among the garrison that the government was to have them evacuated and many men figured that this ship was coming to take them away.

Southern gunners fired on the ship when she came near. Doubleday ran down to tell Anderson who ordered him to have the long roll beaten to assemble the troops for combat, and post the cannoneers near the barbette guns on top of the walls.

By the time the fort's defenders were ready to return the southern fire, a shell had landed too close and the civilian captain, fearing for his ship, turned her round and headed for the open sea and home. War could have begun then, but Anderson, not fully understanding that this was indeed a resupply ship and not wishing to provoke the locals, did not allow the fort's guns to fire, a decision not appreciated by many of the garrison. Gunners at one post witnessed the engineer officer, Captain Foster, leave Anderson and dash his hat to the ground, muttering something about 'trample on it', apparently referring to the American flag.

Anderson did send a note to the governor demanding to know why this ship which was flying a national flag had been fired upon. If the explanation were unsatisfactory, he wrote, he would have the forts' guns fire on any southern vessel within range. The governor replied that Anderson's ire didn't matter; he'd have his guns fire again in a similar circumstance.

On 20 January South Carolina's governor sent a boat under a white flag to the fort. The state Secretary of State and Secretary of War were aboard and they brought a message from the governor demanding that the fort be turned over to state authorities. Anderson declined to meet them, but sent one of his lieutenants to say that surrender of the fort was out of the question. The question was again referred to Washington, where, on 30 January, the state's representative tried again to get US officials to give up the fort. Again their request met with a rebuff.

Many South Carolinians were all for starting a war right away, taking the view that Buchanan's promise to their congressmen not to reinforce the fort had been betrayed by the *Star of the West*'s abortive mission, but they were no longer in control. In February 1861 the crisis at Charleston was taken from state control and handed over to the new Confederate States government. On 26 February President Davis notified his Congress that 'the General Government of the Confederate States is specially charged with the questions arising from the present condition of Forts Sumter and Pickens [in Florida], and the Executive is required by negotiation or other means to obtain possession of those works ...'[10] Davis sent General P. G. T. Beauregard, an engineering officer from Louisiana, to command the troops, now Confederate troops, around Sumter.

Essentially Beauregard was told not to bother the fort if no reinforcements were sent there or if the fort's garrison did not try to bother the local troops at Charleston. The Confederate government would take possession through political negotiations.

On 4 March Lincoln arrived in Washington to be sworn in as the country's sixteenth president, and eventually met his new cabinet members to discuss the situation at Fort Sumter. He decided to wait for the secessionists to make the first mistake; but in the meantime it would be a violation of his oath of office to surrender government property including Fort Sumter. In the meantime, negotiations with the Confederate representatives effectively ended.

In the fort the garrison prepared for the inevitable. They continued to improve the defences, cutting holes through the walls of the officers' quarters to afford protected passage if the fort were under fire. Daily new Confederate gun emplacements being readied for action could be seen across the water. The shortage of supplies began to tell. By 9 April the men were on half-rations. There was no more tobacco and those especially addicted to the weed tried sucking spun yarn as a poor substitute. Some of the officers were lucky enough to have cigars which earlier had been brought by visiting Confederate officers under a flag of truce, together with several cases of claret.

The Confederate government finally realized that the Lincoln government was not going to give up Sumter voluntarily, and Beauregard was ordered to force the fort's surrender and, if it were not immediately forthcoming, bombard it into submission. On 8 April Beauregard notified the defenders that no correspondence from the outside world would be permitted until the garrison's evacuation. On 10 April the fort was entirely out of bread, and rations had to be supplemented by picking through spilled rice that was mixed with splinters of glass from window panes shattered by concussion from artillery practice.

On 10 April, too, Lieutenant R. K. Meade, an engineer officer, discovered that there were too few cartridges to last for any sustained bombardment. He quickly put men to work cutting up all surplus blankets and extra company clothing, mostly flannel shirts, to make powder bags for the guns.

On the 11th Beauregard sent four of his aides in a small boat to say that he would start bombarding the fort if Anderson did not give up right away. If the fort were surrendered, Beauregard would allow the garrison to salute the US flag as it was being lowered, and then depart for any northern port with all private and company property. Anderson rejected these terms, telling Beauregard's aides that he would 'await the first shot, and, if not battered to pieces, would be starved out in a few days'.[11]

This in fact was the crux of the matter. All Beauregard had to do was wait. He telegraphed the Confederate Secretary of War to tell him what Anderson had said. No blood need be shed. War, at least here, could be avoided.

The Secretary of War telegraphed back vague instructions indicating that the General was 'authorized ... to avoid the effusion of blood'.[12] In the absence of more precise instructions, Beauregard felt that he could not simply ignore his earlier orders to fire on Sumter, but he would make one last bid for its surrender. At about 3 a.m. he sent aides to the fort to demand a definite decision and a time, otherwise he would open fire within an hour. Anderson told them that he would evacuate the fort on the 15th unless he received supplies or were ordered to do otherwise. This response was not good enough for Beauregard's aides who were worried that a Union fleet could arrive with supplies and reinforcements at any time. They retired to a casemate and wrote a note calling for surrender within an hour or a Confederate bombardment would begin.

Anderson declined. Seeing the messenger back to his boat, he took his hand and said, 'If we never meet in this world again, God grant that we may meet in the next.'[13]

Beauregard gave the order to open the bombardment. From the ramparts of the fort the anxious garrison watched a grey raw morning dawn. Fog obscured the Confederate batteries and many of the defenders decided that the southerners were bluffing again. They were wrong.

At 4.30 a.m. on 12 April, the first southern gun fired, its shell bursting well overhead, though according to Doubleday, 'The ball from that gun struck the wall of the magazine where I was lying, penetrated the masonry, and burst very near my head. As the smoke from this explosion came in through the ventilators of the magazine, and as the floor was strewn with powder where the flannel cartridges had been filled, I thought for a moment the place was on fire.'[14] Doubleday was lucky; no real damage was done. A Confederate observer, however, said that the first shot burst some 100 feet above the fort.

The men who'd been on the ramparts watched for a few minutes in awe of the high arcing mortar shells, and then ran down the stairs to the safety of the bomb-proof shelters. Civilians in Charleston, many of whom also knew what was coming, sought vantage-points from which to view the spectacle. Mary Chestnut found a place on a rooftop where she wrote that she '... sat down on something looked like a black stool. "Get up, you foolish woman your dress is on fire!" cried a man. And he put me out. It was a chimney, and the sparks caught my clothes.'[15]

Inside Sumter, Anderson mustered his men on the parade ground. He gave a brief speech as the shells were bursting overhead, asking the men to take no unnecessary risks. Then he dismissed them to get breakfast, some water and very poor quality pork, and then to man their guns.

Anderson offered Doubleday the honour of taking the first shot in reply. He pulled the lanyard at about 7 o'clock. At 7.30 Anderson had the drummers beat assembly and divided the garrison into two reliefs, each to man the guns for four hours in turn.

The fort's gunners saw several of their shots strike the Confederates' floating battery, which was of wood covered with iron, but the balls bounced off the iron-clad roof and it was impossible to score hits below the water-line which was protected by a sea wall. At the same time, enemy fire swept the top of the fort's walls so frequently that Anderson ordered the guns there to be abandoned.

Two sergeants, determined to get at least one shot in, disobeyed his order. As no one was about, they sneaked up the stairs to the 10-inch Columbiad. Their first shot, at an iron-clad, was slightly over. Normally it took six men to move the giant carriage and tube; the two men reloaded but were unable to adjust their aim. In the meantime, southern gunners had seen what they were up to and began to aim at them. One of the sergeants ran down the stairs to check that their retreat would be unnoticed, while the other, desperate – the enemy's fire growing hotter – pulled the lanyard. The gun fired, flew up and off its carriage, and landed across the head of the stairway. Unhurt, the two sneaked back to their posts.

Sergeant Thomas Kernan was knocked flat on his back by a chunk of masonry that had been loosened by a bursting shell. One of his fellows asked if he were hurt. 'No,' he replied as he stood up. 'I was only knocked down *temporarily*.'[16]

The duel went on for 34 hours. Since so many of the fort's 66 guns faced out to sea to protect the harbour, only a handful could be brought to bear on the attackers. Also the fort was short of powder bags, even though men continued to cut and sew flannel shirts, sheets and even coarse paper until midnight when they were finally dismissed to get some rest. Thereafter Anderson restricted his return fire to six guns.

At about 1 p.m. on the 12th the defenders saw two US Navy ships approaching the harbour bar, and presently, through the smoke of cannon-fire, a third. But southern guns kept the ships from entering the harbour.

Several times during the day, shells that had been heated in ovens designed for the purpose set the wooden barracks on fire. The garrison's fire-fighting team, led by a civilian carpenter, put the flames out each time before much damage was done. They were helped by cascades of water showering down from two of three iron storage cisterns installed on the tops of hallways, which were riddled with Confederate shot. Shells coming in at high angles tore through the roof of the officers' quarters and plunged two storeys to the ground floor.

During the height of the bombardment a slave rowed across the harbour with a load of supplies for his plantation. Some Confederates met him when he landed and one asked, 'Are you not afraid of Colonel Anderson's cannon?' 'No, sir. Mars Anderson ain't daresn't hit me. He know Marster wouldn't 'low it.'[17] The fort's cannon did relatively little damage. Not one shell landed in Charleston itself, although two rounds hit the roof of the Moultrie House, a hotel near Fort Moultrie.

When evening fell, Anderson ordered the fort's guns to cease fire. High winds blowing in off the ocean splashed waves from a high tide around the fort's walls. Rain beat down. Engineer Captain Foster took advantage of the relative lull to go outside the fort, making his way on the slippery rocks, to check for damage to the walls. He was pleased to find '... that the exterior of the work was not damaged to any considerable extent, and that all the facilities for taking in supplies, in case they arrived, were as complete as circumstances would admit.'[18]

The southern batteries reduced their rate of fire to one round every ten or fifteen minutes, but they maintained this throughout the night. 'During the night of the 12th', the fort's surgeon, Captain Samuel W. Crawford, later wrote, 'the accurate range of the mortars lodged a shell in the parade, or about the work, at intervals of fifteen minutes. It was estimated that over twenty-five hundred shot and shell struck the fort during the first twenty-four hours.'[19]

Weary, hungry soldiers greeted the dawn a little before 5.30. Cooks heated the last of the rice which was served with a bit of pork. The defenders thereafter would have only salt pork to eat. After breakfast the men returned to the guns. The powder bags cobbled together the previous day enabled them to increase their rate of fire. But the enemy cannoneers now had the range quite well, and a definite improvement in accuracy was noticed. One shell hit an embrasure at the right gorge angle, sending pieces of metal and stone inside where a sergeant and three men were wounded. Another shell burst in the fort near one of the casemates and a fragment flew through the casemate opening, severely wounding one of the Maryland civilian employees.

At about 8.30 a.m. heated shot set a bed in one of the enlisted barracks on fire. The weary men rushed to put it out, but it spread too quickly and over too great an area. More hot shells set the officers' quarters on fire. Within hours several separate fires were raging within the walls, flames were rising high and the interior was filling with heavy black smoke.

Foster ran to tell Anderson that the magazine was in danger of being engulfed. The magazine had a flame-proof door which could be closed, but that would cut off the supply of ammunition. Anderson ordered Foster to put some men to work getting powder barrels out and stored in casements.

The men dashed into the flaming wooden building, gasping in the smoke, and managed to get fifty barrels out before the flames reached the copper door which quickly became too hot to touch. Foster ordered it to be shut and had earth piled up in front of it to cool it down. Having done this, the men ran to the relative safety and cool of the casemates, where they lay on the ground, emerging from time to time to fire the guns and show that they were not finished yet. In a matter of minutes the flames, driven by a northern wind, had engulfed all the buildings in the fort. By noon all the woodwork in the upper storey of the officers' quarters and all the barracks were crackling with flames. Black piney smoke, made the more dense because the woodwork had been wet, continued to fill the circular amphitheatre bounded by the fort's walls. Flaming embers blew into the casements and the powder stored there, covered by wet blankets, again became a hazard and Anderson had it thrown out into the water.

Enemy gunners saw the defenders tossing the powder out of an embrasure, and directed their fire there. A lucky shot detonated some of the powder and knocked the gun, whose muzzle protruded from the embrasure, clear out of its carriage. Now the defenders had only a small pile of cartridges for each gun.

Flames spreading throughout the fort reached the piles of grenades that had been stacked in the stair towers, and they detonated in a tremendous explosion. The stair towers collapsed and debris from the upper storeys littered the surviving stairways, making passage through the fort almost impossible.

At about 1 p.m. the flagstaff, which had been hit seven times during the bombardment, was hit again and brought down. Two lieutenants dashed out and retrieved it, and a makeshift staff was rigged up, but the Confederates had seen it fall and before the flag could be re-hoisted Colonel Louis T. Wigfall stepped into a small boat, a white handkerchief tied to his sword as a flag of truce, and had himself rowed out to accept what he perceived as the fort's surrender. Anderson heard that an emissary had arrived and he and a lieutenant dashed to the main gate to meet him, only to find that the gate was jammed shut.

Wigfall's boat had moored at another wall, and he climbed up to a gun port. The gunners manning the cannon refused him entrance, but he begged to be allowed in for fear of being killed by his own cannon-fire. Finally one of them took his sword with the white handkerchief, and then pulled him in.

Wigfall was guided to the batteries where a number of officers had been posted. He told them that he had come from Beauregard. Since the fort's flag was down, the quarters were burning, and the garrison in deep trouble, he suggested that a cease-fire be authorized and that the fort raise a white flag.

An officer replied that the US flag had been raised again and that nobody was going to raise a white flag unless the commanding officer ordered it. As for ceasing fire, the officer said that the Confederate batteries should do that first. Wigfall replied that the batteries at Cummings' Point had already done so, and those on Sullivan's Island would follow suit if a white flag were flown.

By now Anderson had found Wigfall. 'To what am I indebted for this visit?' he asked. 'I am Colonel Wigfall, of General Beauregard's staff. For God's sake, Major, let the thing stop. There has been enough bloodshed.' 'There has been none on my side,' Anderson replied. 'And besides, your batteries are still firing on me.'[20]

'I'll stop that,' said Wigfall, and began to wave his handkerchief-bedecked sword from an embrasure. After a while he said that he was too weary to continue. One of the Union officers told a corporal to take over. He jumped into the embrasure and began to wave the flag, but a shell smashed into the masonry near the embrasure. The corporal jumped back, saying to Wigfall that 'he would not hold his flag, for it was not respected'.[21]

Finally the officers had a white sheet hung from the parapet as a flag of truce while Wigfall and Anderson retired to the hospital to talk. Anderson asked him what terms he could offer. 'Any terms that you may desire,' Wigfall replied, 'your own terms the precise nature of which General Beauregard will arrange with you.'[22]

Anderson agreed, saying that he would accept the terms offered by Beauregard on the 11th. Wigfall said that that would be acceptable, and left at about 3 p.m. to find his boat and return to Charleston. In the meantime, Anderson had the US flag lowered and a white flag run up in its place.

Shortly afterwards another boat bearing three of Beauregard's aides arrived and Anderson met them at the dock by the main entrance. He told them to mind their step as the narrow beach up to the fort was mined. Once inside he told them of his meeting with Wigfall.

The Confederate officers told Anderson that Wigfall was not an official representative; indeed Beauregard had not seen him for several days. Anderson told them that he would immediately replace the white sheet with the US flag: 'Very well, gentlemen, you can return to your batteries.'[23] The flustered aides persuaded him not to do that, saying that they would return to Beauregard for instructions. In the meantime the truce would continue.

The aides' oarsmen must have broken a speed record; they returned at about 7 p.m. to say that the terms were agreed except that concerning the saluting of the US flag – an exception that was later dropped. Meanwhile, Captain Foster toured the fort, counting some 600 shot marks on the face of the scarp wall. According to his survey: 'The only effect of the direct fire during the two days was to disable three barbette guns, knock off large portions of the chimneys and brick walls projecting above the parapet, and to set the quarters on fire with hot shot. The vertical fire produced more effect, as it prevented the working of the upper tier of guns, where were the only really effective guns in the fort.'[24]

At the end the fort's condition was irrelevant. There was little food and ammunition available for a continued fight. Anderson surrendered and the firing ceased. According to the agreement, he and his men would spend the remainder of the day in the fort and formally surrender next day. The ceremony of surrender would include the firing of 100 rounds from the fort's cannon.

On 14 April the weary, soot-stained garrison formally surrendered. Fires were still burning brightly as they began firing the salute to their flag. As the lanyard was pulled for the last round, the gun fired prematurely, sparks from the fires having apparently been into the barrel. The rammer, Private Daniel Hough, was killed, the first man to die from gunfire in the Civil War, and five men nearby were seriously wounded, one of them dying later. Hough was buried with honours in the parade ground. South Carolina's Palmetto Guard took over the battered, smoking fort.

In accordance with the terms of the surrender, the officers and men then boarded a waiting ship, the *Isabel*, to return north. 'Many an eye turned toward the disappearing fort,' Surgeon Crawford wrote, 'and as it sank at last upon the horizon the smoke-cloud still hung heavily over its parapet.'[25]

At the end, the southern decision to fire on Fort Sumter sealed the fate of the new Confederate States. 'No doubt Fort Sumter is taken and its surrender has roused the war passions of the North to a fearful pitch. From all quarters come accounts that the people are arming, and the danger now is that they will go too far. The South has sowed the wind and is likely to reap the whirlwind. The President has issued a proclamation calling for 75,000 troops,' wrote one conservative Philadelphia aristocrat in his diary on 15 April. 'Went to town at 12. Found the city in a state of dangerous excitement. Several well-known persons, who had openly expressed secession opinions, had been assaulted in the streets. At the office of an obscure newspaper at the corner of 4th and Chestnut, the editor had been foolish enough to hang out a Palmetto flag. The office was then attacked by the mob & only saved by the mayor & police. The mob then visited all the newspaper offices & insisted on their showing the American flag. Prominent individuals known to sympathize with the South are threatened.'[26]

Some southerners recognized that the bombardment of the fort had caused them all great problems. North Carolina Senator Thomas L. Clingman told Mary Chestnut that South Carolina was a '... poor little hot-blooded, headlong, rash, and troublesome sister state', adding that he believed that the Fort's forcible surrender would ensure Virginia and North Carolina entering the war on the southern side, but, in the end, the north would 'swoop down on' the seceding states.'[27] He was one of few southerners with such clear vision.

2
The Battle of Ball's Bluff
21 October 1861

The men who formed the armies of both sides in the Civil War were unprepared for the war that was to follow. Unfortunately, most of them had heard tales of how citizen soldiers had beaten trained professionals in the American Revolution. Surely, with little more than a few facing movements and the basic manual of arms, especially loading and firing, soldiers of 1861 should be able to do as well. Not only the new soldiers, but the civilians back home felt this was true. The civilians, their opinions fed by journalists who were just as ignorant of military affairs as they were, pressed for the northern forces to carry the war immediately south.

The result was the disastrous, for the Union forces, battle of Bull Run where, in July 1861, an army under Major General Irwin McDowell, who did not wish to move against his southern opponent until better prepared, but was obliged to do so, met a major defeat. The Union troops fought well enough at first, but stiff southern resistance, fears of 'masked batteries', weariness and thirst after a long, hot march, and terrifying Confederate cavalry and artillery, caused the army to fall apart. The troops fled, the majority barely stopping until they were almost in Washington, the capital city of the United States and their starting-point.

McDowell lost his job, being replaced by Major General George B. McClellan, an intelligent and dashing officer who had driven a badly led and poorly equipped Confederate force from Western Virginia in early 1861. On taking command of the most important army in the eastern United States, McClellan formed camps of instruction to train his seriously demoralized troops. He would make sure that his men were fully trained before any future battle.

Weeks turned into months. Company drills became battalion drills which in turn graduated to brigade drills. Dress parades were held daily. McClellan was seen on his prancing horse going from camp to camp, followed by a staff of handsomely attired and equipped officers. New equipment and clothing was issued. Morale improved and the men began to feel that they were a real army again. They had a tremendous amount of faith in McClellan.

Although McClellan, still popular in the press from his West Virginia campaign, had a temporary political advantage, it would not last forever. Eventually the public and members of the government would demand progress. It was up to him to demonstrate that this fine bunch of parade ground soldiers would be equally fine in combat .

In October 1861, Confederate forces held the town of Leesburg, Virginia, 40 miles up the Potomac River from Washington, DC. They did not pose much of a threat, in terms of a potential invasion of Maryland, but they were a very real embarrassment. However, convinced that the enemy force was considerably larger than his own and was poised to descend on him and destroy the Union army, McClellan believed that an attack from Leesburg was on the cards. Faulty intelligence plagued McClellan throughout his career; he believed that there were almost 27,000 Confederates in Leesburg; in fact there were 2,000.

McClellan could see that the Confederates at Leesburg were somewhat exposed, and that their line of retreat could easily be severed. He decided to send a division towards Dranesville, about a dozen miles south-east of Leesburg, to see what would happen. If the Confederate general at Leesburg, Nathan G. ('Shanks') Evans, were cut of the same cautious cloth as McClellan, he would immediately retreat in the face of this threat. McClellan therefore sent the expedition off in the hope that the Confederates would panic. At the same time, troops in the Poolesville, Maryland, area, across the river from Leesburg, fired cannon across the river as a demonstration against Evans, but he was unconcerned about them or the Dranesville expedition, and stayed in place.

Inadequate Union intelligence meant that McClellan had no idea of the Confederate reaction to the Dranesville expedition. On 21 October, therefore, he ordered the commander of the troops around Poolesville, Brigadier General Charles P. Stone, to make a reconnaissance along the Potomac to see if his Dranesville feint had worked. 'The general desires that you keep a good lookout upon Leesburg,' McClellan wrote to Stone, 'to see if this movement has the effect to drive them away. Perhaps a slight demonstration on your part would have the effect to move them.'[1]

McClellan later wrote, accurately enough as it turned out, that his order 'did not anticipate the making of an attack upon the enemy or the crossing of the river in force by any portion of General Stone's command, and, not anticipating such movement, I had upon the 20th directed Major General McCall to return with his division on the morning of the 21st from Dranesville.'[2]

Charles Pomery Stone, a professional soldier who had seen service in the Mexican War, had been a brigade commander in the Valley of Virginia

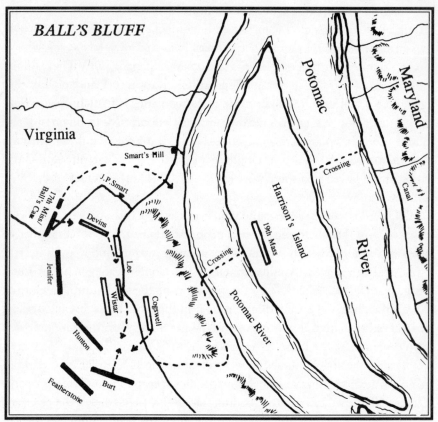

during the Bull Run campaign. After McClellan assumed command, Stone was given command of the Corps of Observation, a division of three brigades located on the Upper Potomac.

Stone's division could invade Virginia across the Potomac – or be attacked from Virginia – by a number of routes. They could cross at Edwards' Ferry below Leesburg, or at Conrad's Ferry above Leesburg, which was already covered by Union artillery. The Edwards' Ferry location had problems in that it was directly across the river from where the Goose Creek, a fairly major waterway, flowed into the Potomac. Moreover, while a road from Leesburg ended at the Virginia side of the Potomac across from Edwards' Ferry, the road end was covered by a steep hill which could be easily defended. The crossing at Conrad's Ferry also met a road to Leesburg on the Virginia side, and it too faced a 100-foot-high bluff, known locally as Ball's Bluff, after the Ball family which lived at its crest. But there at least the landing place was wider and would allow more troops to disembark at any one time. There was a large, cleared field at the crest which would allow the men to form into full regimental lines. Moreover, only a short way downstream from the actual ferry location was a large island, Harrison's Island, in the centre of the river, some 150 yards from the Virginia shore. Stone's men had already occupied Harrison's Island some time earlier.

On 20 October Stone sent some cavalry and the 7th Michigan Infantry to Edwards' Ferry while the 15th and 20th Massachusetts Infantry Regiments were sent to the Potomac across from Harrison's Island. Some of the 15th crossed to the island, the remainder of the regiment waited in Maryland. Stone ordered Colonel Charles Devens, Jnr., commander of the 15th Massachusetts, to send a scouting party across the river and towards Leesburg to find out what was happening there.

Colonel Devens, a prominent lawyer and politician in Worcester, Massachusetts, with no military experience until he was elected major of a rifle battalion at the outbreak of the war, had had no battle experience. He had raised the 15th Massachusetts, which had been mustered into US service on 12 June and arrived in Washington on 11 August. The regiment was sent on to Poolesville, arriving there on 27 August, and had been in that small town ever since. It had never been under fire.

Devens picked Captain Chase Philbrick, who had earlier scouted Harrison's Island, to command the reconnaissance party. He took some twenty men of his own Company H. In the moonlight, they crossed the river and made their way cautiously towards the town, fearful of running into Confederate outposts.

What they actually ran into was – nothing, but they didn't realize this. Two miles from the town (Philbrick thought they were only a mile away) they suddenly froze in their tracks at the sight of the silhouettes of what appeared to be about thirty Sibley tents, which looked like Indian tepees, pointing into a black, starry sky. In fact, what they could see were rows of hay stacks awaiting removal. Without approaching any farther, the patrol made its way back to Harrison's Island. Philbrick told Devens that all they had found was a small Confederate camp about a mile from Leesburg.

Devens sent this report, without thought of verifying it, back to Stone.

Although McClellan had ordered Stone not to precipitate any engagement, Stone reckoned that the capture of this small camp would be a cheap victory, and ordered Devens to send four companies of the 15th to attack it. After taking the camp quickly, the troops would fall back under cover of a company of the 20th Massachusetts which would be posted at the bluffs. Colonel Edward Baker would take his 1st California to Conrad's Ferry.

Two companies of the 1st Minnesota, a handful of cavalry, and an artillery battery were also ordered to Edwards' Ferry. The infantry and cavalry were to cross the river and move towards Leesburg to reconnoitre enemy positions, then rapidly fall back with their intelligence and recross the river. This expedition went as planned, and one prisoner from the 4th Virginia Cavalry was brought back for the loss of one horse.

Devens, who actually ordered five instead of four companies to accompany him to the supposed Confederate camp, started off at about midnight, and ran into problems right away. There were only three boats, each of which could take only thirty men, and autumn rains had so swollen the river that it was an exhausting business making way against the swift current. Consequently it was 4 a.m. before the five companies of men, shivering despite their state-issued gray overcoats, formed up on the Virginia side. As they struck out along the steep narrow path, Colonel Lee brought Companies E and I of his 20th Massachusetts across the river as directed.

The nervous men moved noisily, as recruits will, in the night, snapping branches and tripping over roots. But they arrived unchallenged at the enemy 'camp' which consisted of haystacks. At about 6.30 Devens sent Lieutenant Church Howe, the regimental quartermaster, back to Stone at Edwards' Ferry to say that the expedition had encountered no enemy troops and their presence had been undetected.

Stone decided that he had sufficient troops in a secure enough area from which to conduct further reconnaissance. He ordered ten cavalrymen under a sergeant to join Devens' group as scouts; these got across the river and then apparently lost their nerve. They returned almost immediately without having contacted Devens. The remainder of the 15th were ordered to cross the river and move to Smart's Mill, a stone building half a mile north of Ball's Bluff, which could be easily defended. They would be supported by two mountain howitzers of a regular US Army artillery battery, which were to be sited on a towpath on the Maryland side of the river from where they could sweep the flat fields around Smart's Mill. Stone gave command of all the troops in the Ball's Bluff area to Colonel Edward Baker. His orders were to reinforce the Massachusetts men with his own regiment or, if the enemy were too strong, to bring the New Englanders back to Maryland.

Edward Baker, a one-time US senator from Oregon, was a friend of Abraham Lincoln's. A charming man and a fine speaker, he had had military experience in the Mexican War where he had been twice wounded. At the outbreak of the Civil War, Baker, who was then back east, immediately began forming an infantry regiment, the so-called 1st California, which had one of the oddest origins of any Union Army regiment. Baker set up recruiting headquarters in New York and Philadelphia for the unit, which would be credited to California, with the idea of attracting west coast men who were living in the east. He was elected colonel, and Isaac J. Wistar, who had commanded Indian Rangers in California and Oregon in the 1850s, lieutenant colonel. After Pennsylvania's governor complained about citizens of his state being credited to another state, an important point when states had to meet quotas allocated by the Federal government, the regiment was officially redesignated the 71st Pennsylvania and assigned to what became the Philadelphia Brigade. As long as Baker remained its commander, however, it was known as the '1st California'.

The regiment available to Baker already in the area, was the 20th Massachusetts. A relatively new regiment, it had been recruited at Camp Massasoit, Readville, and had not left for Washington until 4 September. It was made up of Bostonians and Nantucket fishermen who, it was quickly learned, had no idea how to fire a musket. Its commander, Colonel William R. Lee, had been a cadet at the US Military Academy, class of 1829, but had resigned to look after a mentally ill father only a fortnight prior to graduation. Lee had been a civil and railroad superintendent before the war.

Baker's fourth regiment was the 42nd New York Infantry, known as the 'Tammany Regiment' and the 'Jackson Guard'. It had been organized by the Tammany General Committee Society of New York City, and was mustered into US service on 22 June, and sent to Washington on 18 July, from where it had been sent to guard the upper Potomac. Its original colonel having died on 22 July, its commander, Colonel Milton Cogswell, had been in the job only three months. None of these regiments had seen combat before; all had missed Bull Run.

Stone, a professional soldier, probably deferred in conversation to the popular, smooth-talking Baker, a professional politician. Later he said that he had told Baker not to advance unless the enemy were clearly fewer in

numbers, and in any event not to move beyond Leesburg. He said, and
Baker's death in the subsequent battle prevented a rebuttal, that he had
warned Baker of the danger of allowing enemy troops to capture the bluffs
that commanded the river bank, and that he had warned him to be sure that
there was sufficient transport to get all the troops across the river. With
these instructions and warnings, Stone, 'gave him entire control of operations on the right'.[3]

In response to Baker's request for a written order to guarantee his right
to command, Stone wrote: 'Colonel: In case of heavy firing in front of Harrison's Island, you will advance the California regiment of your brigade or
retire the regiments under Colonels Lee and Devens upon the Virginia side
of the river, at your discretion, assuming command on arrival.'[4] Baker, as
was his practice in his lawyer days, stuck this paper in his hat.

While Stone and Baker were talking, the Confederates around Leesburg were busy. A company of the 17th Mississippi Infantry, only 40 men
strong, had spotted Devens' men, and were now approaching the 15th who
were milling around near the phantom 'camp', and opening fire from a
harmless range. Devens directed Captain Philbrick's Company H to
advance on the rebels and drive them off. And now a truly strange thing
occurred. Philbrick's men advanced and the Confederate captain called on
them to halt. The Massachusetts men cried out 'Friends!' and kept on coming. Five or six times this happened before the Confederate captain apparently realized that war wouldn't be bloodless and ordered his men to kneel
and fire a volley. At about 7 a.m. the first shots were fired and the first blood
was drawn. Philbrick's men, shocked by the sudden fire, stopped in their
tracks. A second volley sent them scurrying back to the main body of the
regiment.

There they were reinforced so that an even larger body of the 15th now
advanced towards the Confederates who were drawn up along a fence rail.
For twenty minutes the two sides exchanged volleys, loading and firing by
the regulation manual procedures, drawn up in regulation lines of battle.
Both sides were mostly armed with smoothbore 0.69 calibre muskets,
deadly when close but inaccurate at any distance. Then the Union troops
fell back to the edge of the woods, bringing back one dead and nine
wounded men. The Confederates, kneeling behind a fence, had only three
of their men wounded, and only one of them seriously. Two Massachusetts
men were missing, presumed wounded and overlooked on the field.
Although regimental musicians were supposed to serve as ambulance corps-

men and bring the wounded back to a regimental hospital, their training had been virtually nil, their supervision was minimal and their motivation non-existent. The wounded would have to look after themselves.

Devens sent back word by the ever active Quartermaster Howe that his men had come under attack but that he was not worried. In the meantime, he threw out skirmishers and waited for reinforcements. The remainder of the 15th were already crossing the river, under orders to move to Smart's Mill. On the way, however, their commander, the regimental lieutenant colonel, ran into Howe who told him that Devens was in a 'tight spot', implying that instead of going to Smart's Mill, the 15th should join Devens' men. Spoiling for a fight, they reached Devens' position at about 10.30.

Howe continued into Maryland, found Baker and told him of Devens' situation as he understood it. Baker, a posturing figure, who appears to have seen himself cut in the swashbuckling mode, was not one of the 'stop-and-think-things-through-before-doing-them' school. On hearing of this small firefight, and without waiting to find out how many men on either side were involved, he immediately said, 'I am going down immediately with my whole force and taking command.'[5] Baker sent his own regiment forward, to follow the 15th. Howe went on to Stone's headquarters where Stone appeared unconcerned about Baker's decision to move all the 15th together instead of taking Smart's Mill.

Meanwhile, Devens' men had beaten off a Confederate attack, but Devens himself, apparently a bit shaken, fell back to the position held by the 20th Massachusetts on top of the bluff. Now Howe returned to tell him that Baker had assumed command. But Baker was missing and Howe was sent three times to the river to look for him and get his orders. He did not find him.

There was a good reason for that. Baker had remained on the Maryland side of the river, supervising the California Regiment's passage, and it was about 2 o'clock before six companies had got across. By this time firing was audible to everyone on the Maryland side, although none of the participants was visible. Baker crossed the river as far as Harrison's Island where he wasted much time that should have been spent with his senior officers in planning and executing his next moves, in supervising the lifting of a boat from the canal into the river to help solve the transport problem. Of course the boat problem was serious, but it was in large part caused by his failure to ensure that enough boats were available, order specific details to man the boats, guard the landing areas to prevent unau-

thorized personnel from using the boats out of turn, or prepare a movement schedule.

During this time his only orders were to Colonel DeWitt Clinton Bax-
ter, commander of the 2nd California Regiment, and temporarily in command of the brigade Baker normally commanded, to bring the rest of the
brigade forward.

Little did Stone or Baker know that the area around them was crawling
with Confederate infantry. In all, Evans' brigade, consisting of the 13th,
17th and 18th Mississippi Infantry Regiments and the 8th Virginia
Infantry Regiment, plus four dismounted cavalry companies, was ready to
pounce in strength on the irritating Yankees. Already their probing attacks
were drawing Union blood. Men of the 15th, on the Virginia side, began to
fall in increasing numbers. Private George Simonds felt a blow to his thigh,
and looked down to see his trousers shiny with blood. He took a step and
felt the sloshing of blood in his ankle-length shoe. He turned and, unaided,
headed for the woods to his rear, passing two other men too badly wounded
to move. Eventually he reached a cabin where he found two more of his
messmates, one wounded in the wrist and shoulder. There were no medical
personnel available.

At about 12.30 the remainder of the 20th Massachusetts formed up on
the Virginia shore, 'happy and gay, ready for the fight,' recalled one member. A straggler, filled with the doom that all stragglers spread, called out,
'You will have fun soon after you get to the top.'[6] Lee formed up his regiment in a single line, facing left, along the bluff top, where it was reinforced
by two howitzers and a James rifle, placed in an open field next to the
infantrymen. For ease of movement most of the men took off their gray
overcoats and left them hanging from the branches of nearby trees. When
the Confederates came within range their first volley tore the new overcoats
to shreds.

At about 1.30 Baker received word from Devens that he was facing
some 4,000 troops, but this was an overestimate. Again Baker stuck this
message in his hat, jotting a note back that he had just 'lifted a large boat
out of the canal into the river,' and would, 'as soon as I feel strong enough,
advance steadily, guarding my flanks carefully.'[7]

Although Devens might be excused for thinking that Baker was on his
side of the river and in control of the situation, it was not until about 2
o'clock that Baker actually crossed the river himself. He first met Lee, congratulated him on his deployment and, politician that he was, rode along

the regimental front, calling out, 'Boys, you want to fight don't you? Then you shall have your chance.'[8] He then ordered the 15th to the right on a new line in an open field in front of the bluff, facing west and south, while the 42nd New York was posted on the left. His own 1st California was placed in the centre between the 20th and the 42nd. A reserve of four companies was placed behind the centre, still within range of enemy muskets, but unable to fire safely themselves over the heads of the front line.

That was only one of the weaknesses of Baker's deployment, but it was a fatal one. His position was not good – in an open field, woods to his front to give the enemy protection, and a high, steep bank behind him leading to a river with only a handful of boats to transport the quick, the wounded and the dead. Baker admitted to his old friend Wistar that things were not going well at all, but showed no signs of retreating; instead he greeted Colonel Cogswell of the 42nd with lines from Walter Scott's *The Lady of the Lake*: 'One blast upon his bugle-horn Were worth a thousand men!' and seemed in the highest of spirits.

Cogswell, the only professional soldier among all the colonels on the scene, was in a more serious mood, telling Baker that the wooded ridge past the ravine on the left commanded the entire Union line. 'I advised an immediate advance of the whole force to occupy the hills,' Cogswell later reported.[9] Baker sniffed at this advice, instead telling Cogswell to take charge of the artillery, although omitting any hint of what he wanted done with the guns.

All this time Confederate skirmishers were firing sporadically at the Union line. Their fire was especially directed at the guns and all the gunners were soon wounded. Baker and Cogswell, with several adjutants general and other staff officers, took their places at the guns. Certainly, this was both a waste of command talent and somewhat discomforting to raw troops, to see their senior officers forced to serve as cannoneers.

While the top brass manned the cannon, Confederate soldiers took up positions all along the woods edging the field above the bluff, forming a semi-circle around the Union lines. The Union troops were caught in concentrated fire which poured in on them, blasting holes in the ranks and terrifying the soldiers who had never before seen battle. Baker and Cogswell gave up their cannoneer duties, remounted, joined by their staff, and rode to the left of the line to see how things were going there. There was little to encourage them. Wistar had been hit twice, in the jaw and in the thigh. Blood was running down his beard on to his coat, and down his leg into his boot. He knelt, pulled out a pocket knife, and slashed a hole in his boot to let the blood run out.

Baker ordered Wistar to send two of his already badly disorganized companies forward as skirmishers. Wistar argued against such a move, but Baker insisted. The two companies moved out and, coming under heavy fire, moved just as quickly back. Wistar was hit again, a heavy, painful blow to his right elbow which shattered all the bones at the joint. Bent over, holding his shattered right arm close to his body, he groped about in the high grass for his sword. He then asked Baker to replace the sword in his scabbard. Baker ordered an enlisted man to see that Wistar got on a boat safely, adding in his best oratorical voice, 'The officer who dies with his men will never be harshly judged.'[10]

Dismounting, Baker strode along the line, sword in hand. As he passed the line of the 20th, he called out for its men to lie down. One man said to him, 'But you don't lie down.' Baker paused and looked at the man. 'No, my son, and when you get to be a United States senator, you will not lie down either.'[11]

The 20th were taking a beating. Their officers, clad as they were at this early stage of the war in their frock-coats with golden shoulder-straps and blood-red sashes around their waists, seemed to be special targets. Shortly after the regiment came under fire, Captain John C. Putnam felt a tug high up on his right arm and fell; a heavy, slow-moving lead ball had smashed into it, tearing up tissue and smashing bone. Several of his men dropped their weapons, probably happy for an excuse to get out of harm's way, and dragged the badly bleeding captain off to the rear where doctors would amputate his arm just below the shoulder. First Lieutenant Norwood Hallowell took over his company.

Company C's commander, Captain Ferdinance Dreher, was hit by a bullet which passed through one cheek and out the other. Blood dripping down the front of his dark blue frock-coat, he too made his way to the rear and managed to get across the river to safety. Lieutenant Colonel George Ward, who had brought the remainder of the regiment to join Devens, was hit by a tumbling bullet which smashed many of the bones in his left leg.

Lieutenant Oliver Wendell Holmes was hit after about an hour under fire. Later he wrote in his diary: 'I felt as if a horse had kicked me and went over – 1st Serg^t Smith grabbed me and lugged me to the rear a little way & opened my shirt and ecce! the two holes in my breasts & the bullet, which he gave me – George says he squeezed it from the right opening – Well – I remember the sickening feeling of water in my face – I was quite faint – and seeing poor Serg Merchant lying near – shot through the head and covered with blood – and then the thinking begun – Shot through the lungs? Lets see – and I spit – Yes – already the blood was in my mouth... Just then I remembered and felt in my waist coat pocket – Yes there it was – a little bottle of laudanum which I had brought along – But I won't take it yet; no, see a doctor first – It may not be as bad as it looks – At any rate wait till the pain begins ...'[12]

Baker himself was an heroic figure, striding up and down the battered line, sword in hand. But he made no attempt to manoeuvre his men so as to get out of his predicament. By 5 o'clock it was obvious that he was in deep trouble, and he sent Captain Francis Young, one of his aides, back to Stone to request reinforcements. Then he returned to his heroic posturing, walking about in front of his men. Waiting for just such a chance, a group of Confederates jumped out of the woods not far from him. One of them aimed his revolver and fired four or five times. Baker was dead before he hit the ground. Seeing him fall, several 1st California officers dashed forward, one of them shooting Baker's killer. Three of them, including Baker's nephew, Second Lieutenant Edward Jerome, carried his body behind the Union line, down the bluff, and to the river bank.

Baker had left no single individual in charge of organizing the boatloads of reinforcements. The men had been coming over piecemeal and many were milling around the bank until formed up by their company officers and brought into line. Only two boats were available for bringing reinforcements across and evacuating the wounded, although two boats that had been used to get men to the Island from Maryland remained on that bank. Of the two boats available between the Island and Virginia, one was a ferry that could hold 60 men, and the other, described as 'a metallic life boat',[13] held only sixteen. The chaplain of the 15th Massachusetts appointed himself harbour master and tried to reserve boats for the wounded, but he was unable to make his decisions stick.

Lee assumed command of the forces on the Virginia side of the river, but Cogswell of the 42nd, disputed his date of commission. On comparing dates, Cogswell was found to be senior and took command. While Devens and Lee said it was time to retreat, Cogswell ordered them to prepare to charge and cut their way through to Edwards' Ferry.

Cogswell then rode to the front of the 42nd's firing line, and made some sort of gesture at the 42nd New York. While it was unclear what exactly he meant, or even who he was, since some of the men believed that he was a Confederate officer, the New Yorkers took it as a command to charge. Yelling at the top of their lungs, they dashed forward. The 15th started to join them, but Devens managed to stop the ill-advised dash. Now the men of the 42nd were in trouble. The Confederate infantry had them in a cross fire and they were not well enough trained to disengage under fire, difficult enough manoeuvre even for the best of troops. They began to be cut to pieces.

Discouraged by the news of Baker's death which rapidly spread through the ranks, and seeing their fellows falling right and left, men began to flee. Over the firing a voice was heard yelling, 'Company A, 20th Massachusetts, retreat to the ferry.' The raw soldiers didn't need a second invitation. Regiments and companies disintegrated. It was every man for himself as officers and men dashed back over the bluff and made for the river.

A 20th Massachusetts captain wrote home after the battle: 'For all I knew then, that we should either be killed or taken prisoners. The field now began to look like my preconceived idea of a battlefield. The ground was smoking and covered with blood, while the noise was perfectly deafening. Men were lying underfoot, and here and there a horse struggling in death. Coats and guns strewn over the ground in all directions. I went to the Colonel and he was sitting behind a tree, perfectly composed. He told me there was nothing to be done but "surrender and save the men from being murdered". Most of the men had now got down the bank.'[14]

The Confederate infantrymen, spurred on by the sight of their opponents' backs, pursued them to the bluff and picked them off like targets at a country fair. Captain George A. Schmitt, a teacher of German at Harvard College and the only faculty member of that school to serve in the army, was hit by a bullet that passed through the small of his back. Then he was hit three more times through the leg. First Lieutenant J. J. Lowell was also hit in the leg. Second Lieutenant William Lowell Putnam, said to have been the handsomest man at Harvard College, was shot in the abdomen, a wound virtually always fatal. Although his men managed to get him across the river, he died two days later. His body was sent back to Boston for burial.

For the space of twenty minutes the uneven contest continued. A handful of Union troops formed up as skirmishers to return fire, but most of the troops tried to get back to Maryland one way or another. Many of them huddled along the river bank, trying to shelter from the torrent of Confederate gunfire. The sun began to set, hiding some of them in shadows.

'Here was a horrible scene,' wrote Captain William Barlett of the 20th. 'Men crowded together, the wounded and the dying. The water was full of human beings, struggling with each other and the water, the surface of which looked like a pond when it rains, from the withering volleys that the enemy were pouring down from the top of the bank.'[15]

The wounded were tumbled down the bluff to the muddy bank below and into the two boats. 'When I had got to the bottom of the Bluff the ferry boat [the scow] had just started with a load – but there was a small boat there,' Lieutenant Holmes wrote in his diary. 'I have never been able to account for the fact that the bullets struck in the bank of the island over our heads as we were crossing...'[16]

Holmes was one of the lucky ones. The larger boat, overloaded with wounded and terrified men, became swamped and sank under fire only some fifteen feet from the shore. The boat later drifted away down the river, the man trying to pole it to Harrison's Island having been hit and fallen overboard. The smaller boats disappeared, apparently rowed to the safe side and then not returned; few would venture to return to such a scene. Those left on shore had a choice of swimming the slow-moving river in their sodden woollen clothing, or surrendering.

Oddly enough the Confederates did not seem to think of calling out to the trapped Union men to surrender, nor did many Union troops make the offer. Instead, many of the men made little rafts for their gear which they pushed ahead of them as they swam. Rafts of fence posts were contrived, but most fell apart in the swift current. Some men helped their non-swimming companions, linking arms and pushing off together. A handful of men, dodging low along the shore line, made their way east or west until they reached Union troops at ferries above and below Ball's Bluff.

When the numbers of wounded began to increase, Devens sent Second Lieutenant Willie Grout to supervise their evacuation across the river. He took a boatload over and returned to find total chaos. When he asked Devens what more he could do, Devens simply told him to take care of himself. There being no boats left, he waded out into the swiftly moving river and began the swim to safety. When he was about 75 yards from safety, one of his fellows saw a ball hit him in the head. He paddled for a few more strokes and cried out: 'Tell Company D I should have made it!' before sinking below the surface. His body was found thirteen days later.

Lieutenant Hallowell of the 20th removed the swordbelt from his waist and slung it around his neck. Then he walked out into the water and began swimming to the other side, his sword trailing behind him like a sunken barge. He and his sword made it. Captain Louis Beiral tried to take his sword with him but exhaustion forced him to relinquish it half way across. Private George Suttie wrapped himself in the silk flag of the California Regiment before starting his swim. The silk cloth rapidly filled with water, however, and shivering cold and bone tired, Suttie paused in his swim, bullets tossing up splashes around him, unwound the flag and let it float east to the Chesapeake before continuing. Lieutenant George Macy stopped on the bank, took a picture of his fiancee from his coat pocket and slipped it inside his hat. Then, sword in hand, and naked save for his hat, he swam to safety, although he was forced to part with his sword. A great many didn't make it. One drowned officer was later found by Confederates with $125 in gold in his pockets, whose weight apparently dragged him under.

More than 50 per cent of the 1,700 officers and men who had crossed the river were either killed, wounded or captured. Among the captured were Colonels Lee and Cogswell.

At the evening muster roll, the 15th Massachusetts discovered that they had only 313 survivors of the 625 who had gone into action that morning. The 20th Massachusetts had lost about 218 officers and men killed, wounded or taken prisoner, and these included the colonel, major and adjutant. The 42nd lost nine killed, ten wounded and 135 missing. The 1st California had 270 enlisted men left of the 600 who had crossed on the second day. Twenty-four Union officers and some 300 enlisted men were taken prisoner. According to Lieutenant William Harris, 1st California Regiment, 'The majority of the officers were taken at dusk, and immediately marched under guard to Leesburg, a distance of three miles from the field of battle. Arriving there, the usual rejoicings of an elated and frantic town were performed around us, the town-people appearing perfectly maddened in their yells of ecstasy and derision, crowding and shouldering each other in herds to catch a glimpse of us. "We've got them this time!" "Oh, you infernal Yankees!" "Make way, Jim: I want to see a 'Yank'!" were cries that greeted us on every side; and it was not until we were marched into the presence of General Evans, the Rebel commandant of Leesburg, that the wild uproar of the furious multitude became comparatively silenced.'[17]

The disaster provoked a public outcry. Under political pressure Congress formed the Joint Committee on the Conduct of the War in December specifically to investigate Ball's Bluff. Congressman Benjamin Wade of Ohio, a so-called 'Black Republican' because he came from the radical wing of that Party, was named to head the committee. Stone became a scapegoat for Ball's Bluff, and indeed, all Union failures. Secretary of War Stanton, under pressure himself, and armed with the knowledge that Stone had acquired a pro-slavery reputation, had Stone thrown into jail. After six months locked up at Fort Lafayette, during which no formal charges were ever lodged, he was released. Stone's career was, for all practical purposes, finished although he did hold some minor commands after that. He resigned on 13 September 1864, before the war was over.

3

The Defence of Fort Henry
Tennessee, 6 February 1862

In the west the rivers aimed like daggers into the heart of the new southern Confederacy. The Mississippi cut the south in half, while the Tennessee poured deep into Alabama. The Cumberland led to the Tennessee state capital of Nashville, one of the few industrialized cities in the south. Since the north had the capability of producing and using superior waterborne transportation to bring its troops south down these rivers, and since the Confederate government determined from the outset that it would defend every inch of Southern soil, it would have to build fortifications along these rivers to stop northern invaders.

Initially, the defence of Tennessee was up to the state's active Governor, Isham G. Harris, since the Confederacy had neither sufficient troops nor equipment to send help there once the state had seceded on 7 May 1861. Harris sent a 'widely known' civil engineer, Ada Anderson, to 'locate and construct defensive works on the northward flowing Cumberland and Tennessee Rivers.'[1] Anderson first chose a site on the Cumberland River, and a labour crew from the Cumberland iron works began to build a fort on the site. Then Anderson and his surveying party picked a spot for a fort on the Tennessee just below Standing Stone Creek, across the river from the mouth of Sandy. Both sites, he said, were chosen with care to avoid being inundated by winter flood waters.

Neither fort had progressed very far when Harris appointed Major Bushrod Johnson as the state's chief engineer to replace Anderson. Before any work had begun on the Tennessee River site, Johnson chose a new one, some five miles downstream and connected by a road which ran from river to river to Fort Donelson, due east.

In the meantime, the Confederate Government assumed the responsibility for defending Tennessee. Albert Sidney Johnston, an old friend of Confederate President Jefferson Davis's and commander of the US Army's 2nd Regiment of Dragoons before the war, was given the job of defending the entire western theatre. His staff engineer was First Lieutenant Joseph Dixon, who had served in the US Army Corps of Topographical Engineers before the war. Dixon examined both sites and reported that Donelson could have been better located, but since so much had been done already, it should be completed and additional outer works should be built. As for Fort Henry, it was not sited 'at the most favorable position', but was a strong position. He recommended that it be completed, and another fort be built directly across the Tennessee from it.

Command of both major forts, as well as the projected fort across the river from Fort Henry, was assigned to Brigadier General Lloyd Tilghman, who had graduated from West Point in 1836 but resigned from the army the same year and worked thereafter as a railroad construction engineer. He had seen service during the Mexican War, as both a staff and a line officer.

Fort Henry was the smaller of the two forts. It was five-sided, its western wall being directly on the riverbank. On the southern side, where a bluff ran along the river, a sally-port was constructed. The ground, flat along the river, rose to the south. The eastern salient point jutted into a line of marshy land which ran parallel to the river. The fort was designed to mount seventeen guns, including ten 32-pounders, one 10-inch Columbiad, one 24-pounder and two 12-pounder siege guns, one 24-pounder and two 42-pounder rifled guns. Most of these guns faced north and west, covering the river approaches to the fort. There were also six smaller, iron 12-pounder cannon on field carriages, but these were considered more dangerous to their crews than to the enemy after two of them had burst when tested with the regulation charge.

An outer line of defences was placed along the swamp line, on the bluff south of the fort. Many of the men actually lived in this area, the main fort being too small and wet to be inhabited in any degree of comfort. Other men camped on a hill overlooking the fort directly to its east, just past the swamp line. Another defensive line had been dug around these quarters. A final outer line of rifle pits ran along the top of the hills beyond that, and many of the garrison lived in tents just inside this outer line.

Confederate artilleryman Captain Jesse Taylor, commander of the 11th Company, Artillery Corps of Tennessee, was not at all impressed when he visited the fort in September: 'Arriving at the fort, I was convinced by a glance at its surroundings that extraordinarily bad judgment, or worse, had selected the site for its erection. I found it placed on the east bank of the river in a bottom commanded by high hills rising on either side of the river, and within good rifle range. This circumstance was at once reported to the proper military authorities of the State at Nashville, who replied that the selection had been made by competent engineers and with reference to mutual support with Fort Donelson on the Cumberland, twelve miles away.'

There was worse to come: '... the accidental observation of a water-mark
left on a tree caused me to look carefully for this sign above, below, and in
the rear of the fort; and my investigation convinced me that we had a more
dangerous force to contend with than the Federals, namely, the river itself.
Inquiry among old residents confirmed my fears that the fort was not only
subject to overflow, but that the highest point within it would be in an ordinary February rise at least two feet under water.'[2]

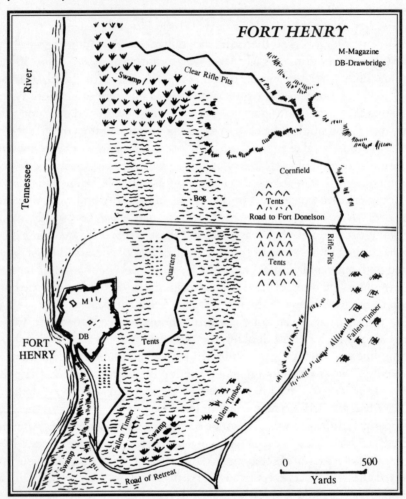

Major Jeremy F. Gilmer, Johnston's chief engineer as of 15 October,
was sent to investigate Taylor's complaint. He reported that Donelson
should have been built elsewhere, but, considering all that had already been
done and the lateness of the season, it was too late to change the fort's position. To beef up its defences, Gilmer ordered that obstructions be placed in

the river. He also ordered Lieutenant Dixon, at Fort Henry, to go ahead with the building of Fort Heiman, directly across the river from Henry, which would protect the position when high waters drove the men from their guns.

On 2 January 1862 Tilghman reported: 'On yesterday I reviewed and inspected the entire command in Henry, and am gratified at being able to report the entire command in a most admirable state of efficiency. Everything will be ready to receive the additional armament now on its way. A heavy rifled gun [32-pounder] arrived at the fort on yesterday and will be in place today. As shown by the weekly report, I have had an addition to the force at Fort Henry in the Alabama troops; seven companies are now on the ground; the remaining three will be in place on Saturday. The companies are tolerably armed. Five of them only were inspected, the others arriving this morning.'[3]

General Tilghman should not have been so self-congratulatory since he had been less than energetic in getting work done on either of the two fortifications. As late as 17 January a visitor found the labour force sitting about waiting for Tilghman to approve the plans for Fort Heiman.

Dismayed on learning this, Johnston ordered Tilghman to, 'Occupy and *intrench* the heights opposite Fort Henry. Do not lose a moment. Work all night.'[4] Then Johnston sent Gilmer back to Fort Henry to make sure that Tilghman had complied with his instructions. On 29 January Gilmer found that the defences of Fort Henry were finally finished, but there was still much to be done at Fort Heiman. Moreover, there were no guns to put into Heiman once it was complete.

In the meantime, however, the forts' garrisons were already in place. Morning reports for December 1861 indicated that Fort Henry was garrisoned by an infantry force of 59 officers and 1,136 enlisted men drawn from the 10th Tennessee, 4th Mississippi and two companies of the 3rd Alabama Battalion. The artillery force of Taylor and Culbertson's batteries consisted of only three officers and 69 enlisted men. A company of cavalry, consisting of five officers and 100 enlisted men, mostly saw service as messengers and manned a picket post some distance along the river to the north. On 21 January 1862 morning reports indicated that there were 140 officers and 2,498 enlisted men in place at Fort Henry.

Fort Heiman was garrisoned by the 15th Arkansas and 27th Alabama Infantry Regiments, two Alabama cavalry companies, a disorganized Kentucky cavalry company, and a light artillery section, for a total of some 1,100 officers and men. Two very small regiments of about 200 officers and men each, the 48th and 51st Tennessee Infantry Regiments, were posted at Paris Landing about five miles above the fort. During the cold, wet winter months many of the men, not yet accustomed to service in the field, were unfit for duty because of sickness.

The magazines held sufficient ammunition supplies to sustain an extended siege; on 18 January 1862 the department's ordnance officer reporting that there were 782 rounds for the 32-pounders, 274 rounds of 12-pounder, 300 rounds of 6-pounder, 100 rounds of 24-pounder rifled, and 150,000 rounds of smallarms ammunition.[5] According to Captain Taylor, however, the powder was of such poor quality that it would not fire a shot much beyond a mile, so his men had to add small-grained, quick-burning powder to each charge to set it off, which diminished accuracy considerably.

The infantry's smallarms posed a problem. At Henry, recalled artilleryman Taylor, the garrison was made up of 'mostly raw regiments armed with shot-guns and hunting rifles'; in fact, the best-equipped regiment of his command, the 10th Tennessee, was armed with old flint-lock "Tower of London" muskets that had 'done the state some service in the war of 1812.'[6] According to Colonel Adolphus Heiman, commander of the 10th, 'None of the cavalry had either sabres or pistols, and were only partly armed with double-barreled shot-guns; no other equipments whatever.'[7]

Henry, however, was not seen as the most threatened post in the defence of Tennessee. On Christmas Day 1862, General Johnston wrote to Governor Harris that he believed he knew the point of attack: 'The vulnerable point is by the line from Louisville towards Nashville, and the Northern generals are evidently aware of it.'[8]

Since, as Johnston indicated, the main concern was with Fort Donelson, Henry was somewhat neglected, but in fact it was by far the most vulnerable of the two. As early as November 1861, an engineer officer on the staff of Federal Major General O. M. Mitchell, Colonel Charles Whittlesy, had suggested to the overall theatre commander, Major General Henry Halleck, that a grand movement should be made by land and water down the Tennessee and Cumberland Rivers into Tennessee. This movement, he suggested, would cause the Confederates to leave Kentucky. Major General William T. Sherman, had made the same observation to Halleck in December 1861.

And indeed that was exactly the Union's plan. First, the northern commanders sent Union naval vessels to probe Fort Henry. The first vessels were just a couple of odd craft that were available; the Federal forces had also been busy during the late months of 1861 and had assembled a fleet of iron-clads up-river. Two of them, *Lexington* and *Conestoga*, would come down-river, anchor just the other side of a small island below Fort Henry, and bombard the fort for an hour or so. Figuring that this was not an assault but a reconnaissance to count the number and position of the fort's guns, the Confederates did not return the fire, although, wrote artilleryman Taylor, the defenders were 'sorely tempted' to return fire.

Their day would come, and soon. On 4 February at 4.30 a.m., a sentinel up-river saw the sparks from the stacks of an advancing flotilla of three Union gunboats and fired a signal rocket announcing their approach. Inside Fort Henry the cannoneers were woken and manned the guns facing up-river. Several steamers, moored at Fort Henry's tiny wharf and used as sick-bays, were sent down-river out of harm's way.

Sunrise was shortly before 7 o'clock; a little later cavalrymen rode in to tell Colonel Heiman of the 10th Tennessee, who was acting commander in the absence of General Tilghman who was at Donelson, that an enemy fleet was on its way. About two hours later the leading Union boats could be seen by the defenders. 'Far as the eye could see, the course of the river could be traced by the dense volumes of smoke issuing from the flotilla indicating that the long-threatened attempt to break our lines was to be made in earnest,' Taylor wrote.[9]

But the Union navy wasn't the only problem. The river, swollen by rain, had been lapping against the fort's sandbag walls for some days previously and now was beginning to flow in over the low walls and pour into the lower magazine. All men save those at the guns were put to work immediately, filling and laying sandbags on top of the walls, and trying to contain the flood damage inside the fort. A temporary, shallow magazine was dug in a high spot inside the walls and covered with sandbags. This latter was vital because by now the lower magazine was under two feet of water and ammunition had to be transferred to the temporary magazine.

The Union navy took its time and it was about noon before five gunboats were in sight, in line some two miles below the fort. Colonel Heiman ordered the infantrymen to occupy the outer line of rifle pits; the artillerymen remained in the fort whose walls were already awash. Not all of them would be needed, because the gunboats were out of range of the 32-pounders, so that only the 10-inch Columbiad and a 24-pounder rifled gun would bear.

At about 1 p.m. the Union ships opened fire. The defenders returned fire, but after only three or four shots the jerry-rigged carriage of the Columbiad broke and there was a danger that if the gun were fired again it might disintegrate. With this mishap half the fort's artillery component was silenced.

The Union ships made no move to attack, but contented themselves with firing on the fort while infantry were landed some distance from the Confederate position. Heiman sent word to Tilghman who arrived with some engineers at about 11.30 that night. At daybreak Tilghman ordered Fort Heiman's garrison to abandon their unfinished post and row across to join the infantry around Fort Henry. He sent out his cavalry to reconnoitre the strength of the Union infantry, and called up two regiments to a position halfway between Forts Henry and Donelson to act as a reserve. Then he waited.

In the late afternoon three Union gunboats, two on the western side of the fort and the other on the eastern side, anchored within range and opened fire. The Confederates held their fire. One Union shot killed a Confederate soldier and wounded three more, so the defenders began to return fire, using the damaged Columbiad as well as the other gun. After only six shots, which appeared to score solid hits on the Union vessels, the boats weighed anchor and withdrew.

Jubilation at the departure of the enemy was premature; word from the scouts was not encouraging. They reported that the Federals had landed some 25,000 infantry in the area, to oppose a force of less than a tenth its size. Tilghman realized that he could not hold Fort Henry against such odds, but he wanted to buy as much time as possible to withdraw the infantry to Fort Donelson where the combined garrisons could defend themselves successfully. The longer he could hold Henry, the more time Fort Donelson's men would have to prepare their own defence. Tilghman called a conference of his unit commanders and asked Captain Taylor, 'Can you hold out for one hour against a determined attack?' Taylor said that he could. 'Well, then, gentlemen,' Tilghman told his other commanders, 'rejoin your commands and hold them in readiness for instant motion.'[10]

The next morning seven Federal gunboats appeared, deployed in two lines. At about 11.30 they closed on the fort, coming within range first of the two larger guns, which opened fire on them at about 11.45, and then the smaller guns which also began firing. The Federals replied, increasing the rapidity and accuracy of their fire until they showed 'one broad and leaping sheet of flame' to the artillerymen inside the fort.[11] According to Colonel Heiman, '... the firing on both sides was without a moment's intermission. Shot after shot was exchanged with admirable rapidity and precision and the enemy's shell struck and exploded in every direction.'[12]

Suddenly steam burst from every open porthole and companionway of one of the Union gunboats, the *Essex*. The crippled boat slowed down, smoke no longer pouring from its funnels. Evidently a Confederate shell had taken effect. Powerless, it slowly dropped out of line and began to drift downstream. It fact, a lucky shot had found the boat's boiler. Twenty-eight officers and sailors had been badly burned in the explosion. The Confederates thought that this had frightened the commanders of the other gun-boats, which appeared to slow down, their fire becoming hesitant.

Luck, however, was on the Union side that day. Hardly had the *Essex* dropped out of the fight, at about 12.30, when the fort's rifled 24-pounder burst, showering shattered fragments of gunmetal everywhere. Most of its crew were hurled to the ground, badly injured and burned in the explosion. Now the only large gun left was the Columbiad; but it, too, suddenly stopped firing. Captain Taylor, who had run to it when the 24-pounder blew up, found that its vent was obstructed by a priming wire that had snapped off. The wire was thoroughly wedged and the captain knew that it would take the best part of a day to get the vent open and the gun working again.

Now that the only two large guns were out of action, the gunboats closed to about 600 yards. 'His rifle shot and shell penetrated the earth-works as readily as a ball from a navy Colt [0.36 calibre revolver] would pierce a pine board,' Taylor recalled.[13] The exposed 32-pounders began to take a beating. Two of them were hit almost simultaneously, one on the muzzle, pieces of iron and wood from which flew about, killing two men and injuring many more. In a matter of minutes only four cannon were capable of replying to the Union guns.

The noise inside the battered fort was deafening. The hands on Tilgh-man's watch had reached 1.30; it was past the hour he had demanded of Taylor. From his position on the walls, he yelled down to Colonel Heiman, asking why so few of his guns were returning fire. Heiman yelled back that casualties and exhaustion had cut the crews greatly and there were no replacements available. 'The general threw off his coat, sprang on the chassis of the nearest gun, stating that he would work it himself, ordering, at the same time, 50 men of my regiment to the fort to assist the gunners. Seeing nobody whom I could send for them, I started myself, the bombardment still going on unabated; but before I could reach the command the boats were so close to the fort that further resistance was impossible,' Heiman later reported.[14]

The gun manned by Tilghman, a 32-pounder, fired two shots at the *Cincinnati*. 'It was now plain to be seen that the enemy were breaching the fort directly in front of our guns, and that I could not much longer sustain their fire without an unjustifiable exposure of the valuable lives of the men who had so nobly seconded me in this unequal struggle,' Tilghman later reported.[15] He ordered a man to mount the walls and wave a white flag in an effort to get the Union guns to cease fire, in the hope that he could get some reinforcements to help man the remaining guns during the ceasefire period Apparently, in the dense clouds of white gun smoke, hanging low in the wet air, the flag was not seen and the Federal guns continued to break up the fort's walls.

Tilghman then called out to Taylor to strike the fort's colour. 'The flag-mast, which had been out of the center of fire,' Taylor wrote, 'had been struck many times; the top-mast hung so far out of the perpendicular that it seemed likely to fall at any moment; the flag halyards had been cut by shot, but had fortunately become "foul" at the crosstrees. I beckoned for it was useless to call amid the din to Orderly-Sergeant Jones, an old "man-o'-war's man," to come to my assistance, and we ran across to the flag-staff and up the lower rigging to the cross-trees, and by our united efforts succeeded in clearing the halyards and lowering the flag.'

The view from the top of the flag pole was amazing. 'At our feet the fort with her few remaining guns was sullenly hurling her harmless shot against the sides of the gun-boats, which, now apparently within two hundred yards of the fort, were, in perfect security, and with coolness and precision of target practice, sweeping the entire fort; to the north and west, on both sides of the river, were the hosts of "blue coats", anxious and interested spectators, while to the east the feeble forces of the Confederacy could be seen making their weary way toward Donelson.'[16]

The guns now fell silent. A cutter with US Navy officers aboard put off from *Cincinnati* to accept the surrender. By now the water was waist-deep on the river side of the fort. Another stream was flowing between the fort and the high ground to the east where the infantry camps and rifle pits had been dug. The *Cincinnati*'s cutter actually rowed into the fort through the sally-port.

When Tilghman surrendered his little garrison of 44 men, five had been killed and another five were missing, probably blown to bits or washed away. Heiman led his infantrymen down the road to Fort Donelson. His dogged resistance in the doomed fort had bought precious time for the Confederates. It would now be up to the defenders of Fort Donelson to prove that it had been worthwhile.

4
The Loss of Fort Donelson
16 February 1862

The two brigades of survivors of the stubborn defeat at Fort Henry reached the other link in the chain defending Tennessee by water, Fort Donelson, but this, despite the breathing-space it had received, was not prepared to face a major assault. Unfortunately the Confederates were unaware of this fact. On 2 January 1862, Brigadier General Lloyd Tilghman, who had commanded both posts until his capture at Fort Henry on 6 February, had reported that, 'A most satisfactory progress has been made in the main fortification, an enclosed work. A very few more days will close up the gap and give us a very good work.

'The heavy batteries are progressing rapidly and will be very efficient. I shall be ready to place all the guns in position as fast as they arrive. I am straining a point to make the armament sufficient to answer the aim we have in view. I look for some of the heavy guns to-morrow. My entire command is now comfortably housed for the winter. The houses are admirably built, well situated, and present an appearance of real comfort that will compare favorably with any command in the field.' But he added: 'I still have near 2,000 unarmed men in my command. I have not men enough armed at this post to man one-half the lines within the fortification, much less to effect anything at the points which command my whole work.'[1]

The work was quite a massive affair. The fort itself had irregularly shaped earthen walls some two and a half miles long surrounding a single square mile of ground. The Confederates built their log cabin barracks, some 400 of them, within these walls. The fort stood on a hill overlooking the Cumberland River. Just slightly above it, on lower ground immediately in front of the swampy banks of a sluggish creek, Hickman's Creek, which fed into the river, the Confederates had constructed a water battery in which they had installed nine cannon commanding the river. Engineers considered the creek impossible for foot soldiers to cross, its wide swampy banks being as good as land mines. The swampy area was heavily wooded. The Confederates also built a smaller water battery just below the fort on the river banks.

Dover, the nearest town, was down-river from the fort. Sparsely populated, it had but two major buildings, the county courthouse and a two-storey tavern mostly used by people involved in legal proceedings when

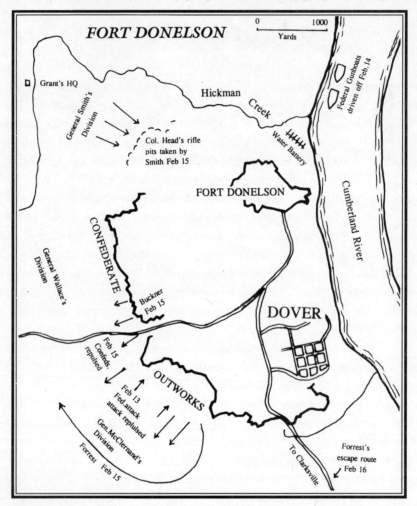

the court was in session. Confederate engineers supervised the building of a line of outer fortifications which began on a bluff overlooking the river just below Dover and then ran along bluffs in clearings all around the area until they reached almost to Hickman's Creek.

On 21 January, morning reports indicated that the garrison consisted of only 89 officers and 1,103 enlisted men, so reinforcements were rushed up but in such strength that they could not all be housed in the fort itself. Tents were set up all along the line of outer fortifications, around Dover, and in clearings between the fort and outer fortification line.

Additional troops who could reinforce Fort Donelson were down-river at Clarksville. They were commanded by Brigadier General Gideon Johnson Pillow. Elderly for the period at 56 years old, Pillow was a lawyer and politician who had served as a major general in the Mexican War. His appointment then had come not because of his military brilliance, but because of his political loyalties to President James Polk, who had been his law partner some years before. When his native state of Tennessee seceded, he was appointed a major general in its forces, but when the state forces were taken into the Confederate Army he received a brigadier general's commission which was bitterly disappointing because he had hoped to retain the state command at the higher rank.

Ambitious and not over scrupulous, Pillow was known at the time as the man who tried to 'supersede General [Winfield] Scott [the army's general in chief] in Mexico'. Indeed, contemporaries spoke of him as being 'jealous' and 'insubordinate and quarrelsome'.[2] At the present time he had sent incorrect reports to General A. S. Johnston, overall theatre commander, in an attempt to retain command of the men at Clarksville, a post which suited him, rather than be sent on an expedition which didn't. His opponent at Donelson, Major General U. S. Grant, dismissed him as being 'conceited, and prided himself much on his services in the Mexican war'.[3]

On 7 February Johnston ordered Pillow to Fort Donelson, with instructions to hold it as long as possible, and then fall back towards Nashville. This presupposed that the fort would fall to naval gunboats and that no Federal land troops would be around to prevent Pillow's retreat.

Then, only a day later, Johnston, totally in the dark as to the real situation on the Cumberland River so far from his headquarters, essentially abdicated his command. He ordered Major General John Buchanan Floyd to assume overall command in the area.

Floyd was virtually identical with Pillow in age and incompetence. He too had been a lawyer and politician before the war. Grant dismissed him as a man who, although 'of talent enough for any civil position, was no soldier and, possibly, did not possess the elements of one'.[4] Floyd had been Secretary of War in the Democratic administration just before the war, and had been accused of transferring arms to southern states in anticipation of hostilities. A Federal grand jury in Washington indicted him for that and for complicity in an embezzlement of public funds. So Floyd was under a cloud, and was determined not to be defeated.

Floyd, however, did not understand Johnston's orders, and his confusion meant that he did not arrive in Clarksville until 11 February. There, under Johnston's orders, he found Pillow, who was yet to go to Donelson, and two brigades, both poorly armed, one under Charles Clark and the other under Simon Buckner.

Brigadier General Simon Bolivar Buckner was the third, and most junior general at Donelson. A West Point graduate who had earned two brevets for bravery in the Mexican War, he had been adjutant general of the Kentucky State Guard. He was commissioned a brigadier general in the Confederate Army only after declining such a commission in the Union Army. A contemporary said of him that, compared to the other two generals, Buckner 'was their equal in courage; while in devotion to the cause and to his profession of arms, in tactical knowledge, in military bearing, in the faculty of getting the most service out of his inferiors, and inspiring them with confidence in his ability, as a soldier in all the higher meanings of the word, he was greatly their superior.'[5]

Floyd ordered Pillow to march the two brigades at Clarksville to Fort Donelson. Buckner would retain command of his brigade, but Clark, junior to Pillow, would turn over his command to Pillow. Clark objected, and in fact refused to surrender his command. Finally, Floyd got Johnston officially to order the change in command. Then, after issuing the official motto for the command, 'Liberty or Death', Pillow, who was quite keen to retain an independent command, headed up-river to Donelson immediately.

Now Floyd began to vacillate. He changed his mind about concentrating his forces at Donelson which most military men thought would at best be difficult hold. He decided to leave only a small force at the fort, and concentrate at nearby Cumberland City. From there he could strike at any Union troops advancing on Fort Donelson on the flank.

Pillow, however, was not about to give up his independent command. He simply declined to send Buckner and his brigade back to Floyd. The two argued by telegraph and courier for vital days, and then, as Fort Henry fell and Union troops moved towards Donelson, Floyd bolstered his case for the successful defence of Fort Donelson by sending a series of overly optimistic telegraphs about his chances to Johnston himself, going over Floyd's head. Fort Donelson, he told Johnston, would be safe if Buckner's brigade were to stay there.

Johnston, nowhere near the actual area and in total ignorance of any-thing but what he was being told, came down on Pillow's side. Unhappily for Pillow's ambition, however, Johnston was so impressed with what Pil-low said that he ordered Floyd to take his troops from Clarksville and join Pillow at Donelson. There Floyd would become the overall commander and Pillow would again be a subordinate. Floyd and Buckner had talked about the overall situation earlier and both agreed that Donelson was little more than a trap. Nevertheless, he obeyed orders, and set out for Donelson. The leading troops entered Donelson's works in the early hours of 13 February. The garrison there now numbered some 15,000 officers and men, but many of them were sick with measles which had spread among the newly orga-nized Mississippi regiments.

But Union troops, from Henry, were on the march as well, and there were a lot more of them, and they were better equipped. Confederate cav-alry under Lieutenant Colonel Nathaniel Bedford Forrest, a rising star among southern officers, went out to try to slow Grant's advance. Although the cavalry fought well enough, their pickets out as a skirmish line to pro-tect the main body, the overwhelming numbers of Union troops pushed the small Confederate cavalry force back with ease. Only the poor terrain, its flooded creeks and ravines confining the Union troops to a narrow, muddy road, allowed the cavalry to slow the advance as long as it did. A larger force of infantry and artillery might well have prevented the Union advance, but neither Floyd nor Pillow, both new in the area and to the troops under their command, attempted any such deployment.

That day saw a major change in the weather which until now had been almost balmy for this part of the country. It began to rain, a warm drizzle at first but as temperatures dropped becoming a cold sleet. Cooking, even the meagre rations the Confederate commissary officers were able to issue, would be impossible in the icy rain.

On this day too the Union Army, three divisions strong under Major General U. S. Grant, fresh from a hard-fought little skirmish at Belmont, Missouri, arrived from the direction of Fort Henry and fanned out to form a besieging line beyond Donelson's outer fortifications, not long after Floyd's arrival. One division, on the Confederate left, attacked and was eas-ily beaten back. Then the Union troops settled in for a siege, digging their trenches within rifle range of the outer works.

Pillow sent two companies of Forrest's cavalry on a sortie against the entrenching Federals and Forrest himself became involved in the action. At one point he saw a Union sharpshooter in a tree in front of him. Taking a rifle from an enlisted man, he aimed, fired and dropped his target.

Union infantry made two sorties on the Confederate lines, more to try them than to break through. Both sorties were easily beaten back, with the loss to Buckner's division of only some 39 officers and men. The ease of these minor successes reinforced the belief of Floyd and Pillow that the fort would easily stand against land-based attacks. They still thought the main threat to Donelson, as at Fort Henry, would be from naval guns on the river.

This belief would soon be put to the test, because 10,000 more Union troops and a US naval flotilla soon arrived on the scene.

At about 3.30 that afternoon four gunboats began a bombardment of the fort from a range of some 2,000 yards. The Confederate batteries remained silent. Slowly the range closed. At a thousand yards, the two largest Confederate guns returned fire. The sailors pressed on. At 400 yards, all twelve guns that could be brought to bear opened up, doing so much damage that three iron-clads had to drop out of the fight, disabled by shots to the pilot-house or machinery. A 128-pound round smashed into the port casement of the USS *Carondelet*, bursting steam lines, and forcing the vessel to withdraw.

The Confederates had not got off unscathed. One naval shell smashed into an open embrasure in the battery, dismounting a 32-pounder cannon by knocking off the cheek of the carriage. Shattered wood and metal flew upwards and a short screw bolt killed the battery commander, and another struck the fort's engineer officer, Captain Joseph Dixon, in the left temple and killed him instantly.

Professionals might have known that the shore batteries were getting the best of the fight; many of the amateurs in the southern army didn't. Forrest, for one, watched the exchange from a clearing overlooking the action. Major David C. Kelley, who had been a minister before joining Forrest's cavalry, soon joined him. 'Parson,' Forrest told him on his approach, 'for God's sake, pray. Nothing but God Almighty can save that fort.'[6]

As the northern boats withdrew, a jubilant Pillow telegraphed Johnston: 'We have just had the fiercest fight on record between our guns and six gunboats, which lasted two hours. They came within 200 yards of our batteries. We drove them back, damaged two of them badly, and crippled a third very badly. No damage done to our battery and not a man killed.'[7]

That evening the sleet turned to snow which continued to fall to a depth of two inches, and this and a temperature of 10° made life miserable for defender and attacker alike. Rifle pits filled with water that froze. Conditions were slightly worse for the defenders because the Union troops had brought their heavy overcoats, though many of them had tossed these away during the spring-like day. The Confederate troops sadly lacked this type of winter wear. In fact many of them had no tents or blankets. They spent the night huddled around fires that produced more smoke than heat.

Given the misunderstanding and mistrust in the high command, it is not surprising that the troops' morale was low and a defeatist attitude was rife. Rumours passed around the campfires. Tilghman, it was said, had surrendered Fort Henry while the Union gunboats were still a quarter of a mile away. Buckner's Kentucky troops, loyal to Tilghman, exchanged angry words and blows with Tennessee troops who called him a coward. So, between the cold weather and the hot words, most of the Confederate garrison spent a sleepless night in Donelson.

'The contest of the day closed,' wrote Major Jeremy Gilmer, Floyd's chief engineer. 'But our forces were much fatigued, having been under arms all day, and this after three or four days' hard labor upon the intrenchments.'[8]

Next day, Johnston, unaware that the Union forces had surrounded the fort by land, leaving no escape route, telegraphed Floyd telling him to 'get his troops back to Nashville' if he lost the fort.[9] But Johnston did not positively order Floyd to evacuate the position. The result was that the habitually indecisive Floyd did nothing. While he was wondering what to do next, Union troops got across the Wynn's Ferry road, the fort's last open land-based line of communications south.

When the Confederates learned that Wynn's Ferry road had fallen, Floyd prepared a plan to attack and retake it. Pillow, however, objected that it was too late in the day to mount such an attack. And all the commanders were more concerned about attacks from the water than the land.

Indeed, the US Navy did return, with five gunboats which blasted away at the water batteries. Confederate gunners were ordered to hold their fire until the boats were at point-blank range, then open up with everything they had. For a little over an hour the boats and water batteries exchanged shots as quickly as they could reload. Confederate gunners cheered as they saw one boat reel from the effects of their fire and drift helplessly away from the fight. More Confederate shells smashed into another boat's side and she too fell out of the fight, followed a few minutes later by a third.

One Confederate gun fell silent as an over-excited gunner drove in his rammer before his mate had withdrawn the vent pick. The pick bent easily, jamming the bore so that the gun could not be reloaded.

The ferocity of the attack so alarmed Floyd at one point that he telegraphed Johnston that the fort would not be able to hold for another twenty minutes, but in fact the boats did remarkably little damage. Captain T. W. Beaumont, who was commanding a battery of four 32-pounders, reported that a few of his men had been slightly bruised by clods of earth thrown up by bursting shells, and one of them slightly hurt by a spent canister round.

'Now boys,' yelled Private John G. Frequa, a water battery cannoneer, 'see me take a chimney [smokestack].' The shot he fired passed through one of the boat's smokestacks and tore off the boat's flag. Frequa tossed his cap in the air, yelling, ' Come on, you cowardly scoundrels; you are not at Fort Henry.'[10]

After this ineffectual firing, the boats eventually retired, having taken rather the worse in the exchange, and the Confederate generals congratulated themselves on their brilliant defence.

The Navy had been beaten, and Fort Donelson would not fall as had Fort Henry. But there was still U. S. Grant and all those blue-clad infantrymen dug in around the fort. The Confederates did not have sufficient supplies for a long siege, nor could fresh supplies be brought to them because the Union forces controlled the waterways as well as the roads leading to the fort. Even Floyd realized now that the real threat to Donelson was not from the river, but from the land behind it. It was time to take Johnston's orders seriously, abandon the fort, and cut a way through towards Nashville.

The plan was simple. Pillow would lead a force against the Union right, which had already been bloodied by its abortive attacks two days before, towards Wynn's Ferry road. At the same time, Brigadier General Buckner would follow up the attack, capturing the road to Nashville, to enable the rest of the garrison to escape. Forrest's cavalry would cover the left. There is some debate as to whether everyone present realized that the end result of the attack would mean abandoning the fort; some of the officers left with the idea that the intention was simply to open a line of communication, while others felt that the idea was first to open and then use a line of retreat. The men thought they were on their way out since they had been ordered to fill their haversacks with three days' rations and carry their blankets, which seemed to indicate movement rather than a spoiling attack or sortie.

Regimental commanders were briefed at about two or three in the morning, and told to get their men ready for the fight. Most of them were given to understand that the plan was not just to open the road to Nashville, but to head off for there leaving the fort empty.

At about 5 a.m. on 15 February, an hour before sunrise, but, according to Forrest, 'in the early gray of the morning',[11] the Confederates launched their attack. Brigadier General Bushrod Johnson, in command of one division, led the spearhead troops. For three hours the Confederates worked their way over the snow-covered ground, firing from behind trees, and from ravines and gullies, against Union troops similarly protected. Slowly they advanced across the icy landscape, slipping and sliding so often that double-time charges were out of the question. Casualties were surprisingly light; the Union troops were not expecting to be attacked, and the bad weather had done little for their morale.

Colonel Gabriel Wharton, 51st Virginia Infantry, reported that his men cheered as they charged, driving the Federal forces easily for two miles. The 26th Mississippi had it a bit harder, being thrown back in confusion by heavy and accurate Union fire, but they rallied and rejoined the advance. In some places the Union troops withdrew slowly, taking advantage of the broken and wooded ground to slow the Confederates with heavy fire.

In the close-quarter fighting many Confederates thought that they had the advantage with smoothbored muskets against the enemy's with rifled muskets. The combination of one 0.69 calibre ball and three buckshot was more destructive at close range than the more accurate, longer-ranged 0.58 calibre rifled musket. At the same time, the wet weather made many of the Tennesseans' flintlock muskets worthless. From time to time the men had to stop, under fire, and try to dry out their flints and frizzens before they could resume. Where possible, those Confederates abandoned their old flintlocks when they could find abandoned Union rifled muskets.

Forrest led the Confederates 'on the left and in advance'. There he 'found the enemy prepared to receive us'.[12] Forrest and his younger brother Jeffrey, who was serving with him, had their horses killed by the fierce gunfire they encountered. Neither of the men was badly hurt, although Jeffrey was battered from his fall and quite sore for some time afterwards.

By 9.30 a.m. the Union troops had fallen back wherever pressed, and Pillow followed up his success up with a general advance all along the line. His men broke through the Union line, while Buckner's men streamed out to take the road to safety. The Union troops fell back, leaving some 300 prisoners and larger numbers of dead and wounded behind, and an L-shaped gap in their line. With the road open, Forrest saw another hole open up on the Union flank. When he sent troops forward, he found the ground over which he would have to attack was heavy marsh, so bad as to provide almost perfect protection to the Union flank.

His troops smashed through the infantry to their front, however, and reached a point defended by four Union Napoleons and two 24-pounder iron cannon, which comprised their entire artillery defence on the Wynn's Ferry road. Forrest ordered a charge, his men firing the shotguns they pre-ferred to sabres in combat. 'I captured the battery,' Forrest reported without elaboration, 'killing most of the men and horses.'[13] His men reported that they found the bodies of some 50 infantrymen who had been supporting the artillery.

Forrest, who had two more horses killed in the fighting that day, reported that his men had wrought 'great slaughter' during the battle, killing some 200 men in a ravine. All along the front, Confederate troops gathered up some 5,000 infantry smallarms, as well as a complete set of band instruments. By 2.30 p.m. the whole front was open, with three roads now available to the Confederates for their withdrawal, but the men were running short of ammunition. Many of them were actually loading the smaller Union ammunition into their smoothbored muskets in a desperate attempt to keep up their fire.

At this point Pillow apparently lost his nerve. He ordered Buckner, whose troops commanded the centre of the line, to withdraw to his original position on the right. Buckner was infuriated. Success was theirs, the way to Nashville was open. But Pillow would not be budged. Buckner then rode off to find Floyd, the attack stalled while this high-level bickering went on. Floyd returned to Pillow's command post with Buckner and the two lower ranking generals argued it out in front of their commander.

Pillow claimed that there were still large numbers of Federal reinforce-ments to their front and that the Confederates just couldn't continue their advance. Moreover, he said, the Confederates were already falling back, fol-lowed closely by Union troops. Buckner said that their door out was still open and a retreat was unnecessary. A good general would have gone to the front to see for himself. Floyd was not a good general. Instead, he ordered Buckner's men back to the original positions. He then had all the sick and wounded, together with the prisoners taken in the attack, put into boats and sent up-river.

Meanwhile, Grant, who had been away conferring with the naval com-mander, returned and ordered a counter-attack on the Confederate left which he thought must have been weakened to bolster the attack on the right. Before Buckner's men had a chance to fall back, Union troops came storming in with the bayonet and carried part of the Confederate advanced line at a point that was defended by only a single regiment. Buckner's men fought for two hours to retake this position, but failed. Apparently inspired by the success on their right, Union troops on the left, where the Confederate attack had fallen, slowed down their retreat, fighting ruggedly.

At the end of the day Union guns were again facing all the Confederate lines virtually in the same positions where both sides had begun that morning.

Still, in the minds of the Confederates, the day had mostly been a success, and had shown that they could escape from the trap at Fort Donelson. The men fully expected to return to the attack first thing in the morning and this time finish the job, but their generals felt that this would be impossible; with the reinforcements that had just arrived, they reckoned that the Union Army now numbered more than 50,000 men. Scouts reported that the Wynn's Ferry road had been retaken and the only other escape route, along a river road to Cumberland City, was under three feet of ice-cold water. It would be impassable for infantry, let alone the artillery, wagons and ambulances with the sick and wounded.

That evening Pillow, who had lost his nerve, called a conference of Floyd, Buckner, Johnson and his chief engineer, Major Gilmer, at the Dover Inn. Pillow and Floyd were convinced that Grant had heavily reinforced his lines and that the battle was lost. It is perhaps surprising to find that Buckner was among those who agreed with him, but it should be remembered that he had been under tremendous stress for some days and was apparently on the verge of a breakdown. None of them had any idea what if anything Johnston was doing with regard to their relief, or even what it was he wanted them to do.

Before coming to a decision the generals sent a scout to find out if the Union troops had indeed reoccupied the trenches they'd lost earlier that day. He returned quickly to say that they had. Floyd and, by now Buckner, said that another attack would be out of the question, doomed to failure. 'Then we can fight them another day in our trenches,' Pillow said, 'and by tomorrow night we can have boats enough here to transport our troops across the river and let them make their escape to Clarksville.'[14]

Buckner was less sanguine about being able to hold an attack that he felt sure would hit first thing in the morning. 'I am confident', he told the group, 'that the enemy will attack my lines by light, and I cannot hold them for half an hour.'

'Why so,' Pillow asked. 'Why so, general?'

'Because I can bring into action not over 4,000 men, and they demoralized by long and uninterrupted exposure and fighting, while they can bring any number of fresh troops to the attack.'

'I differ with you,' Pillow said. 'I think you can hold your lines; I think you can, sir.'

'I know my position, and I know that the lines cannot be held with my troops in the present condition.'

It was clear that Buckner, the best general of the lot, was used up.

Floyd broke the silence that followed. 'Then, gentlemen, a capitulation is all that is left us.'

Pillow, not ready to surrender, said, 'I do not think so; at any rate we can cut our way out.'

'To cut our way out would cost three-fourths of our men, and I do not think any commander has a right to sacrifice three-fourths of his command to save one-fourth,' Buckner said.

'Certainly not,' agreed Floyd.[15]

The group called for their cavalry chief to attend the meeting. Forrest arrived and was shocked at what he heard. He was against surrender, saying that his scouts had found only enemy dead and wounded on their front, but that he would send out more scouts to reconnoitre the battlefield and find an escape route. Forrest later reported: 'I am clearly of the opinion that two-thirds of our army could have marched out without loss, and that, had we continued the fight the next day, we should have gained a glorious victory.'[16]

Forrest was overruled however. Floyd agreed with Buckner and, bowing to their opinion, Pillow agreed that their only choice was to surrender.

While the other generals were discussing the turn of events, Pillow drew his brigade quartermaster and commissary officers aside and told them to be ready to burn all the supplies they had on hand. At what time should this be done the quartermaster asked. 'About daybreak,' Pillow said. 'About 5.30 o'clock.' With that, the quartermaster left to begin his preparations.[17]

Floyd, whose pre-war activities had led to his being accused of high treason, was, not unnaturally, worried as to what sort of treatment he could expect in the hands of the northern troops. He asked Buckner, 'If you are put in command, will you allow me to take out my brigade?'[18]

Buckner agreed: 'I will, provided you do so before the enemy receives my proposition for capitulation.'

In fact, however, Pillow was the second ranking officer. Floyd said to him: 'I turn the command over, sir.'

Without missing a beat, Pillow said to Buckner, 'I pass it.'

Buckner said, 'I assume it.' He then turned to a staff officer in the room: 'Give me pen, ink, and paper, and send for a bugler.'[19]

Then Forrest spoke up: 'I think there is more fight in our men than you think, but if you will let me I will take out my command.' Both Buckner and Floyd agreed to let Forrest make the attempt.

Forrest said to Pillow: 'General, I fought under your command. What shall I do?'

Pillow replied: 'Cut your way out.'

'I will, by God!' Forrest replied.[20]

Buckner wrote a note proposing terms of surrender. He also arranged for white flags to be prepared to be placed along the line during the anticipated truce and for a bugler to sound the ceasefire when the time came.

Then the generals, except Buckner, who was still writing, left the room. Major W. H. Haynes, brigade commissary officer, told Buckner about Pillow's order to destroy the commissary stores. 'Major Haynes,' Buckner said. 'I countermand the order.'[21]

After the conference Forrest rode back to his camp. Meeting his staff he announced: 'Boys, these people are talking about surrendering, and I am going out of this place before they do or bust hell wide open.'[22] He gave orders for the men to get ready to move out.

At about three in the morning of the 16th, Pillow ran into Major Gilmer and told him that the fort would soon be surrendered and he and his staff were going down to the river to find a way to escape. Gilmer said that he would join them. They found a rowing-boat in the town and made their way to Clarksville and safety. Pillow would never again hold a Confederate combat command: he spent most of the remainder of the war supervising the Tennessee Volunteer and Conscript Bureau, until being appointed Commissary General of Prisoners which is how he ended the war.

Sunrise on the 16th was about 6.35, but Forrest's cavalry were ready to move out at about 4 o'clock. Two Kentucky companies and Colonel George Gantt's Tennessee battalion did not join Forrest, for reasons unknown. One soldier told the general that he would not come along because he felt he should share the fate of the others.

'All right,' Forrest said. 'I admire your loyalty, but damn your judgment.'[23]

Then Forrest led his group along the river to a point where he thought they could get through the surrounding Union line. Scouts reported a large body of Union infantry immediately to their front. Forrest and his brother rode forward to reconnoitre and found that the 'infantry' consisted of a row of fence posts silhouetted against the dark sky and giving the appearance of a picket line.

The command remounted swiftly and rode on. Reaching a point where the overflowing Cumberland River blocked their way, Forrest called for a volunteer to ride out into the icy water. Not a man came forward, so Forrest himself plunged in and found the water only 'saddleskirt deep'.[24]

Leaving behind a small rearguard, the command continued on their way. By now the men had been en route for two hours, but contrary to the generals' expectation no enemy troops had been encountered. Forrest reported that 'not a gun had been fired at us. Not an enemy had been seen or heard.'[25] When the troopers reached a small village they halted briefly while farriers shoed some of the exhausted horses. On 18 February they were riding down the streets of the state capital, Nashville.

While Forrest and his men were leaving, Floyd and the two Virginia regiments directly under his command boarded the only steamboat docked at Dover. He ordered a Mississippi infantry regiment to stand guard, to make sure that no one else attempted to board the boat. The Mississippians, fully expecting to be taken aboard after the Virginians, did as they were ordered. When the last Virginian was aboard, however, Floyd had the gangways taken up and the boat steamed off, leaving some very unhappy Mississippians and others behind.

J. J. Montgomery, a member of Lowry's Scouts, ran for the river to try to escape when he heard that the fort was to be surrendered. There he 'found the steamer *Gen. Anderson* waiting to carry off Pillow [Floyd], horses, negroes, and baggage. I went to headquarters and made every effort to get aboard, but appealed in vain, as they were afraid the boat would sink. However, I saw three horses and two negroes with baggage taken on afterwards. It was then early daylight, and I returned to camp with no hope, only to submit to whatever might happen.'[26] In fact, Pillow's horse, baggage and servant were able to board the *General Anderson* and head for safety, as well.

After Floyd reached safety, he lost his commission, by direct order of Jefferson Davis on 11 March 1862.

Colonel John W. Head, who commanded a brigade, learned that surrender was eminent. Sick with a bad cold, which he feared would turn to pneumonia, he asked a surgeon what he should do. The surgeon said that in his condition it was unlikely that he would survive a prison camp. He then asked Buckner if it would be all right for him to escape. Buckner said that it was up to him, but as for himself he thought it his duty to remain and share the fate of his men. Head disagreed and made his escape up-river, leaving his command behind. When he reported to A. S. Johnston with his story, he was told that he would not receive another command and, realizing that what he'd done was contrary to the unwritten code, Head resigned his commission.

Back at Fort Donelson, Buckner sent the following message to the besiegers: 'In consideration of all the circumstances governing the present situation of affairs at this station, I propose to the Commanding Officer of the Federal forces the appointment of Commissioners to agree upon terms of capitulation of all the forces and fort under my command, and in that view suggest an armistice until 12 o'clock to-day.' At the same time he sent couriers to the commanders in the outer line telling them that he had applied for terms and that they should cease fire and raise white flags of truce. Grant's reply was: 'Yours of this date, proposing armistice and appointment of Commissioners to settle terms of capitulation, is just received. No terms except an unconditional and immediate surrender can be accepted. I propose to move immediately upon your works.'

Buckner was shocked. The garrison had fought well and hard, and he had not anticipated such a brusque response, particularly from Grant who had been a close friend in the pre-war US Army. It was unheard of in previous wars, where defending garrisons were allowed to depart with their colours, often their arms, but he had no choice. He wrote back to Grant: 'The distribution of the forces under my command, incident to an unexpected change of commanders, and the overwhelming force under your command, compel me, notwithstanding the brilliant success of the Confederate arms yesterday, to accept the ungenerous and unchivalrous terms which you propose.'[27]

Fort Donelson was in Union hands. With it came the largest group of Confederate soldiers, some 9,000 men, to become Union prisoners of war to date. In fact Grant did allow the captured Confederate enlisted men to bring their belongings and blankets, and commissioned officers were allowed, at least initially, to retain their sidearms.

Victorious Union troops pillaged the Confederate camps although, as even Buckner admitted, Grant and his officers tried to stop them. But this had been their first major victory, and souvenir hunting could not be prevented.

Amidst the confusion, at about sunset on the 18th Confederate divisional commander Bushrod Johnson and one of his staff officers strolled towards the now vacant rifle pits. No sentry stopped them. They continued their walk and soon were on the other side of the Union lines, still without having been challenged. Figuring that they hadn't signed any surrender papers or even been ordered to surrender, the two men escaped the general surrender and prison camp.

The southern public were astounded by this, the first serious defeat of the war. 'At last we have the astounding tidings that Donelson has fallen, and Buckner, and 9000 men, arms, stores, everything are in possession of the enemy!' wrote War Department Clerk J. B. Jones in his diary. 'The Southern people cannot be daunted by calamity!'[28]

Robert Kean, head of the Bureau of War, noted in his diary: 'The way is now open to Nashville; Columbus is cut off, and will of course be, probably has been, evacuated. Bowling Green has been evacuated; our western connections are doubtless cut; vast supplies, especially of pork, doubtless lost or destroyed. Dangers close us round on every side. The timid will begin to croak, the half-hearted to quail and suggest submission, the traitorous to agitate. Redoubled effort, nerve, decision, firmness are essential in all who love the Southern land, and Freedom.'[29]

The end had begun.

5

The Campaign in New Mexico
21 February to 24 April 1862

'There's gold in those hills,' people had said of California since that precious metal was discovered at Sutter's Mill in 1848. And gold is what the Confederacy needed to buy the military and civilian supplies it could not manufacture within its borders. So when the Civil War began a professional soldier, Henry H. Sibley, came up with a plan to capture those goldfields and the silver deposits in Colorado, and thereby extend the young Confederacy from the Atlantic to the Pacific. Sibley, a member of the West Point class of 1831, had been stationed in the New Mexico Territory before the war. He had had a great deal of experience in the west while serving in the US Army's expedition against the Mormons, as a squadron commander in the 1860 Navajo Expedition, and in the Mexican War when he had been breveted for bravery. When Sibley's native state of Louisiana left the Union he resigned his US Army commission, going directly to Richmond to give President Jefferson Davis his plan to capture California

According to Sibley's plan a single brigade, organized in Texas, would move north-west, capturing Union Army supplies from the western forts which would fall like dominoes. His men could buy additional food and clothing from southern sympathizers already living in the west. Indeed, many of these sympathizers would join his ranks. The Union forces in his way, weakened by the resignation of so many southern officers, would offer, he believed, little or no resistance. Sibley would drive north through the silver-lode areas of Colorado through Nevada into Utah, there to connect with the Mormons who were unhappy with the policies of the government in Washington and possibly might form a helpful alliance with the southern government, and finally move on to the Pacific Ocean and the goldfields of California.

Also, according to one of his officers, Major Trevalion T. Teel, 'Sibley intimated that there was a secret understanding between the Mexican and the Confederate authorities, and that, as soon as our occupation of the said states was assured, a transfer of those Mexican states [Chicuahua, Sonora and lower California] would be made to the Confederacy.'[1]

Davis was probably unaware at this time that Sibley was suffering from a chronic ailment which led him to drink to ease his pain. By this point, he was an alcoholic, often drunk when it was least convenient. It was a problem that would haunt the Confederacy's effort in the south-west. Moreover, according to Major Teel, 'General Sibley was not a good administrative officer. He did not husband his resources, and was too prone to let the morrow take care of itself'.[2]

On 17 June 1861 Davis commissioned Sibley a brigadier general and gave him permission to set his plan in motion. Sibley wasted little time, reaching Mesilla, Texas, in December and starting to recruit his brigade immediately. He found it slow going. Most Texans wanted to go to Virginia where they thought the most important battles of the war would be fought. Sibley was unable to supply the men he did recruit as completely as units in more eastern climes. One Union private described Sibley's soldiers in May 1862: 'The Texans are principally armed with a double-barreled shot-gun, two *Navy* [i.e., 0.36 calibre Colt] *Revolvers* and a *two-foot Bowie Knife* to each man. They are the most ignorant set of white people I ever came across in my life,' adding that, 'They are mostly boys from 15 to 20, though there are some very intelligent Germans among them.'[3]

The Union soldier pointed out one problem that Sibley had – obtaining sufficient weapons. Neither the Confederacy nor the state of Texas could supply weapons to his Regiments of Texas Mounted Volunteers. Sibley's ordnance officers bought what they could on the open market, but this meant that his men had a plethora of different types and calibres of weapons, including ' ... squirrel guns, bear guns, sportsman's guns, shotguns, both single and double barrel, in fact guns of all sorts, even down to guns in the shape of cannon called "Mountain Howitzers.".'[4] Indeed, several companies received 9-foot-long lances taken from the Mexican Army in the war of 1846-8 and possibly even from the War of Texan Independence.

Nor were his men clad in anything like regulation Confederate uniforms. Some Texas-made jeans cloth uniforms were issued, but most men marched off towards the Pacific Ocean in the civilian clothes they had brought from home.

On 29 January 1862, his men having been organized and at least rudimentally trained at Fort Thorn, Sibley marched them north, across the Rio

Grande towards his first target, Fort Craig, New Mexico. On 12 February his scouts captured some 21 New Mexico volunteers from that fort. The next day the Texans reached the river where they saw the US flag still flying over the fort's walls. Not wishing to make a direct attack, Sibley drew up his troops on a level plain south of the fort and waited for the Union forces to come out to give battle. The northern commander didn't want to risk his smaller force, which numbered some recruits as well as Regular Army soldiers, and stayed within the fort's walls. After waiting for a while, Sibley recrossed the river and headed north towards Valverde ford. His plan was to cut the Union garrison off from Santa Fe, its area headquarters and source of supplies and reinforcements.

By the 19th, Sibley's men had reached the Rio Grande near Paraje, and by the 20th had encamped on the other side of the river opposite Fort Craig. They were already running short of food: Sergeant A. B. Peticolas, 4th Texas, noted in his diary on the 21st that water was extremely scarce and all they had to eat was dried beef.

Early in the morning of 21 February Sibley's advance guard, led by Major Charles L. Pyron, headed towards the Valverde ford over the Rio Grande. There they found that Union troops had beaten them to it and they came under fire from the other side of the river. At about 11 a.m. Captain Teel, 1st Texas Artillery, led his 4-gun battery to the river bank where they unlimbered and returned fire as the rest of the Confederate troops behind formed into lines. The Union troops had the advantage of numbers, however, and forced the Confederates back with their steady fire. 'Shell and round shot and minié balls came whistling in showers over our heads,' wrote Sergeant Peticolas, 'bombs burst just behind and before, and trees were shattered and limbs began to fall, a horse or two was shot, and presently they brought back one of Teel's artillery men severely wounded. At almost the same time another was shot dead, but in the hail of bullets Teel stood bravely to his post, and his battery returned the fire of the enemy with great spirit.'[5]

Soon the Union artillery shifted its position to the left and Teel's battery followed suit. With that, Union cavalry dashed across the ford towards the gap left by the Confederate artillery. The Confederates quickly remounted and fell back as the Union troopers came on, charging the retreating Texans with drawn sabres. The Texas troops halted and dismounted just in front of an old river channel of the Rio Grande, determined to make their stand there. Sibley, too drunk to maintain control, turned over command of the troops to Texan Colonel Thomas Green.

The men tethered their mules and horses – for both were ridden by the Mounted Volunteers – and took cover wherever they could as the Union troops also dismounted and began to fire into the Confederates. 'One man on my left, in [Captain David A.] Nunn's Company was shot through the back, as he raised to load, by a flank fire, and fell with heart rending groans,' Peticolas wrote. 'Asking some one to load his gun, which was done, he fired at them again, although he had a wound which proved mortal.'[6]

By about 3 p.m. the main Union infantry force came up and joined the cavalry. Fire grew in volume. '[William H.] Onderdonk was shot through the mouth and his tongue nearly shot out,' Peticolas wrote. 'He pulled out a part of it which was hanging ragged to the edge of the tongue and cut it off with his knife. He then gave his knife to Al Field and told him to give it to his brother. He was borne off the field.'[7] The Confederates appeared to be in a desperate situation, their backs to the old river bed, even though they could see that their fire was cutting down Union troops. In desperation, Major Henry W. Raguet led his cavalry on the right flank in a dashing charge. It was met by a hail of smallarms fire and a single artillery shell exploded directly in the middle of the group of cavalry. The bloodied horsemen fell back. The Union commander, Colonel E. R. S. Canby, now figured the battle was his.

He was wrong. Just as Raguet's cavalry fell back, Green led his infantry, armed with Bowie knives and Colt revolvers, directly at the startled Union line. In fierce hand-to-hand fighting Green's men took a Union 6-gun battery, killing the battery commander and many of his men. Major Samuel A. Lockridge, 2nd Texas, led his men forward to the battery, reached out with a hand to touch one of the Union cannon and said, 'This is mine'.

'Shoot the son of a bitch,' the Union artillery chief, Captain Alexander McRae, who was to die in battle here, shouted. A defending Union artilleryman shot Lockridge just as McRae spoke, and the major sagged to the ground, saying, 'Go on my boys, don't stop here.'[8] Another artilleryman thrust a lit match into an open limber chest just as a Confederate attacker aimed his pistol at him. The chest erupted in a tremendous explosion, killing the artilleryman if the pistol shot hadn't. But the rest of the Union infantry, disoriented by the sudden turn of events, fell back, and the Union commander was forced to call a retreat. Confederate artillerymen pulled two howitzers forward and set them up to fire on the retreating Union forces.

While they were falling back, Green was joined by five companies of cavalry. He sent the reinforcements after the retreating Union troops, many of his own men lacking their mules and horses which had been killed in the fire fight by the river bed. Soon a handful of Union troops returned, however, as the Union commander raised a flag of truce to carry off his dead and wounded. In the meantime, many Confederates took advantage of the victory to scour the battlefield for horses, food, superior weapons, military equipment and uniform items such as overcoats.

Union losses amounted to some 68 killed, 160 wounded and 35 missing out of about 3,800 involved. The survivors withdrew to the protection of Fort Craig's walls. Sibley's men lost 36 killed, 150 wounded and one missing from their approximately 2,000 officers and men. Some 43 Confederate and seventeen Union soldiers later died of their wounds.

In what could be seen as an omen of things to come, while the battle at the ford was going on New Mexico militia found and burned some 30 Confederate supply wagons filled with mess kits, blankets, books and regimental records which Sibley had been forced to abandon some four miles south of Valverde. At the time this did not seem an important loss, but added to a number of such losses later it would drastically affect Sibley's campaign.

On the whole, Sibley's plan appeared to be working. The way west was open. The dark side of the victory at Valverde was the discovery, which may have been disheartening to the general, that the Union troops would fight – the campaign would not be a simple matter of marching. Even so, after staying by the battlefield for several days to clean up and care for the wounded, Sibley decided to ignore Fort Craig, and go for Albuquerque and Santa Fe, the two sizeable towns in the area, and then go for Fort Union. The men desperately needed the supplies they were sure to find in the two towns; they were already worrying about a lack of forage for their horses in this part of the country. Union troops, aware of the Confederate supply situation, scoured the countryside to locate food supplies stuffs which they either destroyed or carried off to Fort Craig.

On 26 February Sibley's troops reached the town of Socorro where, lacking forage for all the animals, he converted some of his units to infantry – much to the disgust of his Texas cowboy soldiers. But supplies would be lacking until the army could take a Federal depot. So Sibley started them marching again, in bitterly cold weather and through sand which blew into their faces. There was no wood for fires at night, but the men found 'buffalo chips' [dried bison dung] which they burned instead.

Instead of supplies, however, the Confederates entering Albuquerque on 7 March found only ashes and burning rubble in what had been the largest supply depot in the entire south-west. The Union troops had burned everything they couldn't carry with them to Fort Union, including hay, reported by one southern sympathizer as enough to last the Texas Brigade for six months. Luckily, there were still some civilian-owned stores where the men were able to get food and clothing to replace that worn out in marches over rugged terrain. Moreover, the retreating Union troops hadn't been able to destroy the depot at Cuberco, about sixty miles west of Albuquerque, so Sibley's men did find some foodstuffs, although not enough to sustain them for an entire campaign.

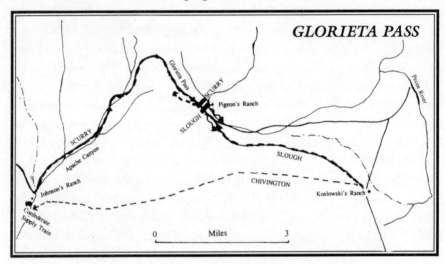

When they reached Santa Fe they found a virtually deserted town. Members of the territorial government had fled through La Glorieta Pass to Las Vegas or Fort Union, and they hadn't been the only ones to leave. Many of the civilians, most of whom were of Mexican origin, had fled from the dreaded 'Texicans', whom they had learned to fear during the Mexican War. There would be no succour there for Sibley's tired men.

The supplies at Fort Union now became the vital target. They learned that Union troops were not going to wait for them there, however, but were advancing towards them. Sibley sent out some of his troops to meet them east of Santa Fe where the terrain would help neutralize the Union numerical advantage.

By 25 March this force had reached the southern tip of the Sangre de Cristo Mountains, some twenty miles south-west of the old Santa Fe Trail west. Sibley sent out a patrol of some 300 cavalrymen and two 6-pound howitzers under Major Pyron to Johnson's Ranch at the far end of La Glorieta Pass. The pass, also known as Apache Cañon, is several miles long, quite narrow at each end but a quarter of a mile across at the centre.

During the afternoon of the 26th Pyron sent a patrol of some 30 men into the pass to see if the Union troops were coming. They never returned – later he learned that they had all been captured – and Pyron's main body was therefore surprised when Union troops came pouring through the cañon. Pyron stayed calm, however, ordering a skirmish line to be formed and getting his two cannon into action.

The Union troops fell back at first under the unexpected artillery fire, but soon their commander, Major John Chivington, sent part of his force through the cottonwood and pine cover along the sloping edge of the cañon, while the others took cover among the rocks. The Union troops worked their way forward to a point where they were able to fire into the Confederate defenders from both sides as well as from the front.

Pyron ordered a retreat of $1^1/2$ miles to a narrow part of the cañon where the rugged terrain would compensate for his smaller numbers. On their way back, they destroyed a bridge across a 15-foot arroyo. This didn't stop Chivington's men long. They soon found the new Confederate line of defences and Chivington repeated his successful tactics of sending men around the flanks.

Again the Confederates fell back, but this time Chivington sent Union cavalry after them, killing a number before withdrawing with some 60-70 prisoners. As dusk fell, the Union commander ordered his men to retire to the nearby Pigeon's Ranch, a well-known place on the Santa Fe trail. The Confederates retired to Johnson's Ranch, from where Pyron sent word back to Galisteo, fifteen miles to the south. Lieutenant Colonel William R. Scurry, on learning of Pyron's situation, left immediately with his 4th Texas to join him, and the remainder of his troops set out directly over the mountains to reach Pylon as quickly as possible.

The night was cold and their route was too steep for the horses to be able to draw the guns so they had to be unhitched and manhandled. Scurry's men reached Johnson's Ranch at about 3 a.m. on the 27th. Exhausted from the march and chilled to the bone, the men fell out to find such kindling as they could and to get some sleep. Sergeant Peticolas and a friend broke into a building on Johnson's Ranch to spend the night out of the wind. 'He and I slept together on the floor with no bedding,' Peticolas wrote, 'and only a few articles of women's wearing apparel which we found scattered round the house.'[9] Still, Scurry now had some 1,100 men under his command, enough, he figured, to fight a successful battle.

In the morning Scurry ordered his men to form a defensive line just beyond the ranch. The infantry dug in behind an embankment and the guns were sited on a hill behind them. Sharpshooters armed with rifled muskets were posted on the walls of the cañon. Throughout the 27th they waited for Chivington to renew the battle, but there was no sign of Union troops. At about 5 p.m. Scurry's baggage train of some 73 wagons arrived and the men were able to get full rations for the first time in two days.

Since the Union commander declined to advance, Scurry decided to take the offensive himself. On the morning of the 28th, leaving his wagons at the ranch, guarded by some 200 cooks, drivers and wounded men, he started down the cañon.

Unknown to Scurry, the Union forces had also been reinforced and they too intended to resume the offensive. The Federal commander, now Colonel John Slough, who had reinforced Chivington, split his force. Some of his troops came directly towards the Confederates, while another group went around La Glorieta Pass to attack from the west in an attempt to trap the Confederates between the two forces.

The Confederates moved out along the road that ran along the centre of the cañon. Peticolas described the terrain: 'The road here down Apache Canion [sic] runs through a densely wooded pine country where you can't see a man 20 steps unless he is moving. The hills slope up from the valley gradually, rising more abruptly as they near the mountains. Heavy masses of rock, too, crown most of these hills, and the timber is low and dense. On the left, the hills rise more abruptly than on the right and the rocks are larger.'[10]

When Scurry's men had reached some way down the cañon, their scouts brought back work of the Federal advance. Scurry sent his cavalry to the rear where they dismounted to form a line of battle. He ordered the artillery forward to a slight elevation in the cañon floor. Pyron's men were placed on the right flank and Raguet's men took the centre. Scurry himself took charge of the left flank.

By about 11 a.m. both sides had formed lines of battle. The Union artillery almost immediately pounded the Confederate guns into silence. The battery commander, Lieutenant Bradford, was hit early on and taken from the field. He was the only officer with the 3-gun battery, and the men took it on themselves to withdraw after he was wounded. When Scurry heard of this he sent a courier to the rear to have the guns brought up again.

Meanwhile, the Union commander advanced a regiment towards the Confederate flanks. The Texans spotted a large number of Union troops working their way forward in a gulch that ran up the centre of an enclosed field on the left. The Confederates jumped over the fence that bordered the field, ran some two hundred yards under enemy fire, and dashed into the gulch. After a hand-to-hand struggle the Union troops fell back in some disorder.

While this was taking place artillerymen under Sergeant Patrick man-handled two guns to the front again, but there was no target in sight; the Union troops were all hidden by terrain and brush. The gunners opened fire in their general direction in the hope of doing some damage.

Scurry sent a force under Major John S. Shropshire towards the right with orders to move forward among the pine trees until they found the enemy. He ordered Pyron's men to support this movement, and the centre troops to charge as soon as they heard firing on their right.

As the troops moved among the pine trees, taking fire from a virtually invisible enemy, Shropshire was hit and killed. Scurry took charge and lead the men towards the enemy at the ranch. Men on the left flank gave cover-ing fire from their positions in the rocks, while the centre troops charged down the road. 'Abe Hanna was shot down on the left in 30 yards of the enemy,' Peticolas wrote. 'Jake Henson, who was on the same side, coming along and seeing Abe down, went to him, gave him water, and began to pick the stones from under him. While in a kneeling position over his wounded friend he was shot and killed, the ball going in at the shoulder and ranging towards the heart. Abe Hanna died about an hour in the night very easily. He was shot in the loins and bled inwardly. He said he felt no pain save that his limbs were numb and dead from his hips down.'[11]

The Union troops fell back to form another defensive position. The Confederates pressed on. 'At this point', Scurry reported, 'their battery of eight guns opened a furious fire of grape, canister, and shell upon our advancing troops.'[12]

The Confederates aimed their attack on the Federal guns, but support-ing Union infantry managed to stop them. Meanwhile, the Union gunners limbered up their guns and fell back. Raguet fell mortally wounded in the final charge that pushed the Federals from the field. As the sun began to set the Federal commander ordered a retreat. The Confederates started to fol-low them, but Scurry had to call it off because of 'the extreme exhaustion of the men, who had been engaged for six hours in the hardest-contested fight it has ever been my fortune to witness'.[13] The Confederates ended up in control of Pigeon's Ranch.

Scurry, who had been grazed on the cheek twice by Union bullets, lost 36 officers and men killed, including some of his best field-grade officers, 60 wounded and 25 missing. Most of the casualties were from the 4th Texas who lost 24 men. The 7th had eight casualties, while the 5th and the artillery had only one each. Scurry had 31 Texans buried that night at Pigeon's Ranch. The Union troops suffered 31 killed, some 50 wounded and 30 missing.

While the battle in the cañon was raging, the second Federal force hiked over the tough San Christobal Trail, across the heights of Rowe Mesa, to Johnson's Ranch where they halted on the crest of a hill overlooking the ranch. One Union soldier wrote how from there they watched 'the unconscious Texans, jumping, running foot races &c.'. After an hour's break to give the men a rest, the Union troops headed down the hill. About two-thirds of the way down a Union officer spotted a Texan and shouted 'Who are you?'

'Texans, God damn you,' came the reply.

'We want you,' the officer said.

'Come and get us God damn you, if you can,' the Texan yelled back as his men loaded and primed an artillery piece.

Meanwhile the Union troops were scrambling down the hill with no semblance of order or formation. Some tripped and rolled down, others leaped like mountain lions from spot to spot. The Confederate guns got off two rounds before the Union troops were in their midst.[14]

The motley crew of defenders was quickly overwhelmed. The chaplain of the 4th, Revd. L. H. Jones, advanced with a white flag to surrender and a trigger-happy Union soldier shot and seriously wounded him.

A group of prisoners taken in the fight at the cañon, guarded by a handful of Confederates, arrived at Johnson's Ranch while the Union troops were destroying Confederate supplies. The Union men who had captured the ranch quickly overpowered the Confederate guards and learned from the freed prisoners that the battle was going against them in the cañon itself. Unable to carry off the supplies, described by a Union soldier as containing 'a great deal of fine officers clothing, fine Mexican blankets and all kinds of military stores, wines, Brandies, pickles, can fruit, oysters, & Navy Revolvers, Double barrel shot-guns &c.', the soldiers set about destroying them.[15] The Federals destroyed virtually all the southern supplies and killed some 500-600 mules and horses with swords and bayonets. They spiked the cannon and burned the carriages. They also set fire to the wagons.

'Each wagon contained from five to twenty-five kegs of powder,' wrote a Union soldier. 'Therefore as soon as the fire would reach the keg of powder the wagons were "no more".'[16]

Then, their commander having received an urgent request for aid from Colonel Slough, they headed back the way they had come to rejoin the main body.

Having collected their wounded and filled their haversacks with anything edible they could find, Scurry's men reached Johnson's Ranch to find a scene of complete desolation. The Union forces had gone, taking some seventeen prisoners with them, leaving behind only dead animals and burned wagons. Anything that hadn't been destroyed had been looted by local civilians.

The Confederates spent a day burying their dead and looking after the wounded. Scouts were sent out, but they found neither supplies nor Union soldiers, so the force retired to Santa Fe to replace their vital supplies. Their retreat was not orderly: the Santa Fe *Weekly Gazette* noted that some 'rode, some walked and some hobbled in'.[17]

As it turned out, there was nothing for them in Santa Fe, either. 'We are resting,' Peticolas wrote, 'but have very poor eating; no bacon nor pork, and very little coffee.'[18] Later he reported that the troops there lived largely on corn meal.

Sibley, who was drunk much of the time, didn't want to give up just yet. Initially he planned to move to Manzano where he could attack Fort Union while maintaining a line of communications with Texas, but this was not to be. Before they could move out, scouts brought word that the Union forces had advanced from Fort Craig and were rapidly moving up the Rio Grande Valley towards them. With enemy forces on both sides of them, Sibley now acknowledged that they had no chance of reaching California and on 8 April began to retreat towards Albuquerque. The Union forces actually reached Albuquerque first, but failed to capture the town from two determined Confederate companies.

The march to Albuquerque was miserable, much of it in a cold rain, and the men had insufficient rations and no adequate clothing. Many of them developed colds and more serious ailments. They straggled into the town over a 48-hour period, 10-11 April, spirits lagging and discipline beginning to disintegrate.

Sibley now toyed with the idea of attacking Fort Union, but feared to do so without adequate food supplies. Instead he chose to retreat, ordering two regiments to start for El Paso on 12 April. The 4th Texas followed on the 13th. Unable to bring all their cannon with them, because of the loss of so many horses and mules at the ranch, the gunners buried eight of the cannon in the Albuquerque plaza; they had already buried several guns at Santa Fe.

On the evening of 13 April the Union forces finally joined up and pursued Sibley's men whom they found at Peralta on 14 April. Rather than attack them with infantry, the Union commander set up artillery and bombarded the southern position. Both sides exchanged shots until at about 2 p.m. a dust storm, common in this part of the world, forced both sides to seek cover. At about 2 a.m. on the 16th, the Confederates retired again towards Texas, the Union commander apparently content to drive them back rather than destroy them. He could not have coped with all the prisoners he would have taken had he captured Sibley's force.

Sibley still thought he had a chance to capture Fort Craig now that its garrison was outside its walls, but the action at Peralta seems to have knocked the fight out of him. He ordered his men off the main road south that led by Fort Craig, instead passing around the Magdalena Mountains to the west of the fort. He ordered the men to burn any excess baggage, allowing each man to carry only a blanket, a set of cooking utensils and the clothes he was wearing.

During the afternoon of 17 April the force began an 8-day retreat though some of the roughest country imaginable. 'The dust and sand has been extremely distressing all day as it blows over us in clouds and almost blinds us as we struggle along through the heavy sand,' Peticolas wrote. 'We left all our most valued articles scattered over the ground in profusion; left the wagons and left our sick men huddled around a fire, with the yellow flag of our hospital waving over them from the corner of a wagon. It was affecting to see the brave companions in arms of these sick men grasping them by the hand and bidding them an affectionate farewell.'[19]

The terrain was largely uncharted and the men had to find their way though a maze of cañons and arroyos. They killed the few oxen they still had with them, and some men managed to kill bears and antelope. Some ate nothing but the bread they'd brought with them during the entire trip.

The Union troops on the other side of the river, whose march paralleled that of the Texans, were constantly in sight. But both sides were too busy just keeping moving to attempt anything like a fight, even had the commanders wanted one, which they did not.

The Confederates dragged along their few remaining wagons, some of which were owned by the many civilian women and children, families of southern sympathizers, who accompanied the column. These continued to slow the soldiers down. On 19 April Private William R. Howell, 2nd Texas, noted in his diary: 'Burn up all our wagons and the pack mules. Also burn 100 rounds cannon ammunition and all the caissons. We travel over an awful rocks mountainous track about 25 miles and camp at Steele's Spring. As this is my first day on foot and me very feeble, I don't get into camp until 10 pm and as all have gone to bed, I can't find my company and have to lay by a fire all night without my blanket.'[20] While the wooden artillery carriages burned, some soldiers dug a pit and hid at least one, possibly three, 12-pound howitzers in it. But they kept nine guns with the column, guns that had to be manhandled over mountains much of the way.

'The brigade presents a singular appearance this morning,' wrote Peticolas on 19 April. 'A great many of the infantry, tired of marching through the heavy sand, have picked up mules, little poor scrawny things, upon which they tie a fold of blankets for a saddle, and with a rope for a bridle strike out, every man for himself, upon the way.'[21]

Water holes were few and far between. In some of them the water was salty, but the men still made coffee with this rank water. Many of the water holes had been poisoned, Mescalero Apache Indians having dumped the putrid carcasses of sheep in them in a further endeavour to destroy the Texas brigade. Water became the prime concern as the column worked its way across the arid terrain. 'I walk hard all day and pass one water hole but not enough water for sick,' noted Private Howell in his diary on 23 April. 'They keep going across a plain. Travel until 9 p.m. and not getting to water, a dry camp is made. I go to bed hungry and thirsty, but being completely broken down, I sleep soundly.'[22]

Union soldiers who followed at a distance found signs of a totally demoralized army. In one place they found three dead Confederates half-buried in hard sand; elsewhere a man's arm that had been gnawed by wolves. Parts of gun carriages, the barrels having been buried, had been abandoned along the way, together with wrecked ambulances, carriages, limbers and caissons. All sorts of personal items had been dropped by men desperate to lighten their loads.

'On passing over the route of these unfortunate men, nearly a year after,' a Union officer later wrote, 'I not infrequently found a piece of a gun-carriage, or part of a harness, or some piece of camp or garrison equipage, with occasionally a white, dry skeleton of a man. At some points it seemed impossible for men to have made their way.'[23]

Finally, on 24 April, Sibley's exhausted, starving men reached the Alamosa River where they found supplies, reinforcements and mail.

Looking back, Teel said the campaign failed because of a 'want of supplies, ammunition, discipline, and confidence'.[24] Sibley could think of no way in which he could overcome these necessities and bring his weary brigade back for another try against a determined, larger Union force. Instead, he continued his retreat back to Texas. The next day the brigade reached the Rio Grande easily. The invasion of New Mexico was over.

6
The Assault on Fredericksburg
13 December 1862

On two occasions Major General George B. McClellan had the Union's Army of the Potomac in a position to end the war. The first time, in early 1862, he had brought the army up the peninsula to just outside Richmond where he was out-generalled and foiled by Robert E. Lee. He had a second chance at Antietam in September when a set of orders showing the disposition of Lee's spread-out army in an invasion of Maryland fell into his hands. Although the two armies fought each other to a stand-still in the bloodiest single day of the war, McClellan did not destroy Lee's army, nor did he make a move to follow up during the subsequent months. Finally, in desperation Lincoln removed the popular McClellan and replaced him with a corps commander, Major General Ambrose E. Burnside.

Burnside, a West Point graduate turned industrialist and carbine inventor, first set about the reorganization of his army. Where McClellan's largest subordinate unit had been the corps, Burnside created four units which he called 'Grand Divisions'. The II and IX Corps were taken into the Right Grand Division, commanded by Major General Edwin V. Sumner. Major General Joseph ('Fighting Joe') Hooker commanded the Centre Grand Division, which consisted of III and V Corps. The Left Grand Division, made up of the I and VI Corps, was commanded by Major General William B. Franklin. The XI Corps was in the Reserve Grand Division, commanded by Major General Franz Sigel.

Burnside decided to send his army to the east of Lee's forces, directly overland by the shortest route between Washington and Richmond, the Confederate capital and the objective of all previous Union campaigns. His entire plan, which he submitted to Washington for approval on 9 November, depended on speed. He first would concentrate his army near Warrenton from where he would send out a feint across the Rappahannock to make Lee think he was moving towards Gordonsville. At the same time, he would move the entire army quickly to Fredericksburg, on that river.

Before setting off he ordered barges filled with provisions, forage and building materials to be towed to Aquia Creek where they could be easily unloaded. Another supply train loaded with two pontoon bridges for

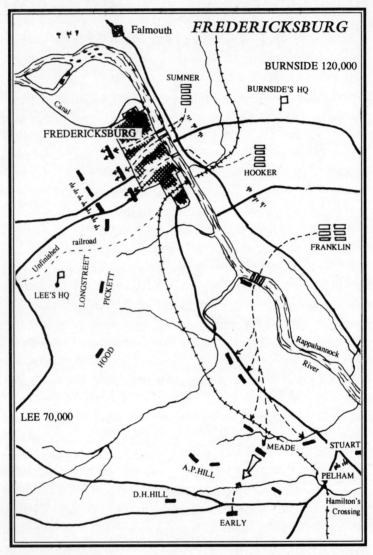

crossing the Rappahannock was directed to Fredericksburg. The army set out on 16 November and by the 19th had reached Stafford Heights on the east bank of the Rappahannock. Opposite them lay Fredericksburg, the home town of George Washington's mother, whose some 5,000 citizens occupied for the most part pleasant brick and frame houses of one or two storeys.

As seen from the Union lines, the town was bordered on its right by a canal running from the river to a point where the river formed a bend. On the left a creek flowed from the heights above the town straight down into the river. The Richmond Fredericksburg & Potomac Railroad passed from the left of the town, where its tracks ran almost parallel to the river, crossed two creeks over bridges, and ran into the town on the southern side. From there it crossed the river going north, but the bridge had been destroyed earlier. Other traffic used a steam ferry which crossed from the centre of the town to a road on the opposite bank of the river.

Burnside's men had reached their position before Lee had had time to react, but, once there, the Union momentum came to a halt. The staff officer responsible for sending pontoons ahead of the army had failed to do his job, having waited until 19 November before sending the pontoon train south, and heavy rains and bad roads thereafter delayed its passage. So there were no pontoons available, and the river was too wide to cross by other means.

The pontoons arrived on 27 November, but the lethargy that had set in in the meantime was not dispelled immediately. Soon after the equipment arrived, General Sumner asked the commanders of the army's two volunteer engineer regiments, the 15th and 50th New York, how long it would take them to get the bridges across the river. They said it could be done in three hours if he would give them the order. After deliberation Sumner said that he would greatly like to do so, but did not wish to make the decision of his own accord for fear that it might conflict with something that Burnside might have in mind.

Burnside seems to have considered crossing immediately, but changed his mind and remained inactive for three weeks before getting the pontons into the river. Later he explained this by saying that his arrangements for the assault had not been completed until 10 December.[1] In the meantime the weather turned. One Union general noted in his diary on 7 December: 'Very cold; plenty of snow. Men suffering; cold outdoors, ice indoors in my room.'[2]

The delay had given Lee time to concentrate his army at Fredericksburg: Lieutenant General Thomas J. 'Stonewall' Jackson's corps arrived from Winchester in the Shenandoah Valley, and Lee's other corps, under Lieutenant General James Longstreet, arrived from Culpeper.

Lee placed his lines along the crest that ran between one and two miles from the river and overlooked the town. His 75,000 men and 300 cannon stretched along a front some seven miles long. Longstreet's corps was positioned behind a 1,200-foot-long stone wall on a road on the ridge known as Marye's Heights. An open plain some two miles wide ran between Jackson's men and the river. Their positions were so strong that one Confederate officer was heard to say that even a chicken could not survive in their fields of fire.

Confronted with a new situation, Burnside seemed unable to make the necessary mental switch. Lee had forestalled him, but he found a new reason for sticking with his original plan. An escaped local African-American told him that the two wings of the widely spread Confederate Army were connected only by a single road, which the Confederate engineers had recently built, just behind the heights overlooking the town. If Burnside's men could cut through the Confederate centre and capture that road, he'd be in a position to turn to either side and destroy a divided enemy. 'I felt satisfied', he reported, 'that if we could divide their forces by piercing their lines at one or two points, separating their left from their right, then a vigorous attack with the whole army would succeed in breaking their army in pieces.'[3] His object had changed from taking Richmond to destroying Lee's Army, a proper enough objective in itself, but one which this plan could not achieve.

While they waited, Burnside's generals discussed the planned attack and most agreed that it would fail. An irritated Burnside summoned a meeting and said that he understood that they opposed the attack. Major General Winfield S. Hancock, nicknamed 'Hancock the Superb' for his spirited fighting in the Peninsula Campaign, said that he thought it would be 'pretty difficult' to take Lee's position on the heights. But Burnside was determined, and his embarrassed generals finally agreed they would do everything possible to make the attack work.

After the meeting broke up, Burnside came upon a nearby group of high-ranking officers, including the assistant adjutant general of the Right Grand Division and the commander of the 9th New York. 'What do you think of it?' Burnside asked the New York colonel. In a spirit more seen in the largely volunteer army of the Civil War than in professional armies of any country or time, the colonel said, 'If you make the attack as contemplated it will be the greatest slaughter of the war; there isn't infantry enough in our whole army to carry those heights if they are well defended.'

Burnside turned to the adjutant. 'Colonel, what do you say about it?'

'I quite agree with Colonel Hawkins. The carrying out of your plan will be murder, not warfare.'

An obviously surprised and irritated Burnside turned and stalked off, muttering something about having victory within 48 hours.[4]

On 13 December, he ordered two corps to the attack. The Right Grand Division was to assault on the right, the Left Grand Division on the left. The Center Grand Division was left as a reserve, ready for the breakthrough that Burnside confidently expected. He had massed some 176 cannon on the bluffs across the river directly opposite the Confederate lines to deliver a pre-assault barrage to clear the way for the infantry.

The two wings were divided by two creeks and almost 3,000 yards, and to achieve their individual objectives would require quite different tactics: the right wing would have to fight their through a town and up a height towards a stone wall; the left to cross cut-up terrain to gain the lower enemy positions – two somewhat different battles which had differing results.

At about 6 a.m. on 11 December, on the right wing, where the largest assault would eventually fall, volunteer engineers began laying down pontoon bridges directly opposite the town, but their task was not easy, and scarcely two-thirds complete when they came under fire from a Mississippi infantry brigade which had moved forward into the town and deployed in and among the houses. The Mississippi troops also occupied a blockhouse directly opposite the pontoons. Beginning to take casualties, the engineers dropped their tools and fled to the safety of the river bank.

As the Federal engineers withdrew, Union artillery opened up on the town. A tremendous bombardment tore up buildings, sending bricks and timber flying. At about 10 o'clock the cannoneers ceased fire, so Brigadier General Daniel P. Woodbury, commander of the army's Engineer Brigade, led a group of volunteers from the 8th Connecticut Infantry to provide covering fire while the engineers resumed their work. Again enemy fire began to drop the engineers. As soon as they reached the bridge, the leading Connecticut infantrymen were brought down and the rest ran back to cover, followed hastily by the engineers.

'I was greatly mortified in the morning,' reported General Woodbury, 'to find that the pontoniers under my command would not continue at work until actually shot down. The officers and some of the men showed a willingness to do so, but the majority seemed to think their task a hopeless one. Perhaps I was unreasonable.'[5]

As it turned out, dense fog which hampered the enemy artillery, and protection afforded by the buildings meant that the Mississippi troops had taken very few casualties from the impressive bombardment. Indeed, even the few civilians who had remained to try to protect their homes when the fighting started, hid in their cellars and escaped largely unharmed.

The artillery opened up again, but after a futile half-hour stopped, and there was a lull while the Union commanders wondered what to do. They decided to try to burn the enemy out. At about 12.30 p.m. all the artillery batteries were ordered to open fire with shell and solid shot in an endeavour to burn the town. After about two hours Union observers could see that they had set several houses ablaze, probably from blasting apart fires set inside houses to keep the defenders warm.

The next phase of clearing the town began. Under a very heavy barrage, three infantry regiments, the 7th Michigan and 19th and 20th Massachusetts, dashed forward and climbed into the pontoons. While being poled across by engineers, one man was killed and several wounded, including the lieutenant colonel of the 7th Michigan. The infantrymen jumped ashore, fixed bayonets and charged into the town. The Mississippi troops, who had been ordered to delay the Federal advance but not to make a full fight of it, withdrew slowly, leaving 31 men behind who were captured within minutes of the landing.

With the river front cleared and in Federal hands, the engineers went back to work and quickly laid three pontoon bridges across the river. The rest of the infantry, followed by support troops such as medical personnel, started across. Confederate troops in and around houses further back, slowed the advance and there was hand-to-hand fighting; in all, 97 Union officers and men fell within fifty yards of the bridgehead. Not until evening was the lower part of the town, almost at riverbank level, cleared of Confederate troops, and the fighting to secure the upper part of the town went on well into the night.

Confederate artillery on the heights above the town had begun to fire on the Union troops crossing by the pontoons as the southern infantry fell back. Wrote one soldier, 'So close indeed did the shells from the Confederate batteries fall to the pontoons that the crossing soldiers were frequently splashed with the water that flew up from the places where they struck the river. It was cooling, but not refreshing.'[6]

Union guns were turned against the Confederate gun positions, firing counter-barrages until about 10.30 p.m. when the darkness concealed all

targets. From then on only sporadic firing was heard; a 9th New York soldier wrote that the streets of the town were silent when his regiment arrived
there between 8 and 9 p.m.

During the hours of darkness the troops broke into houses to avoid
snipers and keep warm; despite the bitter cold, they could not light fires in
the open. Looting began, and soon escalated, the contents of the houses
being tossed out into the streets. Pianos were dragged out to be used as
horse troughs. One officer found a nicely bound copy of *Ivanhoe* in a looted
library and slipped it into his haversack.

Those troops that remained in the streets tore boards and beds from the
houses and wrapped themselves in their overcoats or blankets. They knew
that dawn would bring nought for their comfort. A 9th New York soldier,
returning from picket duty, found a bedstead in an alley and promptly
dropped down on it, without unrolling his blanket in case a sudden formation was called. Damp from the snow beneath it made him so cold that after
a couple of hours he sought refuge by a forbidden fire. The cold night air,
one veteran recalled, was filled with the continuous sound of coughing,
mostly from recruits.

Some barrels filled with tobacco from warehouses that lined the river's
edge had been tossed into the river. Despite the bitterly cold water and the
intermittent shellfire, some of the soldiers dived in and collected them to
sell the contents to their tobacco-starved comrades. Many other soldiers
tried to bring valuables back across the pontoons in the hope of sending
them home, but when their officers found out what was going on, provost
guards were posted to check every man trying to cross, and anything other
than army issue was confiscated.

If this attack were to succeed, absolutely every soldier in blue would
be needed. Men who had had reasonably safe jobs in the rear, such as regimental clerks and cooks, snapped caps on hitherto neglected rifled muskets to make sure they worked. One such conscripted cook in the 116th
Pennsylvania heard cannon firing and asked what that was. 'The rebel
artillery,' he was told. A look of disbelief crossed his face. 'You fellows
needn't think you can fool me,' he said. 'I've heard that noise too often in
Philadelphia; they're unloading boards somewhere.' In a matter of minutes, however, Confederate shells began falling near the pontoon bridges
and, wrote the regimental historian, the cook 'went lumbering to the rear
as though he had forgotten something, and his oleaginous form faded in
the distance'.[7]

Medical personnel set up field hospitals, opening boxes of supplies, laying straw in tents for the wounded, and improvising operating-tables. A divisional hospital was established in a large stone mansion on the riverbank, one of the few houses in which the owner remained, most civilians having fled when the fighting began. One doctor described the owner as 'an old secesh bachelor, very aristocratic in his notions, and highly incensed at the use his house was put to by the "hireling Yankees". But he was taken care of by a guard. His servants cooked for the wounded and our surgeons; his fine larder furnished us delicacies and his cellar rich old wines.'[8]

Meanwhile, the Right Division generals were trying to make sense of a series of conflicting orders from Burnside. At first they were to turn south, cross the creeks between them and the Left Division, and join that division in the attack. This, they thought, was possible since the dark night, and later foggy morning, would hide their movements from the Confederates. But the marching orders never came. The original orders stood.

The battle that followed had no subtlety; there were no clever manoeuvres, only a flat-out charge into almost certain death by a force too large to be destroyed, but too small to overwhelm the defenders.

On the 13th sunrise was at about 7.20 and shortly afterwards the order to begin the assault arrived. But a dense fog, making artillery spotting impossible, filled the river valley, and the generals on the northern side of the river, literally in the dark, delayed the order to move out. While they waited for the fog to lift, the troops were ordered into formation at about 8 o'clock. Finally, at about 10 o'clock, the fog began to lift.

In Sumner's right wing, First Division, II Corps, commander General Hancock briefed his fourteen regimental commanders, ordering them to form the brigades into two lines with a 200-yard gap between brigades. If one line were forced to halt, the next would dash past it, and so on until the heights were carried. The officers returned to their units to brief their subordinates.

While Brigadier General Thomas Meagher was speaking to the men of his famous Irish Brigade, recruited from Irish immigrants in several northern states, Confederate shells fell in their midst, killing and wounding several men of the 63rd and 88th New York Regiments.

Chaplain Thomas Willett, a French-Canadian priest, asked if he could bless the men of the Irish 69th New York, drawn up in battle line and ready to go forward. The colonel readily gave his consent, and received the first blessing himself. Then Willett walked along the line, blessing each man,

Protestants as well as Roman Catholics. Afterwards, the colonel fixed a sprig of evergreen, the brigade's symbol, to the chaplain's hat, adding that he'd 'make an Irishman out of the Father that day'.[9]

Burnside may have thought that his attacks would succeed; the men in the front lines, staring up through the fog to where they knew dug-in southern infantry and artillery were waiting for them, knew it would not. 'I wonder if old Burney expects us to bunt our heads into those rocks?' one soldier asked another as they stood in formation. '"If Johnny Reb had selected a spot to his own liking and invited us to come and be shot he would have chosen this!" said another. There was not a soldier in the ranks but saw the folly of making an attack on those impregnable rocks, and yet when ordered to the attack all went forward willingly, so strong was the spirit of discipline and patriotic devotion in the face of even impossibilities.'[10]

Once in formation the men were told to lighten their loads. They unslung their knapsacks and left them under guard until they could be recovered. Few were seen again. Some officers and men threw away their decks of cards, not wanting their dead bodies to be found with such instruments of the devil as these after the battle. Some commanders now ran through the drill in the manual of arms to keep their officers and men occupied and their minds off what was to come. The final order usually was to load and prime. They were ready to go.

Finally, at about 9.30, the fog lifting, the advance began. The canal on their right being impassable, the men were funnelled straight ahead as they came out of Fredericksburg, deploying from column into line as they emerged. The moment they appeared, the Confederate infantry and artillery opened fire. As the Irish Brigade came into view, a single shell killed or wounded eighteen men from its 88th New York. The colonel of the 116th Pennsylvania was carried to the rear, severely wounded when an exploding shell decapitated a sergeant and killed three other men.

Some of the shell fragments came from Union cannon, whose gunners were setting the fuzes too short. One such shell blew up where the 25th New Jersey was waiting by the river front to go forward. Fragments struck a stack of muskets and shattered one man's leg.

Not everyone went forward. As in every battle, a handful of men from every unit, the traditional malingerers and skulkers, took advantage of the confusion to duck out of the ranks and hide in the ruined houses. The troops of each regiment could see their grim faces staring from porches and windows, and this and the knowledge of what they were going into caused them to advance with something less than parade-ground precision. Veterans admitted that there was some hesitation and unsteadiness as they emerged from the town, but the men closed up and pressed on.

Frequently the advancing troops had to stop, under fire, to tear down fences surrounding gardens and yards between the town and the Confederate lines. Soldiers of the 118th Pennsylvania reached one such fence, 'about five feet high, of three boards, with intervals between them. Opposite the centre and right, the boards had been torn off down to the one nearest the ground. The fatality that had followed the delay in their removal was marked by the bodies of the dead lying there, one upon another. To the left, the boards still remained; the men heroically seized and tore them all away, some climbing over. Thinned out, exhausted, with energies taxed to their limit, in the face of such fearful odds, instinctively the line halted.'[11]

Having got their breath back, the men pressed on, stumbling and falling into muddy ditches, picking themselves up, and jogging on to join their ranks. Ambulance corpsmen tried to help the wounded back into Fredericksburg, only to die themselves in the fury of the fire. In the 48th Pennsylvania every ambulance corpsman but two were killed or wounded. Regiment after regiment got to within 25 yards of the stone wall which was lined with grey-coated Confederate infantry, only to falter under the intensity of the firing. Units, their ranks ripped apart by shellfire, became disorganized. Officers had their horses killed beneath them and could no longer direct their men.

Some of the troops charged through a brickyard, facing additional danger from bricks flying as they were hit by shells. Many of their wounded crawled to the shelter of the kiln to try to escape the hail of bullets. Soon the wounded behind the kiln were piled on top of one another as more and more of them tried to find shelter.

'Officers and men fell in rapid succession,' wrote an officer of the 116th Pennsylvania. 'Lieutenant Garrett Nowlen fell with a ball through the thigh. Major Bardwell fell badly wounded, and a ball whistled through Lieutenant Bob McGuire's lungs. The orderly sergeant of Company H wheeled around, gazed upon Lieutenant Quinlan, and a great stream of blood poured from a hole in his forehead, splashing over the young officer, and the sergeant fell dead at his feet. Captain John O'Neil ... was shot in the lungs, the ball passing completely through his body. But on the line pressed steadily. The men dropping in twos, in threes, in groups. No cheers or wild hurrahs as they moved towards the foe.'[12]

Right: The bombardment of Fort Sumter as seen from a Confederate battery. (*Harper's Weekly*)

Below: The guns on the top level of the walls were the fort's largest, but could not be brought to bear because the walls were being raked by Confederate fire. (*Harper's Weekly*)

Left: Civilians lined the rooftops of Charleston to watch the southern batteries fire on Fort Sumter. Union ships with reinforcements and supplies can be seen just beyond the bar of the harbour, unable to enter because of the Confederate cannon. (*Harper's Weekly*)

Below: A Federal picket post overlooking the Potomac. (*Harper's Weekly*)

Right: Federal troops of General Stone's command, at Edward's Ferry, not far from Ball's Bluff. The Potomac River is seen here, and the heights across the river along the Virginia shore. (*Harper's Weekly*)

Right: Federal troops making a dash from the heights of Ball's Bluff to the Potomac in a desperate attempt to escape.

Below: US Navy gunboats approaching Fort Henry. The Kentucky shore is on the right, the Tennessee on the left. (*Frank Leslie's Illustrated Newspaper*)

THE UNION GUN-BOATS ADVANCING UP THE TENNESSEE RIVER TO THE ATTACK OF FORT HENRY, TENNESSEE.—[SEE PAGE 115.]

Above: Federal gunboats steaming up the Tennessee River towards Fort Henry (centre left). Note that the fort is almost surrounded by water. The incomplete Fort Heiman is on the opposite side of the river, just above Henry. (*Harper's Weekly*)

Below: Federal gunboats capture Fort Henry. The fort is by now almost entirely surrounded by water. The infantry camp's white tents can be seen in the left background. (*Harper's Weekly*)

Right Wing.   Schwartz's Battery.   Taylor's Battery   Battery, Rifle Pits.   Water Battery.   Rifle Pits.   Water Battery.   Fort Donelson.   General Smith's Charge, Iowa Second.

Above: Fort Donelson had a rather better command of the river than had Fort Henry. The horizontal white lines indicate the batteries built along the river. (*Harper's Weekly*)

Below: Top, the Confederate camp's small log cabins spread out well beyond the walls of Fort Donelson. Below, the river as seen from inside the fort. (*Harper's Weekly*)

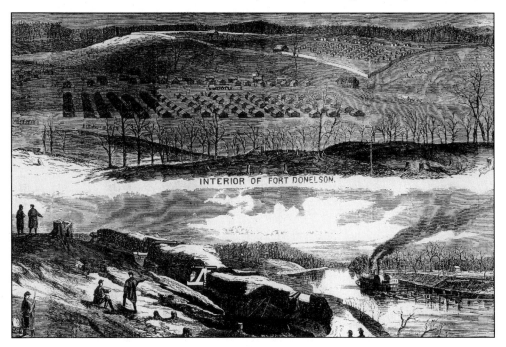

INTERIOR OF FORT DONELSON.

Above: Charge of the 2d Iowa Infantry Regiment on the Confederate works of Fort Donelson towards evening on the Saturday. (*Frank Leslie's Illustrated Newspaper*)

Below: Confederate prisoners taken at Fort Donelson. According to the artist who sketched them, they were dressed in all manner of rags including pieces of carpet. (*Frank Leslie's Illustrated Newspaper*)

Above: Federal batteries bombarding Fredericksburg prior to the assault, in an attempt to drive off Confederate skirmishers who were firing on Union engineers building the pontoon bridges. (*Frank Leslie's Illustrated Newspaper*)

Right: Federal infantry-men use pontoon boats as invasion craft while engineers continue work on the pontoon bridge across the Rappahannock. The odd puffs of smoke in Fredericksburg betray the presence of Confederate snipers. (*Frank Leslie's Illustrated Newspaper*)

Left: Having landed from the pontoon boats, Federal infantry charge up the Rappahannock River bank to drive Confederate sharpshooters out of the town of Fredericksburg. Notice how badly damaged the buildings had been in the earlier, unsuccessful Federal bombardment. (*Harper's Weekly*)

Below: Federal troops advance through the streets of Fredericksburg. Looters have already been at work as evidenced by the items flung into the street. (*Harper's Weekly*)

Above: Fredericksburg as seen from the Union side of the Rappahannock. The destroyed railroad bridge runs to the centre of the town; a file of infantry is crossing one of the pontoon bridges built below the town. Smoke to the left indicates fighting already going on beyond the town.

Below: Confederate defenders at Fredericksburg had a ready-made fortification in the shape of a stone wall which ran along the crest of Marye's Heights. (*B&L*)

Above: Union troops of the Center Grand Division move past the town of Fredericksburg and up Marye's Heights in this eye-witness sketch. (*Harper's Weekly*)

Left: A Federal officer endeavours to avoid the horror of the charge up Marye's Heights by pretending to be wounded, but is stopped by a provost marshal officer at one of the pontoon bridgeheads. The officer made off back towards the sound of the guns.

Left: Waiting can be the hardest part of battle. These Confederate infantrymen wait for the artillery bombardment to stop before beginning the advance known to history as Pickett's Charge. (*B&L*)

Above: The stone wall just in front of the clump of trees along Cemetery Ridge. A handful of Confederate troops managed to get over the wall and advance a little way into Federal lines. Others ducked behind the wall and exchanged shots with the defenders before managing to get away or surrendering. (*Harper's Weekly*)

Below: A wartime sketch of the clump of trees, left, which the men of Pickett's charge used as their aiming point immediately after the Confederates withdrew. Union defenders still line the wall. (*B&L*)

Above: The view from the top of the sea wall of Battery Wagner showing the defensive works, including a moat which attacking infantry would have to cross. Note how far the men just in front of the first wall are from any defenders in the fort. (*Harper's Weekly*)

Left: The 54th Massachusetts Infantry charge through the moat of Battery Wagner to the top of its walls. An officer near the top falls, perhaps one of the many who were mortally wounded in the attack. (*B&L*)

Right: The CSS *Albemarle*, centre, destroys the Union flotilla near Plymouth, North Carolina.

Right: Fort Pillow just after its capture by Union forces. Note the buildings behind the fort which provided protection for the Confederate attackers, and that the heights from which this sketch was made completely dominate the fort's interior. (*Harper's Weekly*)

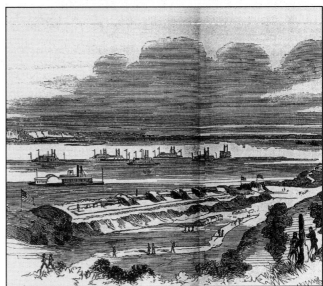

Right: This Goya-like scene depicting the treatment of the Union troops in Fort Pillow after its surrender helped feed Northern animosity towards the southern troops. In the long run, such events did the perpetrators more harm than good. (*Harper's Weekly*)

Left: Sheridan rides to the sound of the guns at Cedar Creek as some of the beaten men of his Union army cheer him. This was one of history's few battles where it can honestly be said that the presence of one man turned victory into defeat. (*Harper's Weekly*)

Centre left: As he drew nearer to the front Sheridan began to find units whose discipline had held and he was soon able to rally them to return to the attack.

Bottom left: The mine under the Confederate lines at Petersburg is detonated, sending tons of earth, men and equipment skywards. (*Harper's Weekly*)

Top right: Federal troops of the IX Corps make a dash from their lines across no man's land and into the Crater, there to be bogged down while the Confederates assemble a hasty defence. (*Harper's Weekly*)

Right: Major James C. Coit, a South Carolinian, who was between the lines under a flag of truce after the Battle of the Crater, made this sketch of the terrain between the crater and the Union lines. The remains of one of his battalion's cannon is lying in the foreground. (*B&L*)

Above: Confederate troops (right) counter-attack Union troops who have halted in the Crater. This post-war engraving captures some of the intensity of that hand-to-hand struggle. (*B&L*)

Right: The interior of Fort Stedman, from a photograph of the time. (*B&L*)

Right: Confederate pioneers chop away abatis outside Fort Stedman as infantry rushe to capture the fort.

The men could do no more. One divisional commander, Major General Darius Couch, watched the assault from the courthouse steeple. 'Oh, great God! see how our men, our poor fellows are falling!' he was heard to say. As he later recalled, 'I remember that the whole plain was covered with men, prostrate and dropping, the live men running here and there, and in front closing upon each other, and the wounded coming back. The commands seemed to be mixed up. I had never before seen fighting like that, nothing approaching it in terrible uproar and destruction. There was no cheering on the part of the men, but a stubborn determination to obey orders and do their duty. I don't think there was much feeling of success. As they charged, the artillery fire would break up their formation and they would get mixed; then they would close up, go forward, receive the withering infantry fire, and those who were able to run to the houses and fight as best they could; and then the next brigade coming up in succession would do its duty and melt like snow coming down on warm ground.'[13]

Burnside refused to give up. In all, the Union commanders launched fourteen charges against the Confederate position along the stone wall at Marye's Heights. After each charge and retreat, the next charge had to pass over more and more blue-clad bodies.

Private Alfred Bellard in the 5th New Jersey, part of the Center Grand Division which was held in reserve, watched as '3 lines of our troops charged up to the stone wall on the double quick, with the shot and shell flying round them like hail stones. It was of no use. They would get close to the stone wall, when they received such a volley of small arms in their faces that they had to fall back, leaving half of their number dead and wounded on the field.'[14]

The terrain was swept with such intensive Confederate fire that many men took shelter in shallow ravines from which they could neither advance nor retreat. Many hid behind dead horses, and would have to wait until nightfall before trying to get back to the Union lines; some of these men lay there for as long as twelve hours. Few ventured to fire. The Confederates were so much better protected than they were, and a single shot from the Union side brought down a hail of retaliatory fire. Some men primed their muzzle-loaders while lying down, jumped up and fired, and dropped quickly to reload. Such games were shortlived however; the Confederate troops soon had their measure and picked them off as they got up.

On the other side of the river, Burnside paced up and down nervously in front of the mansion he had chosen for his headquarters, as he watched his troops being beaten back time and again. 'That crest must be carried tonight,' he was heard to say.[15] But it was not to be. The Union generals launched their last attack at about four in the afternoon, but got no closer to that stone wall than before.

The wounded who could get away in the confusion of the continuing attacks, streamed back into Fredericksburg. Many tried to cross the pontoon bridges, and provost guards checked the severity of their wounds before allowing them to pass.

One officer, a sleeve torn away and a bloody bandage wrapped around his head, was being helped along by two unwounded privates. At the bridge they were stopped by a provost colonel.

'What is the matter with you?' the colonel gently asked.
'I'm wounded,' the officer said, grimacing in pain. The colonel beckoned to a surgeon from the nearby field station over. 'Dress this man's wounds,' he directed. 'I didn't say I was wounded,' the officer said. 'I am sick and want to go over the river to be treated by my own doctor.' The colonel's tone stiffened. 'You can go when this surgeon has examined you and pronounced you unfit for duty.' The officer jumped up, shouting, 'I'll go anyway.' With that the colonel grabbed the officer by the collar, calling for troops to arrest him. The officer twisted out of the colonel's grasp and ran back to the front, followed by his two helpers.[16]

On the whole, however, men did not attempt to evade their duty, but pressed on in what they knew was a hopeless cause.

Finally, such fresh troops as remained were sent forward at sunset, which was at about 4.40, to cover the withdrawal of the survivors. Wrote 9th New York member Edward Wightman: 'Running down a steep bank and through a stream boiling under the shower of shot which played upon it, we climbed a hill over the bodies of dead and wounded men and cast off blankets and knapsacks and, after a moment's exposure to the play of the enemy's battery, formed under the brow of a little ridge, the shot and shell whistling and buzzing over our heads in a most confoundedly malicious manner. Our officers, who had been glad to dismount, now ordered us to lie down, and it was found that we were to support Benjamin's 20 lb. Parrott battery. We did so by lying comfortably where we were and laughing at the screaming bullets until darkness put an end to the contest. Our Orderly Sergeant [Hugo] Schmidt (now, together with Sergeant Cornell, my tent-mate), lying in the second place on my right, was wounded in the back and carried off, and the Lieut. Col. of the 4th R. Island was struck dead from his horse just behind as he led in his regiment to act in concert with us.' Wightman went on to express his astonishment that men could walk at all in such fire without being harmed.[17] There were many miracles that day.

On the left, things were a bit better. By 8.15 on the morning of the 11th, General Franklin had managed to get two pontoon bridges built three miles below Fredericksburg without attracting too much Confederate attention. Some fire was opened on the troops crossing the bridges, but was quickly silenced by artillery and infantry fire.

Franklin began crossing his troops to the southern side early the following day, some 40,000 officers and men being ordered forward even as the attack on the right seemed to be falling apart. According to an eye-witness, the leading troops, of I Corps, were drawn up 'on a plateau near the river; immediately in their front there was a depression several hundred yards in width, which extended to the base of the heights beyond; the Richmond railroad track lay through this hollow, on its western slope. East of the railroad the ground was clear and mostly cultivated fields, but beyond the road, and up the slope to the heights, it was covered with woods. The enemy occupied these heights and the wooded slope, and posted a strong line behind the railroad embankment in the hollow. From the nature of the ground, the movements of the rebels were completely screened from view, whilst every position of the National troops was clearly visible to the enemy.'[18]

Although the attacks were scheduled to begin at daybreak, it was not until 8.30 that the Third Division, I Corps was ordered to send two regiments, the 35th and 38th Pennsylvania Infantry Regiments, forward as skirmishers. They got as far as the railroad cutting, taking cover in the brush and in hollows, and traded shots with the enemy for a full hour before the line behind them received the order to advance.

Initially the Pennsylvanians met with success. Although slowed down by fierce fire, they pushed through the first Confederate line, pursued the retreating southerners up to the stone wall and, hunched and with heads bowed as though making their way against a hail storm, forced their way over the wall.

Trained ambulance corpsmen followed the infantry, giving first aid and bringing wounded back on stretchers to where the ambulances were waiting at field dressing-stations near the bridgeheads. Captain P. I. O'Rourke, 30th Pennsylvania, was in command of a divisional ambulance corps. As the first brigade of his division crossed the railroad and headed up the slope, the brigade commander saw a mounted officer approaching and mistook him for a courier, only to find that it was Captain O'Rourke.

'Why, Captain,' said the colonel, 'I thought you had charge of the ambulance train.'

'So I have.'

'What are you doing then out here on the skirmish line?'

Captain O'Rourke dipped his head as if the answer were obvious and, in a rich brogue, said, 'And, Colonel, will I find the wounded in the rear?'[19]

The Pennsylvanians halted at the stone wall to examine their booty. Private Edward B. Rheem, 36th Pennsylvania, received a sword from an officer of the 1st Kentucky, and the regiment's Corporal Jacob Cart seized the battle flag of the 19th Georgia. But this was to be the high water-mark of Burnside's attack. They dug in there, under fire from three sides, repelling Confederate counter-attacks for an hour before themselves being forced to withdraw. By 2 o'clock they were in retreat, their ammunition exhausted and no reinforcements in sight. The division had suffered 40 per cent casualties.

Nightfall found the ground between the Federals around Fredericksburg and the Confederates above them littered with blue-clad bodies of the dead and wounded. Nervous Confederate infantrymen fired at almost any movement, and few Union men were able to get back to safety.

On the right not one Union soldier had got to within fifty feet of the wall, on the left the slight success had been scotched, and all the Confederate lines were again in southern hands. By nightfall it was obvious, even to Burnside, that the assault had failed and it was called off. 'It seemed', Hancock wryly reported, 'that the defenses of the enemy were too powerful to be taken by an assault of infantry.'[20] Even so, Burnside wanted personally to lead a charge by his old command, the IX Corps, up that bloody slope the next morning, and was only dissuaded by his generals after a long argument.

Later a subordinate general found Burnside alone, obviously badly shaken by the day's events. 'Oh! those men! Oh! those men!' he was muttering. The officer asked what the general meant. He pointed across the river where the ground was still littered with blue-clad bodies. 'Those men over there!' he said. 'I am thinking of them all the time.'[21]

After darkness, the survivors made their way back to the town as best they could. The remnants of units were re-assembled and the rolls were called. Arms were stacked and the men were dismissed to eat and rest. They were warned not to stray because a counter-attack was on the cards.

By about 4 a.m. the battlefield was silent save for the moaning of the wounded. Some Confederates left their positions and came over the wall to help as many of the unfortunates as possible, others came over to plunder.

The temperature fell sharply during the night, which was a mixed blessing in that heart-beats slowed and wounds bled less freely, but this was small consolation to men lying out on snowy or muddy ground, wondering if they would be saved or whether a Confederate bullet would put an end to it all. Some men succumbed, and died of exposure, and some frozen bodies were actually propped up to serve as grisly sentries along the front lines.

Sergeant Edward M. Shriener, Co. K, 44th Pennsylvania, lay mortally wounded and alone. During the night some Confederates seeking warm clothing and full rations which all the Union soldiers had, jostled the sergeant, who groaned aloud. A voice, which he recognized as that of a fellow soldier, Sergeant Charles Hollands, came through the darkness: 'Edward, is that you?'

Now conscious, Shriener gave a secret Masonic sign, which was recognized by one of the Confederates. When they asked him what they could do for him, he asked that Hollands be placed near him. This was done. Next morning, when firing had generally ceased, the Confederate returned and had the two taken back to a Confederate medical facility. From there they were sent on to Richmond where Shriener died; Hollands survived to be paroled, but later died in a Union hospital from the result of his wounds.[22]

The morning after the battle some soldiers came across a seated man wrapped in his blanket, leaning against a wall in the town. '"Wake him up and tell him to move along," one of the soldiers said to another.

The soldier shook him by the shoulder. "I can't," he said, "he's too fast asleep."

"You must."

The soldier pulled the overcoat cape back, intending to give him a vigorous shake. As he uncovered the head, the colourless side-face and triangular hole in the neck told the tale. He was sleeping his last sleep. He must have been struck by a shell the day before, and fallen just where he lay, and some comrade's hand had thrown the cape over his head to hide the ghastly wound.'[23]

Two days later, as a violent rainstorm cloaked the sounds of footsteps and rolling gun-carriages, the Army of the Potomac withdrew across the pontoon bridges. They had suffered 12,553 killed, wounded and missing. Lee's Army of Northern Virginia had lost only 5,309.

It was the lowest point in the life of the Army of the Potomac. One soldier later wrote home: 'The battle did no good at all. Great many lives were lost and for nothing, but I think they have got about enough of the rebs. We shall have to give up to them, the sooner the better.'[24] But in less than seven months they would fight again, in a small town called Gettysburg.

7
Pickett's Charge
3 July 1863

Two years of war in the eastern theatre had, despite a string of resounding Confederate successes, resulted in pretty much of a draw. Early in 1862, the Union Army of the Potomac had thrust through to a position from which the men could see the spires of St. Paul's Episcopal Church in Richmond, only to be stopped in their tracks by the Confederate Army of Northern Virginia under General Robert E. Lee, the man acknowledged by both sides to have been the supreme military genius of the war. Then Lee himself had gone on the attack, north, up through Maryland, only to be stopped at a town named Sharpsburg in September 1862, on the bloodiest day of the war. Stopped, but not defeated. He and his troops waited for a renewed attack which never came, then pulled out, back to Virginia to lick their wounds.

Then the Army of the Potomac moved back south again, again towards Richmond, but this time by the direct route that had brought failure in the spring of 1861. First it attempted simply to steamroller its way through Lee's men at Fredericksburg on a cold December morning in 1862. Then, that having failed disastrously, a flank march was tried, only to stall in a quagmire of rain and melting snow. In May a new Union commander tried the flank again, only to be bluffed, baffled and beaten dramatically by Lee and his invaluable lieutenant, Stonewall Jackson.

Yet Lee did not consider the Union defeat at Chancellorsville satisfactory. First, while reconnoitring between the lines in the dark, Jackson was fired upon by his own men and mortally wounded. Secondly, despite a brilliant strategy, brilliantly executed, which caused entire Union army corps to dissolve and take to their heels, the Army of the Potomac had not been destroyed. It had fallen back sullenly, inflicting great losses on the Confederates, and regrouped to fight again. The longed-for knock-out blow had eluded Lee as it had his opponents.

So, in reality, the situation in the eastern theatre was stalemate. But, in the west, from the very beginning, things started going the Union generals' way and they never slowed down. New Orleans and Nashville, two of the South's major cities, had fallen early on. Union forces hugging the river lines pressed ever deeper into the south. Now, in the spring of 1863, the south had only one major post on the Mississippi River, the river that divided the far west from the rest of the Confederacy. Vicksburg, a city high on a Mississippi bluff overlooking the river below, was ringed with fortifications against a Union army commanded by Major General Ulysses S. Grant. He had already beaten off attempts to relieve the city from the east, and Confederate troops in the area could only look on hopelessly as Grant tightened the noose around the Vicksburg garrison.

Were Vicksburg to fall, the entire Mississippi River would be in Union hands. What was the high command to do?

The Battle of Chancellorsville, fought in May, was not only Lee's greatest victory, but it was won despite the absence of a large part of the Army of Northern Virginia. In fact, the Confederates considered Chancellorsville to have been two separate battles: the Second Battle of Fredericksburg where, for some time before being forced back, little more than a division stood off at least a Union corps; and Chancellorsville Court House, where little more than a skeleton force of Lee's Army of Northern Virginia defeated virtually the entire Army of the Potomac with the exception of its troops at Fredericksburg. Lieutenant General James Longstreet's First Corps, almost a third of Lee's Army, missed the entire battle, being in North Carolina.

This proved that Lee could defend Richmond even when lacking as much as an entire corps. Therefore, the obvious thinking was to send one of the Army of Northern Virginia's corps west to join the forces sent to relieve Vicksburg and save the city.

Indeed Longstreet himself suggested that he and his corps be sent to join a new army that would be assembled at Tullahoma, Mississippi, which would then '... march through Tennessee and Kentucky, and threaten the invasion of Ohio. My idea was that, in the march through those States, the army would meet no organized obstruction; would be supplied with provisions and reinforcements by drawing those friendly to our cause, and would invariably result in drawing Grant's army from Vicksburg to look after and protect his own territory.'[1]

Like any general, Lee didn't want to lose a single man from his command, and he made a different suggestion: that he strike north, as he had done the year before, but this time, heading deep into Pennsylvania itself. The 1862 raid had been in large part an attempt to recruit Marylanders whom the Confederate government had been assured were ready to join the cause in large numbers. In this the government had been mislead; few Marylanders were willing to leave the safety of their homes to join Lee's dirty troops. But now this proposed raid would have a different and two-fold purpose.

First, the raid would relieve pressure on Vicksburg. The US Government, in Washington on the Maryland-Virginia border, had always been very sensitive to threats against its capital. When McClellan moved from the east against Richmond in the Peninsula Campaign, he was forced by politicians in Washington to leave large numbers of troops behind to protect that city, even though most military men realized that the closer threat to Richmond would be a sufficient safeguard for Washington.

Secondly, taking the war into lush Pennsylvania would relieve some of the burden from the farmers in northern Virginia who had had to bear the brunt of supplying food to Lee's Army. In Pennsylvania the army could live off the enemy, in much the same way as Napoleon's army in Spain had lived off the land. Moreover, flying a Confederate battle flag in the north could boost the hopes for European recognition as well as dampen northern morale. A successful raid in 1863 could help turn the 1864 election against President Abraham Lincoln and his Republican Party, and bring peace-party Democrats into power. There would be a strong possibility that a peace treaty recognizing the Confederate States as an independent nation could be signed with a Democratic government.

Jefferson Davis, President of the Confederacy, agreed with Lee's proposal. 'It was decided by a bold movement to attempt to transfer hostilities to the north side of the Potomac,' Davis wrote. 'Thus it was hoped, [Major] General [Joseph] Hooker's army [of the Potomac] would be called from Virginia to meet our advance toward the heart of the enemy's country. In that event, the vast preparations which had been made for an advance upon Richmond would be foiled, the plan for his summer's campaign deranged, and much of the season for active operations would be consumed in the new combinations and dispositions which would be required. If, beyond the Potomac, some opportunity should be offered so as to enable us to defeat the army on which our foe most relied, the measures of our success would be full; but, if the movement only resulted in freeing Virginia from the presence of the hostile army, it was more than could fairly be expected from awaiting the attack which was clearly indicated.'[2]

The emphasis in Davis's, thinking, however, was clearly on Lee's Army making nothing more than a giant raid, with no large battle unless some opportunity arose that made a victorious outcome easy and inevitable.

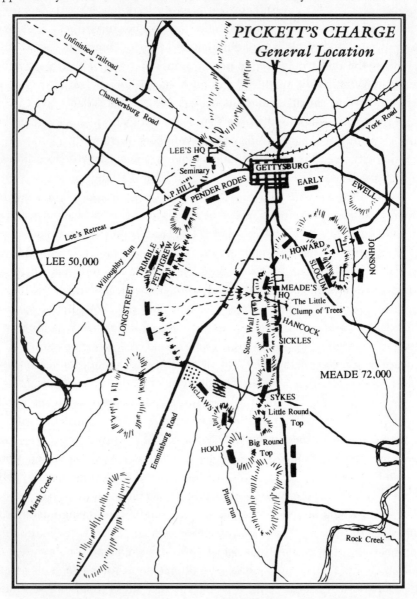

So it was that, in June, while the Union Army of the Potomac was rebuilding itself in its camps after Chancellorsville, Lee's Army struck north. Stuart's cavalry masked the movement along the eastern flank, but became separated once into Maryland. Lee's main force, moving north along the Shenandoah Valley, was out of touch with its cavalry and largely dependent on individual scouts, signal and engineer officers riding out to find the enemy.

Lee divided his army, keeping the corps within easy march of each other, but heading the troops in different directions to take advantage of as much provender as they could find in Pennsylvania. Confederate troops reached Carlisle, which had been the US Cavalry's training depot until the outbreak of war, and burned buildings there. Others pressed eastwards, reaching the Susquehanna River in York County, at Wrightsville, just across the river from Lancaster County and within easy march of Philadelphia and Baltimore. Many Pennsylvania civilians fled east just ahead of the advancing Confederate army.

Finally, troops in Lieutenant General Richard Ewell's corps headed towards the crossroads town of Gettysburg, where shoe factories promised a chance to replace well-worn leather. There, on 1 July, they ran into scouting units of Union cavalry. The blue-jacketed cavalrymen dismounted and, with their multi-shot carbines, slowed Ewell's advance as Union artillery and infantry arrived on the scene. The Union forces deployed into battle lines and put up a tough defence against the on-coming Confederates.

Lee, who had been conferring with Lieutenant General A. P. Hill, one of his corps commanders, at Cashtown, heard the firing, and rode as quickly as possible towards the sound of the guns. When he arrived he found that, as one of his staff officers, Walter Taylor, wrote, 'Heth's division was already hotly engaged, and it was soon evident that a serious engagement could not be avoided.'[3]

Ewell's men, in tough, see-saw fighting, finally drove the Union troops back through the town, but then halted, just short of the point where additional troops had formed a defensive line on Culp's and Cemetery Hills. Many southerners deeply regretted the lack of a Stonewall Jackson who, they felt sure, would have driven on even without Lee's orders to take those hills that commanded the area around them.

But a thrusting, aggressive attack was not the type of fighting that appealed to many Confederate commanders. Longstreet wrote that he and Lee had discussed the conduct of any battle that might occur: 'The plan of defensive tactics gave some hope of success, and, in fact, I assured General Lee that the First Corps would undertake the defense if he would guard its flanks, leaving his other corps to gather the fruits of success.'[4]

Longstreet went away from that meeting with the belief that he had carried his point with Lee, a man who avoided confrontations with his subordinates. But Lee, who had been the almost perfect student at the US Military Academy, had learned his lessons well. And one of these lessons was that a defensive battle was a lost battle. 'Every army which maintains a strictly defensive attitude must, if attacked, be at last driven from its position,' wrote the philosopher of war most studied in those days, Baron Antoine Henri de Jomini, in his book, *The Art of War*, the basic military text of the age. Moreover, Jomini had written: 'A general who stands motionless to receive his enemy, keeping strictly on the defensive, may fight ever so bravely, but he must give way when properly attacked.'[5]

In any event, Longstreet was not on hand by 1 July, and the corps available to Lee was Ewell's, which had come from Chambersburg, and A. P. Hill's, from Cashtown. Hill was sick and relatively inactive during the battle that was to follow, while Ewell was satisfied on that first day to take only the town and not the heights beyond.

Longstreet and his corps arrived on 2 July and Lee ordered him to strike at the enemy's left flank, anchored by two tall hills, Little Round Top and Big Round Top, while other Confederate troops would assault the left flank on Culp's and Cemetery Hills. A foolish mistake by the Union III Corps commander, whose experience had been more political than military before the war, exposed that corps to Longstreet's attack. So much of Longstreet's force fell on the exposed III Corps, while a handful of Union troops held on to the Round Tops in the face of other Confederate attacks.

On the Confederate left, dug-in Union troops, given the chance to build breastworks when Ewell failed to continue his advance of 1 July, drove off Confederate attackers with heavy losses.

The evening of 2 July found the Union army still in its position, its right on Culp's Hill and its left on the Round Tops, and a battered Confederate army facing it. But not all the Confederate troops had yet seen combat. A division of Longstreet's Corps, commanded by Major General George Pickett, had been on the march and had only just arrived by the evening of 2 July.

At 5 p.m. on that day Longstreet and Lee met to discuss the next day's battle. Lee told Longstreet: '... to my surprise, that he thought of attacking General Meade upon the heights [Cemetery Ridge in the centre of the Union line] the next day'. Longstreet, a bit inflexible in his thinking, said that he thought that they had agreed before they even began this raid into

Pennsylvania not to attack Union troops but to draw them in and destroy them from defensive positions .

'If the enemy is there tomorrow, we must attack him,' Lee, ever seeking the one knock-out punch, replied.

'If he is there', Longstreet said, 'it will be because he is anxious that we should attack him. A good reason, in my judgment, for not doing so.'[6]

Longstreet's plan was to pull the southern troops around their right, where they could attack if they found a weak point, or they could draw the Union troops after them and force them to take the offensive. Lee, however, thought that such an attack in the centre could split the Union forces and he could go on to beat them in detail. 'He seemed under a subdued excitement, which occasionally took possession of him when "the hunt was up," and threatened his superb equipoise,' Longstreet felt.[7]

So, with nothing really settled, the two generals parted. Longstreet, convinced that a movement to the right would give the best chance for success, sent out scouts to find a route. They returned saying that this would be possible.

That evening, too, Longstreet told his assistant artillery chief, E. Porter Alexander, that next morning Pickett's Division would attack the enemy, probably near where that day's fighting had been on the Confederate right. Then they parted to make their final arrangements.

In the morning, Longstreet later wrote, without orders, he 'was about to move the command,' to the right when Lee rode up. Longstreet remembered that it was just after sunrise, 4.30 local time.[8] The two generals discussed the situation briefly and Lee announced what had probably been his intention all along: Longstreet would attack the Union centre. Longstreet said that his scouts had found the terrain passable to the right and he thought that that was where any movement should take place.

'No,' Lee replied. 'I am going to take them where they are on Cemetery Hill. I want you to take Pickett's division and make the attack. I will reinforce you by two divisions of the Third Corps.'

'That will give me fifteen thousand men,' Longstreet said. 'I have been a soldier, I may say, from the ranks up to the position I now hold. I have been in pretty much all kinds of skirmishes, from those of two or three soldiers up to those of an army corps, and I think I can safely say there never was a body of fifteen thousand men who could make that attack successfully.'[9]

Longstreet's outspokenness manifestly annoyed Lee, who usually kept his feelings well hidden. Longstreet saw the black look cross Lee's face, and kept quiet while his orders were detailed. Longstreet would attack with two divisions, those commanded by Major General John B. Hood and Major General Lafayette McLaws. Longstreet, still unhappy with Lee's decision, pointed out that both these divisions had been badly bloodied the previous day when they had seen heavy fighting on the right flank.

Lee agreed that they were probably too badly winded for a successful attack. Instead, he suggested using Pickett's Division with men taken from Major General Henry Heth's Division of Hill's Corps who would not be needed on the relatively quiet left flank. As Lee's aide Walter Taylor, who was present at the conference, understood it, 'The assault was to have been made with a column of not less than two divisions, and the remaining divisions were to have been moved forward in support of those in advance.'[10]

Lee ordered Hill to release command of Heth's Division, with about 4,500 men, and two brigades of another of Hill's divisions, Dorsey Pender's, to Longstreet for the attack. Meanwhile, the generals involved in the attack began reporting to the informal command post. Showing them where he wanted their men to be, Longstreet assigned Pickett's Division, some 4,300 men, to the right; two brigades, James Kemper's and Richard Garnett's, in front, supported by Lewis Armistead's. Cadmus Wilcox's Brigade was to fall in in echelon and guard Pickett's right. Heth's Division, supported by brigades commanded by Alfred Scales, some 500 men, and James Lane, with some 1,200 men, would be on Pickett's left. Then Longstreet told Alexander, who had been up since 3 a.m. overseeing battery positions with an eye to attacking on the right, and had been present at Longstreet's meeting with Lee, to lay down an artillery barrage on the enemy line.

The point where the attack was aimed, Cemetery Ridge, was in fact merely a slight rise in the gently undulating terrain stretching to the Confederate line at the edge of the woods, a mile and a half away, with a break in the centre of the area separating the two armies. There the Emmitsburg Road, edged with rail fences on each side, broke the clear-cut defensive lines. The ground itself was relatively clear farmland, with clover in some areas and corn elsewhere. A small clump of trees made a convenient point of aim in the centre of Longstreet's objective. A short fence of stones, the fruit of years of ploughing, ran parallel to the Emmitsburg Road, and the Union troops used this as their basic defensive line which was pretty well parallel to the Confederate line.

The Union Army had posted a solid line of infantry there and filled the ridge with artillery. From across the fields, Confederate observers could make out flags of the II Corps, one of their army's toughest fighting organizations.

Alexander, dressed for the heat of battle in a plain grey shirt and trousers with a torn knee, arranged some 75 cannon from five battalions in a curved line 1,300 yards long, to bear on these Union troops. He earmarked nine 12-pounder howitzers, useful for short-range work, to accompany the infantry advance. Another 60 cannon of Walker's Battalion were placed on the ridge as far as the Hagerstown Road. Two long-range Whitworth guns were sited to the north of these guns. Finally, another twenty guns of Walker's and Latimer's Battalions, together with several other batteries, had been assigned to prepare the way for the infantry.

There were considerably more cannon available, including 25 rifled guns and sixteen 12-pounder smoothbore Napoleons of the Second Corps and fifteen howitzers of the Third Corps that could have added their weight to this group. Moreover, these guns were positioned for enflade fire on the Union target and Union guns on Cemetery Hill that would take the Confederate advance under flank fire. They would have been invaluable, but the Army of Northern Virginia's Chief of Artillery, Brigadier General William Pendleton, was not actually a field commander, and the general, an Episcopal clergyman in civilian life, was of unsuitable temperament for field command. In practice these guns were directed by their respective corps commanders, and during this attack, far from playing a dramatic role, they were silent, save for one battery which fired a few dozen rounds.

The signal for Alexander to begin his barrage would be two guns fired by the Washington Artillery near the Peach Orchard. He began getting his artillery into position, while the infantrymen filed into the woods behind the gun line, most of them being in position by noon. There they dropped off their equipment and grounded their weapons. The day was hot, a July sun blazing in a nearly cloudless day. An observer noted that it reached a high of 87° that day. The men, glad to be in the shade, took off their jackets and waited. Those who had food in their haversacks, mostly 'corn dodgers' and pieces of bacon, ate what for many would be their last meal.

While they waited, Lee, Longstreet and Pickett rode along their front. The men were under strict instructions not to cheer, as was their habit, for fear of betraying their presence to the enemy nearby, but they stood in silence and took off their broad-brimmed felt hats or smart kepis as the generals passed by. The ride took some minutes, as Pickett's first line was some 2,500 feet long, while each of Heth's were some 2,000 feet long.

Armistead's brigade front covered 1,500 feet, while Pender's two brigades had a front of some 1,650 feet.[11] When Lee reached Brigadier General Isaac Trimble's front, he saw that many of the men were wearing bandages as a result of the previous day's fighting.

'Many of these poor boys should go to the rear,' he said. 'They are not fit for duty.' Then he added sadly, 'I miss in this brigade the faces of many dear friends.' Finally, as he rode on down the line, he glanced back at the silent, standing troops and said in a low voice, 'This attack must succeed.'[12]

Then Lee rode over to the sector of the line held by Hill's Corps. Finding an elevated point about the Confederate centre, he dismounted and waited to watch the assault. A British military observer, Colonel A. J. L. Fremantle, Coldstream Guards, saw him there: '... sometimes talking to Hill and sometimes to Colonel Long of his staff. But generally he sat quite alone on the stump of a tree. What I remarked especially was, that during the whole time the firing continued, he only sent one message, and only received one report.'[13] At one point during this time, Hill requested that he be allowed to advance his entire corps alongside Longstreet's attack, but Lee refused, saying that Hill's Corps would be the only reserve the army had if the attack were to fail.

While at work, Alexander received a note from Longstreet: 'Colonel. If the artillery fire does not have the effect to drive off the enemy, or greatly demoralize him, so as to make our efforts pretty certain, I would prefer that you should not advise Gen. Pickett to make the charge. I shall rely a great deal on your good judgment to determine the matter & shall expect you to let Gen. Pickett know when the moment offers.'

Alexander was shocked. It was obvious that Longstreet, whom he knew was not in favour of this attack at all, was placing the responsibility for its success on his shoulders. He jotted a note back to Longstreet: 'General. I will only be able to judge the effect of our fire on the enemy by his return fire, for his infantry is but little exposed to view & the smoke will obscure the whole field. If, as I infer from your note, there is any alternative to this attack it should be carefully considered before opening our fire, for it will take all the artillery ammunition we have left to test this one thoroughly, & if the result is unfavorable we will have none left for another effort. And even if this is entirely successful it can only be so at a very bloody cost.'

Longstreet wasn't prepared to be so easily forced into a decision so desperately against his inclinations. His reply came back swiftly to Alexander: 'Colonel. The intention is to advance the infantry, if the artillery has the desired effect of driving the enemy's off, or having other effect such as to war-rant us in making the attack. When the moment arrives, advise Gen. Pickett, and of course advance such artillery as you can use in aiding the attack.'

Alexander showed Longstreet's note to a brigade commander, Ambrose Wright. 'He has put the responsibility back upon you,' Wright observed.

'General,' Alexander said. 'Tell me exactly what you think of this attack.'

'Well, Alexander, it is mostly a question of supports,' Wright said. 'It is not as hard to get there as it looks. I was there yesterday with my brigade. The real difficulty is to stay there after you get there for the whole infernal Yankee army is up there in a bunch.'[14]

So Alexander returned to his job of seeing that all the guns under his command were in position and ready when the alerting shots were fired. From there he wrote his last note to Longstreet: 'General: When our artillery is at its best, I will advise Gen. Pickett to advance.'[15]

The marshalling and deployment of Civil War armies was a time-con-suming affair. Most of these men had been on the move since before day-break, but it was not until about 1 p.m. that Longstreet was satisfied that his preparations were complete. He then jotted a note for the commander of the Washington Artillery: 'Colonel. Let the batteries open. Order great care and precision in firing. When the batteries at the Peach Orchard can-not be used against the point we intend to attack, let them open on the enemy's on the rocky hill [Little Round Top].'[16] The artillery commander wrote on this order that he had received it at 1.30 p.m.

The order for the first gun to signal Pickett's Charge went to Captain M. B. Miller of the 3rd Company. His first gun fired immediately, but the friction primer failed to ignite the charge in his second gun. Quickly the gunner jumped forward, inserted a new primer, hooked it to his lanyard, and jerked. The second signal gun fired.

With that, all the Confederate artillery erupted with a giant roar, then each crew settled into an average of one round per minute. Union gunners immediately replied so that the entire Union line '... from Cemetery Hill to Round Top seemed in five minutes to be emulating a volcano in eruption,' Alexander wrote.[17]

In the heat of the day, the noise of gunfire, exploding shells and limber chests was overwhelming. The cannoneers, at least, could keep busy, their preoccupation making them oblivious of the din, but the infantry sitting in the woods behind them had no such diversion.

Some bright soul, however, had thought to bring out the few regimental bands still in the Confederate army to boost the men's morale. 'When the cannonade was at its height,' Colonel Fremantle recalled, 'a Confederate band of music, between the cemetery and ourselves, began to play polkas and waltzes, which sounded very curious, accompanied by the hissing and bursting of the shells.'[18]

'The smoke soon darkened the sun,' Second Lieutenant John H. Lewis of the 9th Virginia in Pickett's Division wrote, 'and the scene produced was similar to a gigantic thunder-storm, the screeching of shot and shell producing the sound of the whistling blast of winds. Man seldom ever sees or hears the like of this but once in a lifetime; and those that saw and heard this infernal crash and witnessed the havoc made by the shrieking, howling missiles of death as they plowed the earth and tore the trees will never forget it. It seemed that death was in every foot of space, and safety was only in flight; but none of the men did that. To know the tension of mind under a fire like that, it must be experienced; it cannot be told in words.'[19]

In the almost windless day, the heavy white smoke of black powder lay like clouds on the ground. Sulphur fumes made breathing uncomfortable to artillerymen and infantry alike. Worse, Union artillery fire, overshooting Confederate guns, did a great deal of damage among the waiting infantrymen. In Kemper's Brigade some 200 officers and men were wounded during the cannonade alone; one company of fifty men suffering nineteen casualties.

Private Jere Gage, 11th Mississippi, disembowelled by a bursting shell, was carried to the regimental hospital with the front of his abdomen torn away and his left arm hanging by a thread. A surgeon started to give him some opium to ease his pain, stopping first to ask if he had any last message. 'My mother, O, my darling mother,' Gage gasped. 'How could I have forgotten you.' A friend guided his hand to write his last message, a 'dying release to Miss Mary ... you know who' and a farewell to mother and sisters. Then he touched the letter to his torn side and added the last words, 'This letter is stained with my blood.' Only then did he take the opium and accept its sweet release.[20]

The Union artillery fire was not, however, directed at the waiting infantrymen but at the Confederate guns, and, as usual, it was excellent. The gunners found the range of Milledge's Georgia Battery, on the flank of Cemetery Hill, after the battery had fired one round, and swept it, killing and wounding men and horses and blowing up caissons. One shell passed through six standing horses.

A cannoneer with the Rockbridge Artillery saw 'a shell plow into the ground under Lieutenant Brown's feet and exploded. It tore a large hole, into which Brown sank, enveloped as he fell in smoke and dust. In an instant another shell burst at the trail of my gun, tearing the front half of Tom Williamson's shoe off, and wounding him sorely. A piece of it also broke James Ford's leg, besides cutting off the fore leg of Captain Graham's horse. Ford was holding the lead-horses of the limber, and, as they wheeled to run, their bridles were seized by Rader, a shell struck the horse nearest to him, and, exploding at the instant, killed all four of the lead-horses and stunned Rader.'[21]

But Confederate morale remained high. During the firing one gunner broke out in song: 'Backward, roll backward, O Time in thy flight,' he sang. 'Make me a child again, just for this fight!' A nearby gunner quickly added, 'Yes, and a gal child at that.'[22]

The Confederate artillery fire was not nearly so successful. The Union guns were on the crest of the ridge, their infantry crouched behind the wall below the crest. The Confederate gunners were having to fire too high to cause much damage to the infantrymen; many rounds overshot the crest and their fall could not be spotted by Confederate observers. Then too many gunners set their fuzes too long and the shells exploded well beyond the targets, causing damage, but mostly among clerks and cooks, generals and their staffs, and medical personnel and ambulances.

The Confederate artillery did manage to blow up a dozen caissons in the Union reserve artillery park, which added to the fireworks and convinced the gunners that their fire was effective. The minutes ticked by. Originally, Alexander had thought that the barrage should last not longer than 30 minutes at most, so that he would still have enough ammunition to support the attack, but after about $1^{3}/_{4}$ hours of firing, time that went much faster for Alexander than for the men waiting to move out, he sent a note to Pickett: 'If you are coming at all you must come at once, or I cannot give you proper support, but the enemy's fire has not slackened at all. At least 18 guns are still firing from the cemetery itself.'

Meanwhile, the Union artillery chief decided to break off counter-battery fire to save his ammunition for the forthcoming attack. He ordered many of his guns to withdraw beyond the crest, there to wait and be ready to move forward again when Confederate infantry appeared. Through his glasses, Alexander saw the movement. Never before, in artillery duels, had Union artillery been known to withdraw to save ammunition, so he thought that the Federal batteries at the front had run out and were about to be replaced. Here, if there were to be any that day, was the window of opportunity to launch the attack. Alexander sent a second note to Pickett: 'For God's sake come quick. The 18 guns are gone. Come quick or I can't support you.'[23]

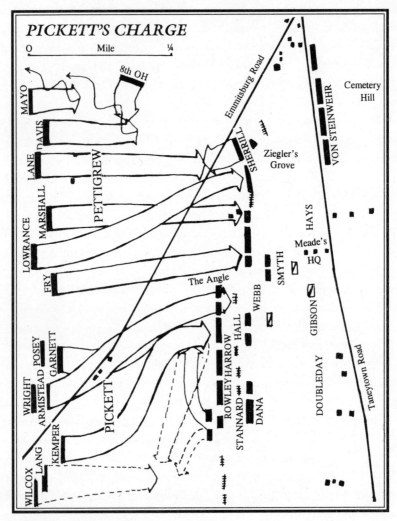

PICKETT'S CHARGE

Alexander's courier found Pickett with Longstreet. Pickett scanned the message and handed it to Longstreet, asking: 'General, shall I advance?'

Longstreet, apparently overcome with emotion, held out his hand to Pickett, who grasped it. Pickett clasped his other hand over their two folded hands. Longstreet bowed his head, writing later that, 'The effort to speak the order failed, and I could only indicate it by an affirmative bow.'[24]

'Then, General,' Pickett said, 'I shall lead my division on.'[25] He started off, then stopped and taking an envelope with a letter to his wife from his pocket, handed it to Longstreet asking him if he would be good enough to mail it for him. Then he leaped on his horse and rode off, appearing, Longstreet thought, fully confident of success. Longstreet mounted and rode to Alexander's post.

It was now about 3 o'clock and silence, broken only by the odd cannon firing, settled over the field. Now it was the infantry's turn. They were ordered to fall in in two ranks and shoulder arms. Officers were required to advance dismounted; exceptions were made for those physically unable to go far on foot, and these included two colonels and two generals, Garnett and Kemper. In one company, a captain led his troops in a hymn; in another a white-haired chaplain offered prayers. The troops received their last-minute instructions to keep closed up to their respective colours, carried at the centre of each regiment, not to stop to load or fire, and to keep their dressing in the ranks – no one to charge until ordered.

Once the division had emerged from the woods, Pickett rode to the centre and made a short speech which ended: 'Charge the enemy, and remember old Virginia.' Only those nearest to him heard his stirring words. Most unit commanders delivered an exhortation. Armistead's speech ended: 'Men, remember your wives, your mothers, your sisters and your sweethearts.'[26] Then, having given the order to advance, he 'turned, placed himself about twenty paces in front of his brigade, and took the lead. His place was in the rear, properly. After moving he placed his hat on the point of his sword, and held it above his head, in front of him,' recalled an officer in his command.[27]

While the infantry were forming up, Longstreet reached Alexander. There his acting artillery chief told him that he was rather too short of ammunition to support the infantry efficiently. 'Go and halt Pickett right where he is,' Longstreet ordered him, 'and replenish your ammunition.'

'General, We can't do that,' Alexander said. 'We nearly emptied the trains last night. Even if we had it, it would take an hour or two, and meanwhile the enemy would recover from the pressure he is now under. Our only chance is to follow it up now to strike while the iron is hot.'

There was a pause as Longstreet scanned the enemy in front of them through his binoculars. 'I don't want to make this attack,' Longstreet said. 'I believe it will fail. I cannot see how it can succeed. I would not make it even now, but that General Lee has ordered and expects it.'[28]

At that moment the command 'Forward march!' was given. It had begun.

As the infantry passed between the cannon, the artillerymen raised their hats and cheered. Alexander saw his old friend Garnett, wished him good luck, and rode back to organize the artillery to advance in support. By now, too, Union artillery had re-entered the affair, and began firing into the advancing grey mass. Both the mounted colonels were hit before they had got past the Emmitsburg Road. The infantrymen began to take casualties. In the 9th Virginia a Private Byrd was wounded in the arm and asked to go the rear. 'Lieutenant,' his sergeant said, 'they have winged our Byrd'. In the 28th Virginia an officer saw his son mortally wounded, kissed him and laid his body carefully on the grass, then raised his sword and continued the advance.[29]

After some eight minutes, Pickett's men reached a slight depression where they halted and re-dressed the ranks before continuing. In the meantime, artillerymen were following the infantry forward. One of them was a South Carolina artillery battalion commander, Major John Haskell: 'Having no special orders beyond that I was to help where I could, I moved about halfway to the heights. At that point I saw to our right, about five hundred yards away, possibly a little more, an immense body of the enemy's infantry, apparently deploying to take Pickett in the flank. I at once came into action and opened fire on them.'[30]

The enemy fell back initially as Union artillery opened up on Haskell's guns. Their fire disabled two of them and wounded a number of his men. At the same time, the returning Union infantry opened fire on the advancing Confederates near Haskell. His ammunition was quite quickly exhausted, but rather than pull back immediately, he had his cannoneers help their own wounded and the wounded from nearby infantry units on to limber chests and litters and then they left the field, their disabled guns in tow. 'Soon all were out,' he wrote, 'but while waiting I was struck in the side by a heavy piece of shell. It was half-spent and striking my swordhilt did not go into my body, but knocked me from my horse. For a time it disabled me so that I was assisted to a large barn which was just on the left of my guns during the duel of the morning.'[31]

Things weren't going well on the left flank either. The Virginia brigade, only some 600-strong, led by Colonel John M. Brockenbrough, had been a bit slow off the mark in joining the others. On the extreme left of Pettigrew's line, Union troops caught it in a terrible fire, from the front and in the flank. A Union regiment advanced on their left, turned to face them and opened volley fire from their side. Before its men had even reached the fence-lined Emmitsburg Road, the unit had virtually dissolved. Most of its men ran towards the rear carrying their flags with them while others crowded to their right, staying with the advance but trying to get away from that terrible fire from two angles.

Most of the troops in Lane's brigade turned to their left to cover the gap left by the missing Brockenbrough's brigade and to stop the Union attack. Several of Lane's regiments, however, did not receive orders to do this and kept on straight ahead. The left was beginning to fall apart.

'The crash of shell and solid shot, as they came howling and whistling through the lines, seemed to make no impression on the men,' 9th Virginia Lieutenant Lewis, who was a file closer during the attack, recalled. 'There was not a waver; but all was as steady as if on parade. Forward was the command, and steady, boys, came from the officers. Great gaps were being made in the lines, only to be closed up; and the same steady, move-forward; the division was being decimated. Its line was shortening, but as steady as ever, the gallant Armistead still in the lead, his hat working down to the hilt of his sword, the point having gone through it. He seemed to be as cool as if on drill, with not a sound of cannon near. We were nearing the Emmitsburg road. There were two fences at that road, but they were no impediment. The men go over them, and reform and forward again. At this point the crash of musketry was added to the roar of artillery. Men were falling in heaps. Up to this time no shot had been fired by this division.'[32]

The advancing units did not reach the road, which ran at a 40° angle to the two front lines, simultaneously. Pickett's men got there first, paused to throw down the fence rails and then re-formed on the other side. From there they advanced slightly to the left oblique, both to avoid enemy fire from their right and to form on Pettigrew's advancing troops. Many men crouched down in the relative safety of the roadbed and went no further. Others turned and headed for the rear, joining a parade of wounded.

Along Pettigrew's line, the fence seems to have been more sturdy and the men had to climb over it, making good targets as they rose against the skyline. His men, too, had to re-form on the other side of the fences that edged the road.

Fremantle, riding to Longstreet's command post from Lee's, '... began to meet many wounded men returning from the front. Many of them asked in piteous tones the way to a doctor or an ambulance. The further I got, the greater became the number of the wounded. At last I came to a perfect stream of them flocking through the woods in numbers as great as the crowd on Oxford Street in the middle of the day. Some were walking alone on crutches composed of two rifles, others were supported by men less badly wounded than themselves, and others were carried on stretchers by the ambulance corps ... They were still under a heavy fire; the shells were continually bringing down great limbs of trees, and carrying further destruction amongst this melancholy procession.'[33]

Finally Fremantle found Longstreet, seated on top of a rail fence, and said, 'I wouldn't have missed this for anything.' 'The devil you wouldn't!' Longstreet, who could see signs of the lines falling apart, replied. 'I would like to have missed it very much, we've attacked and been repulsed: look there.'[34]

His words seem premature; at this point Confederate troops were still driving towards that clump of trees. Pickett didn't think he'd been repulsed; he sent word back to Longstreet that the position could be carried but that he would need reinforcements to hold it. But Longstreet, from a distance, had a better view, seeing the Union troops now surrounding Pickett's flanks and firing into the advancing men. Pickett's courier arrived almost at the same time as did Fremantle, and Longstreet said to him: 'Captain Bright, ride to General Pickett, and tell him what you have heard me say to Colonel Fremantle.'

The captain started to return to Pickett's command post, but was stopped by Longstreet. 'Captain Bright! Tell General Pickett that Wilcox's brigade is in that peach orchard.' He pointed towards the right. 'And that he can order him to his assistance.'[35]

By the time the captain found Pickett his division had finished its oblique march and was now parallel to Pettigrew's men, both divisions still advancing. Now the Union gunners switched to canister, shotgun-like blasts of heavy balls in tin cans which devastated infantry ranks. Pickett himself halted at the Codori house and big barn where he would be in a better position to observe the charge and supervise the reinforcements he expected to be able to feed into any successful breech of the Union lines.

Organization began to fall apart as officers fell to enemy fire, both artillery and steady infantry volleys. The 8th Virginia's flag fell four times, each time to be picked up by another volunteer and carried forward. Every man in the 1st Virginia's colour guard was hit. Private William Monte, 9th Virginia, said, 'What a sublime sight,' before looking at his watch and remarking, 'We have been just nineteen minutes coming.' Hardly had he spoken when a shell fragment ended his time forever.[36]

General Kemper rose in his stirrups, pointing forward with his sword, and shouted, 'There are the guns, boys, go for them!' This was his last order; a bullet dropped him seconds later.[37] Some of his men managed to get the mortally wounded general to the rear. Most of his surviving men went forward, pressing to the left and becoming mixed up with Garnett's Brigade. In turn, many of them worked their way into Armistead's Brigade, as orderly formations fell apart. Others, realizing that they had no chance, crouched behind rocks to return fire.

Private William Goodykoontz, Co. A, 24th Virginia in Kemper's Brigade, made it to within 20 feet of the stone wall when he was slammed to the ground by a Union bullet. For a couple of seconds he lay there, catching his breath, checking how badly he was wounded, and trying to figure a way to get back through the rain of bullets and artillery fire passing over his head. He looked back the way he had come and saw that the ground was covered with parallel windrows of stubble. He also noticed that the Union firing was fairly regular, with a few seconds interval between volleys. The moment a volley had been fired, he made a dash for the nearest windrow, threw himself down behind the slight pile of earth and waited for the next. In this manner he made it to safety.

About twenty yards from the clump of trees and the stone wall in front of it, the mass of advancing Confederates were brought up short, stunned by the weight of ammunition being brought to bear. Then the Union regiment at the wall broke and ran, and several hundred Confederate troops, Armistead in their midst, leaped over the wall and seized the two cannon that had been causing such havoc.

'Armistead dashes through the line, and, mounting the wall of stone, commanding follow me, advances fifty paces within Federal lines, and is shot down,' Lieutenant Lewis wrote. 'The few that followed him and had not been killed fall back over the wall, and the fight goes on. Death lurks in every foot of space. Men fall in heaps, still fighting, bleeding, dying. The remnant of the division, with scarce any officers, look back over the field for the assistance that should have been there; but there are no troops in sight; they had vanished from the field, and Pickett's division, or what is left of it, is fighting the whole Federal center alone.'

Nearby Union troops rallied and dashed forward to engage the handful of Confederates who had taken possession of their cannon, and Garnett, who one eye-witness said was wearing 'an old blue overcoat' though another said that his dress was a 'fine new gray uniform', fell to their fire. A Union souvenir hunter later clipped the three stars and wreath insignia from his collar.

'We see ourselves being surrounded,' Lewis went on. 'The fire is already from both flanks and front; but yet they fight on and die. This cannot last. The end must come; and soon there is no help at hand. All the officers are down, with few exceptions, either killed or wounded. Soon a few of the remnant of the division started to the rear, followed by shot, shell, and musket-balls.'[38] Lewis found himself the only officer in his regiment still on his feet and called out that each man should look out for himself. He himself stayed at the wall for as long as he thought there was any hope and was taken prisoner.

Of the 26th North Carolina men who had started out with Armistead, 88 per cent were lost, only 90 men returning safely to Confederate lines. The regimental colour-bearer and a sergeant reached the wall and huddled behind it, looking back for help that didn't come. A Union soldier called out, 'Come over on this side of the Lord.' The two men stood up with raised hands and were taken prisoner.[39]

In fact help was on the way in the shape of Wilcox and his 1,050 men. But it was too little and too late, by a good ten minutes. Hill also ordered one of his brigades forward, but it too could not possibly reach the Confederates at the wall in time to save them. Alexander watched Wilcox's men advancing into what appeared to be certain death: 'The men, as they passed us, looked bewildered, as if they wondered what they were expected to do, or why they were there. However, they were soon halted and moved back. They suffered some losses, and we had a few casualties from canister sent at them at longer long range.'[40]

Other, nearer, Confederates from the Brigades of Scales, Trimble and Lane, tried to reach the wall, only to be driven back by increased fire. An aide asked Lane if he should try to rally the men for another try. 'No,' Lane said. 'The best thing the men can do is to get out of this; let them go.'[41]

Back near the Codori house Pickett saw his men die, surrender, or make their way back to the Confederate line. He mounted and headed back himself. Major W. T. Poague, commanding an artillery battalion which was ready to advance in support of a successful attack, stopped Pickett and asked, 'General, is that Virginia flag carried by one of our men or by the enemy?' He received no reply.

'What do you think I ought to do under the circumstances?' he tried again. 'Our men are leaving the hill.'

'I think you had better save your guns,' Pickett finally said, then rode off again.[42]

Longstreet meanwhile had ridden to the guns and prepared them to receive the counter-attack he was sure would follow. As the fighting at the clump of trees died down, so did musketry across the entire front. Now the disorganized mass of Confederates, retreating singly and in small groups, found themselves in danger from the artillery fire which harried them the while. Lee rode out alone to meet and rally them. A few of them yelled that they were ready for another go, but most were mentally and physically drained. 'Are you wounded?' Lee asked one man.

'No, General,' the soldier replied, 'only a little fatigued; but I am afraid there are but few so lucky as myself.'

'Ah! Yes, I am very sorry the task was too great for you, but we mustn't despond. Another time we shall succeed. Are you one of Pickett's men?'

'Yes, General.'

'Well, you had better go back and rest yourself. Captain Linthicum will tell you the rendezvous for your brigade.'

Lee spotted Pickett and ordered: 'General Pickett, place your division in rear of this hill, and be ready to repel the advance of the enemy should they follow up their advantage.'

The exhausted Pickett blurted out: 'General Lee, I have no division now. Armistead is down, Garnett is down, and Kemper is mortally wounded.'

'Come, General Pickett, this has been my fight, and upon my shoulders rests the blame. The men and officers of your command have written the name of Virginia as high today as it has ever been written before.'[43]

Some officers tried to form a line at the point where the Confederate cannon had opened up to begin the charge, but Union gunners concentrated their fire on them and the men broke for the rear, throwing their equipment away as they ran. Finally, officers set up a new line in the ravine behind the guns and, out of sight of the Union guns, tried to rally their units and prepare for the counter-attack which didn't materialize.

That night roll calls showed that the attacking Confederates in Pickett's Division had lost 1,125 killed, 4,550 wounded, and 792 prisoners, a total of 62 per cent of the attacking force. Archer's Pettigrew's and Davis' commands lost men in at least as high a proportion. All but two of the colours of Pickett's Division were in Union hands, as were four colours from Archer's Brigade.

That night a general summoned to Lee's headquarters found the old man so exhausted as to be almost unable to dismount. 'General,' the shocked man said, 'this has been a hard day on you.'

'Yes, it has been a sad, sad day to us,' Lee finally said. There was silence for a while, broken only by the occasional shot in the distance as a horse was put out of its misery. In their minds perhaps the generals could even hear cries of the wounded. Then Lee spoke again in a loud, agonized tone: 'Too bad! Too bad! Oh! Too bad!'

8
The Assaults on Battery Wagner
10–18 July 1863

If there were one symbol of secession, one cause of the war, in the minds of the average Union soldier, it was the hated city of Charleston. It was there that the first convention calling for secession had been held; there that the first shots on Sumter had been fired. The city had to be captured. Major General Quincy Adams Gillmore, a trained engineer, was in charge of the military side of the attempt. Looking over his maps, Morris Island caught his eye. Some 2,600 yards from Fort Sumter – within easy range of a 10-pound Parrott rifle – the island dominated the right-hand approach to Charleston Harbour; its capture would close the harbour and be a major step in taking the city.

The Confederates had also realized its importance and had built several forts on the island, and dug a series of rifle pits along the lighthouse inlet on the southern side. Battery Gregg was built on a promontory at the very northern tip of the island, and behind it across the promontory was built a larger fort known as Battery Wagner, after Lieutenant Colonel Thomas M. Wagner, 1st South Carolina Artillery, who had been killed at Fort Sumter. The walls of the fort were of sand contained within palmetto log shoring. Earlier combat had shown that solid shot was absorbed relatively easily by the soft palmetto wood, and shells buried themselves in the sand walls to explode dramatically but relatively harmlessly. An outer wall, separated from the inner wall by a shallow moat filled with sea water, formed a bridge stretching 800 feet across the width of the island from shore to shore. There was a heavy traverse and a curtain covering a sally-port facing the ocean. The fort was armed with eleven cannon, including 32-pounders for channel defence and siege guns to sweep the narrow beach over which attacking infantry would have to pass. A large bomb-proof shelter was built within one minute's reach of the defensive positions on the walls.

'We did not know that the island at its narrowest point between us and Battery Wagner, and quite near to the latter, had been worn away by the

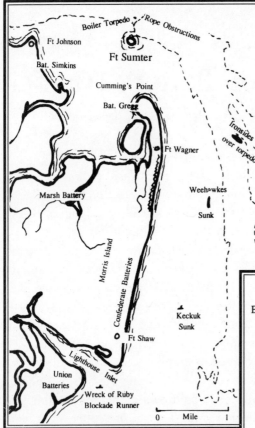

encroachments of the sea to about one-third the width shown on our latest charts, and so much reduced in height that during spring-tides or heavy weather the waves swept entirely over it to the marsh in rear,' Gillmore wrote. 'Against us the fort presented an armed front about 800 feet in length reaching entirely across the island, while our advance must be made over a strip of low shifting sand only about 80 feet wide, and two feet above the range of ordinary tides.'[1]

Wagner was garrisoned by the 31st and 51st North Carolina Infantry Regiments, the Charleston Battalion, two companies of the 1st South Carolina Infantry, serving as artillery, two companies of the 63rd Georgia Heavy Artillery, a section from the Palmetto Battery, and a section from Blake's Battery, for a total of some 1,700 men. The commander was Brigadier Gen-

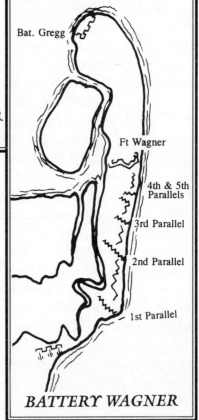

BATTERY WAGNER

eral William B. Taliaferro, a lawyer who had seen commissioned service in the Mexican War and, in the Confederate Army, under Stonewall Jackson until being sent to Charleston after the Battle of Fredericksburg.

On 9 July Gillmore ordered Brigadier General Truman Seymour, a professional artilleryman of the West Point class of 1846, to take the island with his infantry division. Seymour sent 'a small brigade' under Brigadier General George C. Strong, to land on the south side and attack towards Battery Wagner. Preparations took a couple of days. At about 3 a.m. on 10 July the troops were ready in boats across the inlet from the island, hidden from the Confederates by the tall swamp grass. Just before sunrise, mainland based cannon and four US Navy monitors opened fire on Battery Wagner. At 7 a.m. Gillmore ordered the artillery to cease fire, and Strong's infantry to attack.

As the longboats carrying men of the 6th and 7th Connecticut Infantry emerged from their hiding places along the lighthouse inlet, the Confederate cannon opened up on them, raking the inlet with canister. Strong's boat was splattered by two near-misses from a row of canister, but the general was unhurt. Lieutenant Colonel Daniel C. Rodman, commanding a battalion of the 7th, called out to Strong from a nearby boat, requesting permission to charge the batteries.

'Go!' shouted Strong.

The 6-foot-tall Rodman rose in the stern of his boat, pointed his sword to the shore, and urged his men to press on towards the bank where several enemy cannon were firing. Getting ashore in a matter of minutes, they rushed the rifle pits, as the Confederates fled before them. Men of Company I found a loaded howitzer, turned it and fired two rounds of canister at the backs of the fleeing Confederates. Confederate gunners desperately tried to bring an 8-inch howitzer in the second row of rifle pits to bear on the advancing troops, but were overrun before they had a chance to fire.

While this was going on, the 6th Connecticut landed on the right, in front of another battery, jumping off in knee-deep surf and dashing ashore with fixed bayonets. The Confederate gunners got off a single round, which flew harmlessly over the heads of the attackers, before being overrun. Within minutes the Union infantry had taken the battery, some 125 prisoners and a regimental flag.

Without pause the Connecticut regiments advanced along the beach towards Battery Wagner, and got to within some 300 yards of the walls

before Confederate cannonfire forced them to take cover. By 9 o'clock Federal forces were in control of three-quarters of the island and had a line of
skirmishers within musket range of the Confederate fortifications. The two
regiments had captured eleven cannon, a great quantity of smallarms and
ammunition, a regimental colour, and several hundred prisoners for the loss
of ten casualties, all in the 6th.

But Batteries Wagner and Gregg were still in southern hands and Gillmore had to be satisfied with that. 'The intense heat, which prostrated
many of the men,' he later wrote, 'forced a suspension of operations for the
day.'[2] Gillmore had expected tougher opposition; his men probably could
have pressed on and taken Wagner, but their commanders were not ready to
do so. They decided to consolidate their gains, and postpone the assault for
a day. It was a bad mistake.

At 2.30 a.m. on the 11th, Union troops were sent to assault the walls
again, the 7th Connecticut being charged with leading the attack. Strong
personally briefed the men, ordering them to advance silently until fired
upon by enemy sentries. Then they were to rush the fort. 'If you fire,' he
told the attackers, 'aim low, but don't stop to fire; trust in God and give
them the bayonet.' Private Stephen Walkley, Company A, 7th Connecticut,
later wrote: 'When I learned what we were to do my knees shook so that I
thought I should drop.'[3]

The advance was halted by a single shot followed by a volley from the
walls. This shook the attackers and they stopped for a minute, until their
sword-waving officers got them moving forward again. Enemy fire grew
stiffer as they dashed over the outer wall and through a foot of dank seawa-
ter to the inner wall. At the row of sandbagged parapets on top of the inner
wall they exchanged fire with the Confederate infantrymen while waiting
for support to arrive before jumping down into the fort.

Sergeant John A. Porter, Company B of the 76th Pennsylvania
Infantry, was one of those in the supporting force. 'We were roused up
and formed for the assault,' he later wrote. 'We came up in what is known
as a "close column". When we struck the rebel pickets, they fired on us.
Up to this time, all was still as death; then we raised a cheer and started
on a double quick. A few moments brought us to the foot and all halted;
it looked liked a hopeless case. Here we were on the edge of a ditch about
twenty feet across the top and perhaps ten feet deep, covered with two or
three feet of water in the bottom. Their gunners were covered, out of
sight, and so arranged that the ditches could be swept with grape or can-

ister. While we were considering what do to, "Boom!" came a charge of grape right in our faces. We were near enough to look into the gunner's eyes, if he had shown himself. I dropped down on one knee and commenced to watch with great fierceness the gun in front of me. This little move of mine was before we got the first charge, but it was not my gun that fired. Soon there was a terrible crash and men began to fall all around me. There was no time until I heard Lieutenant [Martin] Stambaugh say out in a loud voice, "The order is to fall back!" He was right at my side when he gave the order, and the order had hardly left his lips when he dropped with a bullet in his brain.'

The attackers were forced back without even breaching the fort's walls. 'When the order came to fall back,' Sergeant Porter wrote, 'there was a general break for the rear, and no wonder. There was no prospect to get forward, and the guns were piling us in heaps in the front. I was on the extreme left of the regiment, and the right was in the direction of the sea beach. Most of the regiment broke and ran straight for the rear. I cast a hasty glance around and saw rough uneven ground in the rear. It was likewise covered with a kind of stubble. The beach was smooth, so I struck across the face of the fort to get there. A little to the rear were some sand mounds I wanted to take advantage of. I was so completely fagged out by former exertions that when I started to run, for the life of me I could not get into a faster gait than a dog-trot. When I reached the beach, I could not go faster than a walk to save my life; and I just leisurely walked off.'[4]

On the left, the 9th Maine also ran into the heavy smallarms fire of infantry, and case and canister fire from three heavy cannon. Halted for a moment by the shock of the fire, they advanced, only to face an even heavier fire. They, too, were forced back, shattered.

Once the two supporting regiments had been dealt with, the defenders were free to turn their attention to the 7th Connecticut, still holding its own along the sandbag parapets. Rodman decided not to wait to be mown down or forced to surrender. He ordered an immediate retreat. In the morning sunlight the men's dark blue blouses and sky-blue trousers standing out against the white sand, made perfect targets as they ran down the inner wall, through the moat, and up the outer wall. Rodman, among the last to get off the wall, had been encouraging his men on when he fell with a wound in his side. Lieutenant Charles Greene went to his aid. As he was helping Rodman up, Rodman was hit again, this time in the leg. Then Greene was shot.

But Rodman made it to safety; one of only 88 surviving officers and men from the force of ten officers and 185 enlisted men who had taken part in the assault. 'Ah, my brave fellows,' Strong said as he watched their repulse, 'you deserved a better fate.'[5] Losses in other regiments were also heavy; the 76th Pennsylvania had lost 208 officers and men, the 9th Maine 34 and the 3rd New Hampshire one killed and one wounded.

'This repulse demonstrated the remarkable strength of the work and the necessity of establishing counter-batteries against it, which, with the co-operation of the fleet, might dismount the principal guns and either drive the enemy from it or open the way for a successful assault,' Gillmore wrote.[6]

The Union troops erected five batteries in the sand, armed with 27 rifled cannon and fourteen mortars, within 1,700 yards of Wagner's walls. Infantry kept Confederate skirmishers away as pioneers dug rows of redoubts closer and closer to Wagner. Early in the morning of the 14th, a Confederate raiding party sallied from Fort Wagner in an attempt to capture or kill the workers in the trench lines. Union infantry was ready, and the Confederates were driven off with the loss of one Union soldier killed, two wounded, and one man taken prisoner. Rain fell for several days while the men were working, which slowed progress somewhat, but the works had been completed by the 17th.

The next day was clear, with a pleasant sea breeze blowing. At noon, the guns in the new batteries all opened fire, joined by cannon on USS *New Ironsides* and five monitors anchored offshore, a total of 60 guns, and the bombardment continued for eight hours. Twice the Confederate flag was shot down; twice it was replaced, under fire, by the fort's brave defenders.

In the meantime a second infantry assault was being planned. General Seymour gathered his commanders at a point overlooking the bombarded fort to discuss the prospects. Brigadier General George C. Strong thought it had a good chance, but Colonel Haldimand S. Putnam thought it had no chance. 'I did not think we could take the fort so,' he later said, 'but Seymour overruled me. Seymour is a devil of a fellow for dash.'[7] While they were watching, Wagner's guns fell silent at about 4 p.m. but the Union commanders were unable to determine whether they had been withdrawn or the gunners were merely seeking safety in the bombproof shelter below. As it turned out, the guns were in good shape, and the Confederates had lost only eight men killed and twenty wounded in the tremendous bombardment.

Seymour having the deciding vote, and Strong backing him up, the attack was on. Strong's Brigade, consisting of the 6th Connecticut, 9th Maine, 54th Massachusetts, 3rd New Hampshire, 48th New York, and 76th Pennsylvania, would make the main attack. Colonel Robert Gould Shaw requested the honour of having his 54th Massachusetts Volunteers, all of African descent, lead the assault, probably to prove how well they could fight.

'You may lead the column if you say yes,' Strong told Shaw. 'Your men, I know, are worn out, but do as you choose.'[8]

The 54th was the first combat unit of African-Americans authorized during the war. Originally the armies that fought on both sides were all white and it was not until the Emancipation Proclamation was issued that the recruiting of African Americans was authorized. Massachusetts Governor John Andrew was the first to take advantage of this, and called for the organization of the 54th. Shaw, their colonel, had been a lieutenant in the 2nd Massachusetts Infantry and had been wounded at Antietam.

Although Nathaniel Page, a special correspondent for the *New York Tribune*, told the American Freeman's Inquiry Commission in May 1864 that Seymour had said that he would have Strong's brigade make the attack to 'put those damned niggers from Massachusetts in the advance; we may as well get rid of them one time as another,' there is little evidence to support this. Indeed, Seymour, the son of a Vermont Methodist minister, was himself severely wounded at Battery Wagner and went on to lead black units again, including the 54th and the 8th and 35th United States Colored Troops at the Battle of Olustee, Florida, on 20 February 1864.

For whatever reason, the 54th was picked to lead the assault, even though its ranks were greatly depleted by sickness and casualties sustained during a recent skirmish, and by men detached for guard and fatigue details. While the commanders discussed the forthcoming attack, the 54th crossed to Morris Island and moved up into position, which involved a two-day march through the swamps in rain. The men were tired and hungry, rations being rather short, when they arrived at the departure line. Their officers and NCOs had not seen any plan of the fortifications they were to assault – in fact no one in the regiment had had any experience or training in assaulting fortifications. There were no engineers on hand to guide them to suitable positions, no pioneers were sent out to destroy the many devices in front of the fort designed to slow down attacking forces. The 6th Connecticut, the second regiment in the assaulting column, was drawn up behind the 54th.

Shaw, having received his last briefing from General Seymour, saw an old civilian correspondence acquaintance, Edward L. Pierce of the *New York Daily Tribune*, one of a large party gathered to watch the assault. He gave the journalist some personal papers and letters to deliver should he not survive the attack. Then he rode to the head of his regiment, the lead regiment in the brigade. 'I want you to prove yourselves,' he said, looking over the black faces in his command. 'The eyes of thousands will look on what you do tonight.' He then dismounted and sent his horse to the rear.

'Ned,' he said to his second in command, Lieutenant Colonel Edward Hallowell, 'I shall go in advance of the men with the National Flag, you keep the state flag with you. It will give the men something to rally round. We shall take the fort or die there. Goodbye! If I do not come back, take my fieldglass.' Hallowell, who thought that Shaw had been depressed earlier on by a belief that he would die in this battle, thought he seemed '... happy and cheerful, all of the sadness had left him and I am sure he felt ready to meet his fate'.[9]

Shaw took a position at the right of the column, beside one of the colours. He was dressed in regulation sky-blue trousers, with a dark blue waist-length jacket, the silver eagles of his rank within gold borders on each shoulder, and was wearing a black, broad-brimmed slouch hat. A crimson silk sash was wrapped around his waist under a sword belt from which hung a British-made field officer's sword with his initials worked into its hilt. A lighted cigar was clenched between his lips. Hallowell took a position at the left, beside the other colour. The field musicians were sent to the rear to serve as stretcher-bearers under supervision of the regiment's surgeon and hospital steward.

'The time of evening twilight was selected for the storming party to advance,' Gillmore wrote, 'in order that it might not be distinctly seen from the James Island batteries on our extreme left, and from Fort Sumter and Sullivan's Island on our distant front.'[10] To keep the identity of the unit indistinct, the regimental colours were furled; the commander of the colour company noticed the cased colours and, apparently not having been otherwise ordered, had them unfurled for the assault. On the 18th the sun set at about 7.30; the moon, only a sliver at that time of month, would not rise until about 8.40.

General Strong, a dapper yellow handkerchief tied around his neck, rode up to the head of the 54th and halted. Those near him heard him say: 'Boys, I'm a Massachusetts man, and I know you will fight for the honour of the State. I am sorry you must go into the fight tired and hungry, but the men in the fort are tired too. There are but three hundred behind those walls and they have been fighting all day. Don't fire a musket on the way up, but go in and bayonet them at their guns.' Then he pointed to the US flag and its black bearer. 'If this man should fall who will lift the flag and carry it on?'

Shaw took the cigar from his lips. 'I will,' he said. Those men who heard this exchange cheered.[11]

As darkness began to fall, at about 7.45, the Union guns fell silent and a signal flare from Gillmore told the infantry to launch the attack. A curious Confederate, emerging from the bombproof at Wagner, saw the flare and signalled to the gunners at Fort Sumter and Battery Gregg that Wagner was about to be attacked. Then he alerted the battery's defenders, who flocked to the walls. The 51st North Carolina took up positions along the curtain. Two companies of the Charleston Battalion, outside the works, covered the gorge. The 31st North Carolina lined the walls on the fort's left, including the south-east bastion.

Meanwhile, on the beach, Shaw drew his sword from its scabbard and, facing his men, yelled, 'Attention! Move in quick time until within a hundred yards of the fort; then double quick, and charge!' He paused for a moment, his eyes sweeping over the faces of the men staring at him, then, 'Forward!' he commanded, and turned and began to make his way to where the enemy was waiting.[12]

From a nearby hill, the 7th Connecticut's chaplain and adjutant watched the men move off. The adjutant later wrote that all they could see or hear was 'a few minutes of comparative silence, and then a burst of flame from the walls of the fort, otherwise indistinguishable in the darkness, and the sharp crackle of musketry ... Heavy discharges of artillery followed in rapid succession, flashing like heat lightning; while the little jets of fire from the rifles made a sparkling frieze along the dark parapet.'[13]

At first there was little firing from the Confederate position, although cannon in Fort Sumter and on Sullivan's and James Islands opened up on the densely packed ranks. Exploding shells joined the sounds of the surf pounding the beach, gulls crying above them, and the steady sound of heavy feet digging into loose sand. There was little talking in the ranks, any remarks being quickly silenced by the officers and NCOs. A heavy fog began to roll in from the ocean, adding to the sense of isolation, and dampening the sounds of battle. Ahead of them, shells from the Union land batteries and US Navy ships were pounding Wagner's walls. When the regiment got to within some 1,600 yards from the fort, Shaw halted the column, and formed a full regimental front. Most of the Confederate guns were still silent. The regiment marched forward again for about four hundred yards, and the Federal artillery ceased fire for fear of hitting blue-clad troops.

Shaw raised his sabre and called for an advance at the quick time, then, seconds later, at the double quick. This was the signal for a hail of shot and bullets from the fort. From Gillmore's vantage point he saw 'a compact and deadly sheet of musketry fire was instantly poured upon the advancing column by the garrison, which had suddenly issued forth from the security of the bomb-proof shelter.'[14]

'It was now dark,' a surviving officer later wrote. 'The gloom made more intense by the blinding explosions in the front. This terrible fire which the regiment had just faced, probably caused the greatest number of casualties sustained by the Fifty-fourth in the assault; for nearer the work the men were somewhat sheltered by the high parapet. Every flash showed the ground dotted with men of the regiment, killed or wounded. Great holes, made by the huge shells of the navy or the land batteries, were pitfalls into which the men stumbled or fell.'[15]

As in the previous attack, the men of the 54th paused, shocked by the sheer volume of the enemy fire. Many fell back through the ranks of the 6th Connecticut behind them, before being rallied and brought forward. The 6th, however, pressed on. Their commander, Lieutenant Colonel John L. Chatfield, was twice wounded in the hand and leg, and had to lie in the open for two hours. A private scraped out a slit trench to help protect his colonel, then later helped him to the rear. The regiment's colour-bearer, Gustav de Bouge, was killed, but the blood-stained white state flag of the 6th was picked up and brought forward, over the wall and into the first line of casemates and bombproof shelter.

Here the Connecticut men halted and, joined by men of the 48th New York, opened fire. For three hours they fought tenaciously, but finally the handful of survivors, unable to advance and with no prospect of being reinforced, were forced to retire over the wall.

Shaw rallied the 54th which came forward again, heading for the parapet to the left of where the 6th had breached the defences. The flashes from musketry and cannonfire lit the night sky. Men fell at every turn, the wounded curling up small in the endeavour to protect themselves from the bullets and shot that were tearing up the sand around them. Captain Cabot J. Russel, the 19-year-old New Yorker in command of H Company, was killed near the base of wall. Captain William H. Simkins, Company K, nearby, saw him fall and stopped to help him; he too was shot and fell dead over Russel's body. The black soldiers pressed on towards the fort, heads bent and muskets pressed to the chest as if they were struggling to make their way through a fierce rainstorm.

From his position in the second assaulting line, Hallowell saw Shaw running forward, the flashes from the gunfire reflecting off his silver sword blade. 'I saw him again', he wrote, 'just for an instant, as he sprang into the ditch; his broken and shattered regiment were following him.'[16] Shortly afterwards Hallowell was wounded in the groin. Private Frank Myers, Company K, saw Shaw as the colonel got to the bottom of the fort's walls, splashing through the surf as he ran, leaning forward against the hail of bullets aimed at him. He dashed up the wall, his silhouette was seen against the night sky, lit by cannonfire. Suddenly he bent at the middle, dropping his sword, and falling, killed, into the fort.

Beside Shaw, the colour-bearer, Sergeant John Wall, fell, and a regimental sergeant, William H. Carney, a Virginian who had been recruited in the whaling town of New Bedford, Massachusetts, grabbed the flag and led the way to the top of the walls where he planted the flag.

He was followed by others of the regiment, who fought a hand-to-hand engagement on the top of the parapet. Once they had cleared the top of the wall, they began firing at the muzzle blasts below them, but, silhouetted against the glare of the continual detonations, they began to be picked off in increasing numbers and were forced to drop below the parapet. The defenders dashed forward and dropped fuzed shells and grenades down on the crouching men.

'One brave fellow,' Captain Luis Emilio recalled, 'with his broken arm lying across his breast, was piling cartridges upon it for Lieutenant Emerson, who like the other officers, was using a musket he had picked up. Another soldier, tired of the enforced combat, climbed the slope to his fate; for in a moment his dead body rolled down again. A particularly severe fire came from the south-west bastion. There a Confederate was observed, who, stripped to the waist, with daring exposure for some time dealt out fatal shots; but at last three eager marksmen fired together, and

he fell back into the fort, to appear no more.'[17] This engagement continued for about an hour, but it became clear that the men could not remain
there much longer if they hoped to survive. Some men again tried to get
up the walls, but most made their way back across the moat and up the
outer wall.

Sergeant George K. Stephens, Company B, 54th, later wrote: 'When
our column had charged the fort, passed the half-filled moat, and mounted
to the parapet, many of the men clambered over and some entered by the
large embrasure in which one of the big guns was mounted, the firing sub-
stantially ceased there by the beach, and the rebel musketry firing steadily
grew hotter on our left. An officer of our regiment called out, "Spike that
gun!" Whether this was done I do not know, for we fired our rifles and
fought as hard as we could to return the fire on our right.

'But the rebel fire grew hotter on our right, and a field-piece every few
seconds seemed to sweep along our rapidly thinning ranks. Men all around
me would fall and roll down the scarp into the ditch. Just at the very hottest
moment of the struggle a battalion or regiment charged up the moat and
halted, but did not attempt to cross and join us, but from their position
commenced to fire upon us. I was one of the men who shouted where I
stood, "Don't fire on us! We are the Fifty-fourth!" I have heard it was a
Maine regiment. This is God's living truth! Immediately after I heard an
order, "Retreat!" Some twelve or fifteen of us slid down from our position
on the parapet of the fort.

'The [US] men-of-war seemed to have turned their guns on the fort,
and the fire of the Confederates on the right seemed to increase in power.
The line of retreat seemed lit with infernal fire; the hissing bullets and
bursting shells seemed angry demons.

'I was with Hooker's division cooking for Colonel B. C. Tilghman, of
the Twenty-sixth Pennsylvania Regiment, in the battle of Fredericksburg,
when General Burnside commanded. I traversed the Hazel Dell Marr, the
Stone House, when all the enemy's artillery was turned upon it; but hot as
the fire was there, it did not compare to the terrific fire which blazed along
the narrow approach to Wagner.'[18]

As the troops fell back, Sergeant Carney pulled up the flag he'd dug into
the top of the fort walls and carried it back to safety, being wounded twice
in the fire that fell all around the retreating 54th. For his exceptional bravery he was awarded the Congressional Medal of Honor, the first
African-American to be so honoured.

Several hundred yards away from the fort, the 54th's senior surviving officer, Captain Luis Emilio, the regiment's ninth ranking captain, rallied the survivors. Three companies of the 3rd New Hampshire, led by Major Josial G. Plympton, also got across the outer walls and through the moat, only to be pinned down by heavy fire just outside the inner wall. Finally, with no possibility of advancing farther and no sign of reinforcements, the survivors of the 3rd were the last troops of Strong's Brigade to retire from the field.

Strong himself was wounded while leading his brigade up the south-eastern bastion of the fort in much the same way that Shaw had earlier been killed. As Strong was being carried off, Gillmore stopped the ambulance to ask the attendants if he were badly hurt. Strong recognized his superior's voice, and called out, 'No, General, I think not; only a severe flesh-wound in the hip.'[19] He was taken to Beaumont and seemed to be responding well to treatment, but he decided to return to New York to recuperate. There he developed lockjaw and died.

The attack continued. Colonel Haldimand S. Putnam's Brigade was rushed to the fort. The 100th New York Regiment of this brigade approached the south-eastern bastion, halted and fired a volley into troops they thought were counter-attacking Confederates, only to find the men were survivors of a Union regiment, probably the 54th. Cannonfire had felled General Seymour, hit in the foot while rushing reinforcements up to the fort. One of his aides, Lieutenant S. S. Stevens, of the 6th Connecticut, was killed by the same canister shot.

Like Strong's, Putnam's men were soon pinned down, but rather than sound the retreat, he begged his men to remain where they were until reinforcements would enable them to force their way over the walls. 'Hold on for a minute, brave men. Our reinforcements are coming,' he was saying as he was hit in the head by a bullet and fell dead.[20] The survivors of Putnam's Brigade were falling back, just as a third brigade, led by Brigadier General Thomas G. Stevenson, was coming up. The 97th Pennsylvania in the latter brigade was ordered up. Some 200 yards into their advance they were met by hundreds of wounded and demoralized troops streaming back; the brigade commander halted the regiment and ordered it back to its former position to prepare for a counter-attack. But there would be no counter-attack. There had been enough death for one day.

Strong's Brigade had 32 killed, 474 wounded, and 329 missing. The 6th Connecticut alone lost 141 officers and men killed, wounded or missing from the 300 who had set out. Total losses in the 54th Massachusetts were

256 officers and men. Putnam's Brigade had 37 killed, 391 wounded and 212 missing. Total Union casualties were 1,575. Confederate losses totalled 174 all ranks.

The Union army never again tried to take Wagner by assault. The siege continued until 6 September when, seeing that the Union lines enfiladed the entire south wall of the fort, the Confederate commander ordered Wagner evacuated. It had never been captured.

9
The Capture of USS *Satellite* and USS *Reliance*, 23 August 1863

Not all dramatic defeats involved great loss of life or heroic leadership. Consider, for example, the relatively easy, bloodless cutting-out expedition which ended up in the capture of two US Navy gunboats *Satellite* and *Reliance*. These two craft were among those deployed along the coast and on the many waterways to interdict the passage of goods to the south. One of the most important patrolling areas was at the mouth of the Rappahannock River where it flows into Chesapeake Bay.

Although the crews of these patrolling vessels were always in danger from the sniper's bullet or, occasionally, fire from shore-sited cannon, for the most part their duty was monotonous in the extreme. Day after day, up and down, sweeping the same old shoreline with high-powered glasses for a sight of Confederates. The lack of action tended to make officers and men lethargic, and unless the boat commander were a stickler for training (and the fear of snipers caused many to neglect this) crews were often less than fully ready for combat.

Two such boats were *Satellite* and *Reliance*, on patrol in the Rappahannock River in Northern Virginia. *Satellite*, the larger of the two, had been built in New York in 1854 and was acquired by the Navy in its rush to get armed vessels on all southern waters at the outbreak of war. A 217-ton steam boat powered by side wheels, she was some 121 feet long with a beam of 23 feet. She was armed with two cannon, an eight-inch and a 30-pounder. Her normal complement numbered 43 hands. She had had a pretty uneventful war, although she was credited with the capture of the Confederate submarine *Alligator* in June 1862, and four other vessels in 1863, the last of them, *Three Brothers*, on 17 August.

Reliance was a 90-ton, screw-driven vessel which, unlike *Satellite*, had been built for Navy use. She and her sister *Resolute* had been launched on 4 June 1860. They were both about 90 feet long with a beam of 17 feet, and each had a complement of 17 hands. Initially they were to have been armed with one 24- and one 12-pounder, but by 1863 *Reliance*'s armament consisted of one 30-pound Parrott rifle and one 24-pound howitzer. The *Reliance* had also had a relatively uneventful war, although her crew did get some gunnery practice when engaging Confederate land-based batteries at Aquia Creek in the spring of 1861, and she had taken part in a naval expedition up the Rappahannock River to Tappahannock, Virginia, in April 1862. She was also credited with three prizes captured during patrols between August 1862 and March 1863.

Since then, the two ships had been patrolling the Rappahannock River in concert and had been out for some time. Coal stocks were low and a third vessel, USS *Currituck*, which usually accompanied them, had left them to return to their home port to embark more coal for the three of them.

The daylight hours of 22 August 1863 had been cloudy and grey, and wind and rain had whipped-up choppy, white-capped waves in the Rappahannock where the two ships were on routine patrol. Confederate deserters had disclosed the fact that a group of some 500 southern soldiers and sailors were in the vicinity, and the crews of the two ships were on full alert although the rough dark night would not favour any military activity. Acting Master John F. D. Robinson, captain of *Satellite* and senior officer of the two ships, dropped anchor about a mile and a quarter from shore, in the mouth of the Rappahannock at a point known as Butler's Hole.

Robinson was not a professional naval officer. Indeed, the navy had problems in enlisting a sufficiently strong officer corps throughout the war. There were not enough professional officers in the regular navy to staff all the boats and ships required to protect commerce, blockade the southern coast, and patrol all the inland waterways. Moreover, while the army could tap the thousands of men who before the war had served as amateur soldiers in the many volunteer militia units across the nation, the navy had no such resource because there was no corresponding naval militia. So the navy had to commission men with maritime or technical experience in such fields as medicine or engineering as 'acting' officers. After commissioning these men had no formal naval training in an officers' cadet school; they went directly into service bearing the insignia of their new ranks. Robinson was one of these new officers, having received his commission as an acting master on 12 March 1862.

After dropping anchor, Robinson ordered Acting Ensign Henry Walters, commander of *Reliance*, to anchor some 200 yards away. Walters' commission was even more recent than Robinson's; he had been made an acting ensign, the lowest commissioned rank, on 19 January 1863.

Walters didn't like the order. 'Although the *Reliance* was a commissioned vessel of war,' he wrote, 'she was a very small tug propeller, with but one serviceable gun [a 24-pounder] mounted aft, and with a crew reduced by promotion and discharge to 10 men forward, and 4 firemen, the officers besides myself being one master's mate and two engineers.'

'The *Reliance* was very low in the water, her rail being no higher than a large cutter's gunwale, and therefore, with an enemy well organized, and so greatly outnumbering us, the capture, while lying at anchor, was not a very doubtful venture.'[1] But orders were orders, and reluctantly Walters dropped anchor.

Because of the constant threat of capture by shore parties, the Potomac Flotilla, which had overall command of all naval vessels on the Rappahannock, had issued strict instructions to vessels intending to anchor by night. Boarding nettings were to be secured in place; anchors had to be ready for slipping at short notice; steam pressure was to be kept up so that vessels could get under way immediately; guns were to be kept loaded with canister, an excellent short-range anti-personnel weapon, and smallarms were to be kept ready for instant use, rather than locked up under the master's control. And, as usual in all naval vessels, watches were to be kept throughout the night.

Aboard *Reliance*, a slip buoy was attached to the anchor cable and the ship's single working gun was loaded, but not primed. The watch was not armed, indeed this was not stipulated, but the arms chest was unlocked. The fireman, Daniel J. Cole, slept, as was his custom, on a settee in the engine room and could be quickly roused if necessary.

Satellite's complement at this time numbered six officers, two petty officers, and 24 ratings. Her anchor chain was shackled, but a hammer was kept nearby to drive out the restraining pin. The ship's boilers had some 20 pounds of pressure. The usual watch, consisting of two armed seamen and an officer, was on duty, and on this occasion the duty of Officer of the Watch had fallen to Acting Master's Mate William Fogg.

While the crews of both ships had acted according to the letter so far as the Flotilla's security orders were concerned, neither could really be called totally ready for action.

In *Reliance*, seamen had been allowed to sling their hammocks so low on the quarter-deck that they interfered with the movement and aim of the one serviceable gun, and in fact a couple of chairs and a table had been placed next to the gun. Things were a bit more ship-shape on the larger *Satellite*, although Fogg had been known to catch a bit of sleep, against all orders, while on duty.

Unseen by the men who were preparing to turn in for the night, Confederates on the shoreline, in the driving rain, were watching across the pitching waters. Confederate States Navy First Lieutenant John Taylor Wood, commanding a force of some eleven officers and 71 men, was on the river bank, hidden by the woods which ran down to the water's edge. With him was a group of hand-picked volunteers from the CSS *Virginia* and Wheat's Louisiana Zouave Battalion. His sailors and marines had four boats concealed at the river bank, each large enough to take fifteen men.

If there were one man in the Confederacy who was capable of conducting such a cutting-out operation as was now planned, it was John Taylor Wood. Nephew of President Jefferson Davis, he had been an instructor in gunnery at the US Navy Academy before the war. Joining the Confederate Navy at the war's outbreak, he had seen service as a Second Lieutenant aboard CSS *Virginia* during her famous dual with USS *Monitor*. After that battle he had been assigned to shore duty, commanding navy guns at Drewy's Bluff that had repelled a Union attempt to capture Richmond on 15 May 1862. Then he had talked the Navy Department into letting him lead small raids against blockading Union ships. In his first exploit, he had taken thirteen Confederate seamen out in a small boat on the night of 7 October 1862 and captured and burned the steamer *Francis Elmore* which was lying at anchor off Lower Cedar Point in the Potomac River. In January 1863 he had received another commission, as colonel of cavalry, and was appointed to serve as a liaison officer between the two branches of service, army and navy.

The night grew stormier. The Confederates, shielding their weapons and ammunition against the heavy weather, waited until after midnight.[2] When the last light flickered out aboard the anchored ships, they climbed into their boats and rowed out to them. Within hailing distance, they drew up in line. CS Marine Corps Second Lieutenant Francis L. Hoge, of the *Virginia*, in command of two the boats, had headed for *Reliance*, while Wood took the others on to *Satellite*.

The forward lookout in *Satellite*, Nelson Frazier, hailed the approaching boats: 'Who is there?'

'Second cutters!' came the immediate reply.

'Come alongside.'

When the Confederates drew closer Frazier could see their sword blades glinting through the rain. 'Who are you?' he yelled again.

'Privateers,' came a rather more truthful reply.

'Boarders!' Frazier exclaimed, as Fogg, attracted by the noise on deck, appeared at his side.

'Boarders,' Fogg agreed, and he turned and ran aft. There the executive officer, Acting Ensign Rudolph Sommers, also aroused by the noise, was just coming out of his cabin.

Sommers acted quickly. 'Immediately I seized my cutlass and pistol,' he later wrote. 'I stepped on deck; my attention was attracted to the noise aft. Still thinking the noise was made by our own men, before I could reach the quarter-deck (in which direction I was going), I received a shot in my neck. The boarders, observing that I was armed, attacked me with their cutlasses, and, being closely pressed, I freely used my pistol as a sling shot, during which time I received three cuts over my arm, when, being overpowered, I was placed in my room with a sentry over me.'

Boatswain's Mate Jack Tye was another quick-thinking sailor. He darted towards the boat's bell, with the intention of alerting the engine room, but he was spotted and mortally wounded in the shoulder before he could get to the bell. Master-at-Arms William Bigham dashed to the armoury and managed to pass out three pistols, but without any percussion caps, so they were of little use save as clubs. Bigham was reaching for a pike when one of the Confederates felled him with a cutlass blow to the head.

Other members of the crew had also fallen. Master-at-Arms Samuel Chin, one of the rare African-American petty officers, was wounded. Paymaster's Steward N. H. Stavey was shot in the arm. Fireman Thomas Damon lay dead on the deck.

By now the rest of the crew had pulled on clothes and were racing for the deck, but the well-rehearsed boarding-party were firmly in control. Some held the hurricane deck, others the forward deck, and some had broken down the locked companion-way door and were making their way below. *Satellite*'s crew was quickly rounded up and placed under guard.

Indeed, the crew were out of bravery at all levels. Fogg had run to alert the captain when the Confederates stormed aboard. 'Boarders, sir,' he panted as Captain Robinson opened the door a crack.

'Well, drive them off, sir,' Robinson replied, slamming the door in Fogg's face and disappearing from the fight.

Acting Second Assistant Engineer Isaac Johnson, who was in charge of the engine, left his stateroom in time to see Sommers fall, his arm bleeding severely. Not wishing to share the same fate, he quickly stepped back inside and slammed the door. Fogg and Acting Third Assistant Engineer Christopher McCormick were nowhere to be seen during the fight, although Acting Third Assistant Engineer John Mee did remain at his station as ordered.

As the mêlée died down, not a single shot having been fired by the defenders, Confederates pounded on Captain Robinson's door. 'I surrender,' he shouted, arms raised high, as they smashed the door open.

'If you don't come out and stand on the gun carriage and halloo out you surrender the ship, we'll blow your brains out,' one of the Confederates said.

Robinson quickly came out to the quarter-deck, shouting as loudly as he could that he surrendered the ship. The largest of the two ships, and the most easily defended, was in Confederate hands.

Things were not going quite so well for them aboard *Reliance*.

Her lookout, John Hand, had spotted the Confederate boats when they were some 75 yards off and had demanded identification. They chose not to reply to his first hail. He called out again, and as they drew near a Southern voice replied, 'Putnam'.

Something about the voice was not right and Hand yelled 'If you come closer, I'll fire!' Anthony Spisenger, in charge of the watch, heard the exchange and joined Hand. When the Confederates were some ten yards off Hand fired his rifle at them and then ran aft, while Spisenger shouted 'Rebel boarders!' and began firing.

While the crew were tumbling out of their hammocks, Hand rejoined Spisenger, who was still firing, accompanied by a Confederate Army deserter named Lawson who had earlier surrendered aboard *Reliance*, and another seaman, John Watson. The four of them kept up a steady fire, but the Confederates closed *Reliance* and scrambled over her low bulwarks. Once aboard they dropped to the deck and a brief, fierce firefight ensued. Lieutenant Hoge was hit in the neck by a pistol ball and was unable to continue in command of the boarding-party. Midshipman H. S. Cooke, also hit twice but only slightly, waved his men on, firing his revolver as they darted forward to engage the Union defenders who were maintaining their fire.

Reliance's commander, Walters, was up and running the moment his feet hit the deck. He dashed forward, yelling to the men there to slip the cables – which they did not do – and he was cut in the hand by a Confederate cutlass. He then headed for the pilot-house, intending to take his ship out into the main channel, but at the door a bullet slammed into his stomach and tore out of his back.

Later he reported that he had 'succeeded in crawling to the wheel and blowing the whistle for help from the *Satellite*, not knowing she had been captured so quickly'. He had then passed out.

Aboard *Satellite*, John Taylor Wood heard the firing and the whistle sounding and ordered a boat-load of his men off to reinforce their fellow-boarders in *Reliance*.

'In the meantime,' a court of inquiry later found, 'the enemy were captured one by one, and some spotty firing, without order or command, was still carried on by the men of the *Reliance*. Thomas Brown, acting master's mate and executive officer, was, in the early part of the attack, awakened, and as soon as he came out of the cabin went forward on the starboard side, passing within 4 or 5 feet of the arms chest without arming himself, until he reached the engine-room door, when he cried out several times to the enemy that he surrendered, making no resistance at any time during the attack.'

At the beginning of the struggle, Acting Third Assistant Engineer Alexander D. Renshaw had hidden himself beneath the engine-room deck and stayed there until the fighting ended. Acting Second Assistant Engineer James McCauly did not take part in the fighting, but when he saw that there was no chance to save the ship, he sabotaged the engine in the hope that they would be unable to move before other Union ships arrived to reclaim *Reliance*.

When the third boatload of Confederates arrived, they scrambled over the low rails and quickly overcame the few remaining Union sailors. The Confederate deserter, perhaps lucky in the long run, was killed in the fighting.

Hoge had been seriously wounded, but Midshipman Cooke and another enlisted man were only slightly wounded and were able to stay on their feet. Two Union men were killed, including the deserter, and four wounded. Both ships were now the property of the Confederate States Navy.

Given the poor visibility and the absence of other Union vessels, and the fact that the engine gearing had to be repaired, Wood decided to spend the night where they were. In the morning he brought his two prizes into Urbana where the Union prisoners and the wounded men from both sides were put ashore, the Union men to spend only a few days in captivity before being paroled. The Union naval command, having no vessels nearby, were unaware of the loss of these two ships.

Wood planned to use them to capture other US Navy boats on the river, but they were both short of coal and there was little available nearby. Even so, he split as much coal as he could get between the two and set out next day. 'The *Reliance*, not working well, was ordered back,' he later reported. 'A fresh breeze from the southward, with rough water, prevented the accomplishment of anything.' The advantage of surprise on the 23rd had been lost.

The weather had improved on the 24th and Wood set out once more. His ships soon fell in with, and captured, three unsuspecting schooners, and he replenished his bunkers with their coal, ready for action again on the 25th.

By now, however, the US Navy knew that two their vessels were missing. 'There is some mystery about the capture of these vessels, or the most disgraceful neglect of duty I have ever heard of,' reported Lieutenant Commander Samuel Magaw, commanding officer of the Potomac Flotilla.

Stung by this loss, Magaw gathered a sizeable force, including two ironclads, and moved towards where the ships were now berthed. On their approach, Wood had one of the schooners stripped, and fled with the other ships up-river to Port Royal where the shallow waters would keep the larger Union ships at a distance.

While the US Navy were milling about down-river, the US Army swung into action. Major General George G. Meade, commanding the Army of the Potomac, sent a cavalry division with two batteries of light artillery, to Port Conway, across the river from Port Royal.

When Wood's small flotilla reached Port Royal, the blue-jacketed gunners were in position and immediately opened fire. Wood saw that he was badly outgunned and had no chance of getting his ships away. Therefore, as he later reported, 'steamers and vessels were stripped and scuttled. While this was being done the enemy from the opposite side shelled the steamers and our position for four hours without injury. Three guns landed from the steamers were in position and replied.'

On the morning of 2 September 1863, cavalry commander Brigadier General Judson Kilpatrick reported back to Meade: 'The enemy have abandoned the boats. Elder has riddled the *Satellite*. She is fast sinking. The *Reliance* is receiving a heavy fire from both batteries.'

In the hurried stripping, under fire, a 32-pound gun was lost overboard, but the remaining guns were shipped to Richmond for Confederate Navy use. All the machinery was removed except the boilers, after which the ships were scuttled. The careers of the ships' captains were also scuttled by this affair. Acting Master Robinson was dismissed from the service on 21 November, less than a month after losing his ship, and Acting Ensign Henry Walters of the *Reliance* was dismissed from the service on the same day. *Satellite*'s executive officer, Acting Ensign Sommers, who had served well in the emergency, was promoted to acting master on 8 December 1864. He was honourably discharged on 27 August 1868.

Of the various engineering officers, Acting Second Engineer Johnson, who had sat out the fight in his stateroom, was not dismissed, but his naval career was effectively finished and he resigned on 30 December 1864. Of the other two engineering officers in *Satellite*, Acting Third Assistant Engineer McCormick, who was not seen during the fight, stayed in the Navy until honourably discharged on 29 March 1866, and Acting Third Assistant Engineer Mee, who had remained at his post throughout the fight, nevertheless received a simple discharge on 27 December 1864. Acting Third Assistant Engineer Renshaw, who had been reported as hiding aboard *Reliance* during the fight, overcame the difficulties his conduct had created, and remained in the Navy until honourably discharged on 8 December 1866.

On the Confederate side, Lieutenant Wood went on to cut out USS *Underwriter*, the largest of the gunboats, near New Berne, North Carolina, in February 1864, Midshipman Cooke serving with him during this exploit. Wood then received a sea command, that of CSS *Tallahassee*, which captured some thirteen northern vessels off the North Atlantic coastline during the second half of 1864. He was promoted to the rank of captain on 10 February 1865. He was back in Richmond in time to be at the president's side when he learned of the fall of Petersburg and fled with him, to be captured with President Davis on 10 May 1865. Unlike Davis, however, he managed to escape, by bribing a guard, and reached Cardenas Bay, Cuba, on 11 June 1865. He then set up a merchant commission house in Halifax, Nova Scotia, where he died on 19 July 1904.

10
The Siege of Plymouth, North Carolina, 17–20 April 1864

One of the problems in pacifying an area as large as the south, from the Union government's point of view, was to decide which was the better option: to concentrate large garrisons in major towns or forts from which they could control neighbouring towns; or to put a small garrison into every town of note. Along the North Carolina coast the latter course was adopted because by early 1864 US Army troops had already captured many of the coastal ports, and had been left in 'penny packets' in several of them to guard against much needed supplies from Europe reaching southern hands. There were garrisons at New Berne at the head of the Neuse River, at Washington on the Pamlico River and at Plymouth. These towns were some 30 miles apart.

The northernmost of these garrisons was at Plymouth, North Carolina, a small town on the Roanoke River which runs into Albemarle Sound along the North Carolina Coast. It had fallen early to Federal troops, and in 1864 was garrisoned by some 2,834 officers and men under the command of Brigadier Henry W. Wessells who, at 55, was elderly by Civil War command standards. He had been noted for gallantry in the Mexican War, but thereafter his career had stalled, and he had served in the west without promotion for fourteen years. He had been wounded slightly during the Seven Pines fighting around Richmond in 1862, where he had commanded a brigade. Recovering from his wound, he had been named commander of the District of the Albemarle on 3 May 1863.

The town, only three blocks deep and four blocks wide, situated on a high area with swampland reaching in fingers towards the town, was defended by a string of forts, redoubts and entrenchments. Fort Grey, on the south bank of the Roanoke River, west of the town, had been sited to protect the town against attack from down that river. A mile away on the south-western edge of the town lay Fort Wessells, on a road that ran around the town, on a high spot of land between two swamps. A redoubt placed halfway between the fort and the town covered its line of retreat. Battery Worth had been built right at the river's edge, on the western side of town. Fort Williams, the strongest post in the entire series of works, was at the centre of the southern sector of the defensive line, while Conaby Redoubt and Fort Comfort covered the eastern sector.

The US Navy was present near Plymouth to aid in its defence. Indeed, naval gunfire was a basic component of the defensive planning. The eastern

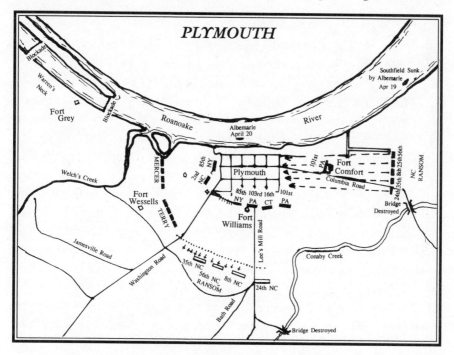

and western sectors, through which were the only clear approaches to the town, could easily be swept by ships' guns, which made any attack from those quarters very chancy at best. The only other way to approach the town was directly from the south, over what was largely swampland.

Four river gunboats, *Miami*, *Ceres*, *Whitehead* and *Southfield*, were docked at the town's edge, and an armed transport, the *Bombshell*, was available in a pinch. The flotilla was commanded by Lieutenant Commander Charles W. Flusser, an intelligent career naval officer who had received his first commission in 1847.

The *Miami*, the flotilla's flagship, was a side-wheel gunboat built for narrow and shallow coastal waters, and could go either way quickly without having to put about. She was well armed with six 9-inch smoothbores, a 100-pound rifled gun and a 24-pounder. She carried a crew of 134 hands.

The *Ceres* was a small 4th-rate side-wheel boat, mounting two 30-pounders and two smoothbore 24-pounders. She carried a crew of only 45.

The *Whitehead* was another small, 4th-rater, but she was a screw-driven vessel, not a side-wheeler. Her crew of 45 men had only one 100-pound rifled gun and three 24-pound howitzers at their disposal.

The *Southfield*, a side-wheeler, had been built in 1857 as a civilian ship and acquired by the US Navy in December 1861 when the Navy was putting everything that could float under the flag to blockade Southern ports. She was armed with only six guns, a 100-pound Parrott rifle and five 9-inch smoothbore guns. Her crew numbered 61 all ranks.

The Union garrison included not only artillerymen to man the guns in the forts, but a number of infantry regiments. The 85th New York Infantry had been serving since December 1861 and had seen a great deal of hard fighting, including the Peninsular Campaign, before being sent to the Carolina shore.

The 101st and 103rd Pennsylvania Infantry Regiments were both mustered in February 1862, and had also seen Peninsular Campaign service. The 103rd was missing its Company C which was stationed on Roanoke Island. In 1864 the men of both regiments were looking forward to their first furlough after two years of active service.

The 2nd North Carolina had been raised at New Berne in November 1863 from among loyal Union natives of North Carolina; they had not seen a great deal of action, having been stationed in this relatively peaceful theatre since their enlistment. Only two companies of the regiment were in the Plymouth garrison.

The 16th Connecticut Infantry had arrived in the town in January, together with the 15th Connecticut which had been sent on to New Berne. The 16th was an experienced regiment, in service since August 1862, and its men were veterans of many battles, including Antietam and Fredericksburg.

In Richmond, General Braxton Bragg, discredited in the popular mind after his disastrous campaigns in the west, but still popular with his pre-war friend Jefferson Davis, was officially in charge of 'the conduct of the military operations in the armies of the Confederacy'.[1] Bragg came up with a plan to sweep the North Carolina coast clear of these annoying Federal garrisons. It called for a joint Confederate Army/Navy operation, using one infantry division and an ironclad to attack each garrison in turn and capture them all.

Bragg chose Brigadier General Robert F. Hoke, a North Carolina native and graduate of the Kentucky Military Institute, to command the military element of the operation. Hoke's troops would consist of his own brigade, with two more brigades, commanded by Matt W. Ransom, another native North Carolinian and a lawyer before the war, and James L. Kemper, a Virginian who had seen service as a captain of volunteers in the Mexican War. All three brigades were presently part of the Army of Northern Virginia.

The Confederates had a trump card: the ironclad CSS *Albemarle*, which had been laid down in North Carolina waters in April 1863 and commissioned on 17 April 1864. Her commander and, as much as any, her builder, was Lieutenant Commander James W. Cooke, who had been badly wounded in naval battles at Roanoke Island in 1862. She featured an octagonal 6-inch casemate on a flat hull powered by two horizontal non-condensing engines. She was lightly armed, having only two 6.4-inch rifles, but she had been designed as a ram rather than as a gun platform.

Commander Flusser was aware of the threat posed by *Albemarle*, but thought his flotilla could beat her. His plan, were she to attack his ships, was to join *Miami* and *Southfield* together with a number of chains to form a gigantic gun platform that would ensnare *Albemarle* between the two, and then destroy the Confederate ship by gunfire or by boarding.

In early April Wessells heard that Hoke's division was approaching Plymouth, and on the 13th he and Flusser received news of *Albemarle*'s imminent arrival off Plymouth. Wessells was not convinced that Flusser's flotilla could fend off the Confederate ironclad, and telegraphed the commander at New Berne and Major General Benjamin F. Butler, an excellent politician turned poor general, at Fortress Monroe, Virginia, for reinforcements. His pleas fell on deaf ears, although additional troops already stationed at nearby Washington, North Carolina, could have been made available.

Hoke's men were in position near Plymouth on 16 April, and spent an uneasy night before moving forward to the attack at 4 a.m. on Sunday the 17th, '... an ideal spring day ... neither too warm nor too cool for comfort'.[2] Sunrise was at about 5.15 and a Union cavalry patrol set out to reconnoitre the town's outskirts. Shortly afterwards troops in the town, just dismissed from their morning formations to make breakfast, heard a 'murderous volley' from the direction of woods outside the town.[3] Then sentries along the line of earthworks saw the cavalrymen galloping back, some leading horses with empty saddles.

The drummers sounded the long roll and men dashed to their action positions, but Hoke was not going to oblige them with an infantry assault. After three years of war, even the lowest private knew that an assault against entrenched infantry was bound to fail.

Instead, Hoke brought artillery up and his infantrymen stood and watched as his cannon opened up on Fort Grey. Cannon fire smashed into the fort, which had been equipped with a 100-pounder and two 32-pounders for use against enemy ships rather than for a counter-battery role. The fort soon began to get the worst of the one-sided battle.

'Last night almost continual skirmishing was kept up,' Private S. J. Gibson of the 103rd Pennsylvania noted in his diary. 'The Rebs seem determined to have Ft. Gray but so far have been repulsed with considerable loss & the loss of 1 piece of Arty.'[4]

Wessells took advantage of the attacks centred against Fort Grey, away from the town itself, to get the mob of civilian dependants, mostly women who followed the regiment as washerwomen and for other reasons, and their children, aboard the Union steamboat *Massasoit*. A number of sick and wounded soldiers were also embarked to avoid falling into the hands of the Confederates. Many left reluctantly, having heard that *Albemarle* was on her way, and she was invulnerable, and if *Massasoit* ran into the Confederate ram they would be dead ducks.

'Ladies,' Commander Flusser said to one frightened group. 'I have waited two long years for the rebel ram. The Navy will do its duty. We shall sink, destroy, or capture it, or find our graves in the Roanoke.'[5]

Another transport ship, the *Bombshell*, attempted to reach Fort Grey, to bring ammunition and evacuate any wounded, but she came under fire before reaching the river bank, and was holed twice below the waterline. She just managed to get to her wharf at Plymouth where she settled on the bottom.

Apart from this success, and some casualties in the fort, the Confederate artillery had caused relatively little damage to Fort Grey's works.

A second boat, the *Ceres*, was sent towards Fort Grey, to add some weight to the counter-battery fire, but again the Confederate artillery, especially one 32-pounder overlooking the river, brought their fire to bear and within minutes nine of her crew were dead or wounded, and *Ceres* was severely damaged and had to withdraw.

Meanwhile, the Confederate infantry, deployed into skirmish lines, were darting forward under whatever cover they could find, to trade musketry with the Union infantry within the town's entrenchments. At Fort Williams, the 24th New York Battery kept up a steady fire against these will-o'-the-wisps. Then a gunner was ramming home a round when his Number Three prematurely inserted the primer and pulled the lanyard. The resulting explosion hurled the shot and rammer out of the muzzle and the unfortunate gunner lost one arm and the other was shattered. Black powder and pieces of cloth and buttons were burned deep into his body. Still alive, he was carried away by his fellows and survived until 26 April.

Finally, at about 12.30 p.m. on the 18th, Ransom's brigade charged Fort Williams, at the centre of the Union line, and got to within 300 yards of the earthworks before concentrated musketry and cannon fire drove them off. Their desperate charge showed the town's defenders what they were up against. 'It was very evident to us that we must either be killed or go to "Libby" [prisoner-of-war camp]' later wrote 16th Connecticut Lieutenant Bernard F. Blakeslee.[6] The Confederates, badly bloodied, fell back to their starting-positions.

While Ransom was urging his men on towards Fort Williams, Hoke sent his own brigade against Fort Wessells. Captain Nelson Chapin, commander of the men of the 85th inside the fort, dashed from point to threatened point to rally his beleaguered men. Again and again the Confederates reached the very base of Wessells' walls where the defenders hurled heavy hand-grenades at them while a steady fire was brought to bear. Captain Chapin fell mortally wounded. After the fourth or fifth attempt (those involved not surprisingly had lost count) some of the Confederates managed to leap over the walls and the defenders began to retreat towards the town, stopping from time to time to return fire.

The survivors of the 85th made it safely to their own lines, where they threw themselves exhausted to the ground and waited for a renewed attack. None came. The Confederates were almost as exhausted as the men of the 85th. They rested in the shelter of the fort while Hoke had artillery brought up and knocked holes in the fort's walls through which to aim his guns at the town.

In the early hours of the 19th, the Confederate behemoth, *Albemarle*, slowly made her way up the river towards the waiting Union vessels. At about 3.30 a.m. sparks blowing skywards from her stack could be seen by the Union sailors and by the Union artillerymen in Fort Grey who immediately opened up on the Confederate ship. But all the rounds fired, even from the 100-pounder, bounced harmlessly off her sides. Within minutes *Albemarle* had passed the fort and was out of range.

At the same time, the linked Union ships started down-river to a point where the Roanoke bends to the north-east. Here Flusser thought to trap *Albemarle* between his two ships, but Commander Cooke was suspicious and kept his vessel close to the southern bank. Suddenly, he put her helm hard over and headed straight for the two Union ships in mid-channel at top speed. Shot from the Union ships' forward guns bounced off the 6-inch armour as she came at them.

Then *Albemarle* struck a glancing blow across *Miami*'s bows, and rammed *Southfield* heavily in her starboard side. The tethering chains snapped like twigs, and the boats were driven apart. *Albemarle* now engaged *Miami* at short range and her heavy rounds caused casualties and damaged the ship. *Southfield* meanwhile was taking in water badly through a gaping hole in her hull.

Now the Union sailors' priority was to save their ships. While *Miami* began to drift away, *Southfield*'s pumps were manned but the ship was already foundering. *Albemarle*'s chain-plates on her forward deck were wedged in *Southfield*'s framing and her bows began to sink ever deeper until water was pouring in through her forward portholes. Her commander reversed his cranky engines with as much pressure as the boilers could take, but within ten minutes *Southfield* had settled on the bottom, dragging *Albemarle* with her. Having hit the bottom, *Albemarle*'s engines were able to back her out and she bobbed up like a rubber duck, her decks several inches awash, but otherwise relatively undamaged.

When *Southfield* was going down, her captain, Acting Volunteer Lieutenant C. A. French, and 42 of her crew jumped from her sides and swam or rowed towards *Miami*. Most of the others went down with the ship. A few managed to swim to the shore where they were quickly captured by Confederate infantrymen.

Miami, now alongside the Confederate ironclad, continued to bounce her shells off *Albemarle*'s sides. One shell, with a 10-second fuze, fired by the 100-pounder which was aimed by Commander Flusser himself, bounced back off the ironclad into the Union ship, landed on the deck almost beneath the commander's feet and, while he was still grasping the lanyard, and in a state of shock, exploded, tearing him to pieces. 'Our 100-lb rifle was fired and struck her plumb, but the shot ... produced no

more effect than one of those little torpedoes we have Fourth of Julys,'
wrote the ship's assistant surgeon later. 'They killed our commander, C. W.
Flusser, and wounded Ensign Harris, Engineer Harrington, and ten men.
Capt. Flusser was awfully mangled had 19 musket balls and pieces of shell
in different parts of his body, one arm was blown off.'[7]

With the flotilla commander down, the crew rallied to try to board
Albemarle, but some two dozen Confederate sailors and marines, clearly
well-trained for just such a defence, climbed the ram's turtle-like shell, to its
flat top from where they fired volley after volley into *Miami's* decks below
them. As soon as a man had fired, he would pass the musket down and
receive a loaded one. The Union crew was largely driven below decks.
Clearly unable to board or damage the iron-clad, *Miami* steamed away from
Plymouth, followed by the other equally useless Union gunboats. The Confederate ship pursued them for a while, but then returned to help the army
capture the town.

After the battle, *Albemarle's* commander reported that she had taken 44
hits from US cannonfire, only one round of which had done any damage
worth noting.

In the meantime, the Confederate army had kept up a steady artillery
barrage on the town and its defensive works. Ransom's Brigade moved
along the axis of the Columbia Road, which ran east almost parallel to the
river, while Confederate pioneers built a pontoon bridge across Conaby
Creek under cover of darkness. By midnight all the Confederates were in a
line at right angles to the Columbia Road, facing the lines around Fort
Comfort, in position to begin the next day's offensive.

'Morning comes after a night of terror,' Private Gibson wrote on the
19th. 'The Rebs are before us, behind us, and on each side of us. They have
carried Ft. Wessells on our right & turned its guns on us. their "RAM" has
sunk the G. B. Southfield and driven off our fleet. Now we are "gone up"
unless we get reinforcements, but we will die "game". Bombardment con-
tinues all day. Work under a galling crossfire all day & at night Co "B" have
to go on picket. The night is made lively by bursting shells and the sharp
rattle of musketry.'[8]

Sunrise on the 20th was at about 6.30. Private Gibson noted in his
diary: 'Our flag still floats defiantly, but we cannot hold out much longer,
the Rebs have got all their artillery in position and have carried the forts on
our left. Just at daylight the "ball opens". I am on picket in front of the
works. My chance for getting in looks rather blue.'[9]

The Confederate attack began with a charge across a cow pasture north, on the river side, of the Columbia Road. Rebel yells – those terrifying high-pitched screeches which so demoralized the men on the other side of the field – mingled with artillery explosions. 'At 7 a.m. the enemy has gained the town & are now in our rear,' Private Gibson wrote.[10] The attackers quickly swarmed over the walls of Fort Comfort and the Conaby Redoubt, driving the defenders, the 101st Pennsylvania, into the streets behind them.

Men of the 16th Connecticut and 103rd Pennsylvania, together with survivors of the 101st, were thrown into a hasty line in the town's centre. 'Forward!' the order came, to drive the five regiments of the Confederate brigade back and regain the old works. Wrote Private Gibson: 'We form & advance to drive them out. Then commences a most terrific streetfight.'[11]

The three understrength Union regiments failed to push back the victorious Confederates. Instead, the men on both sides broke into houses and fired from their windows, while others ducked behind fences and trees to keep up a steady stream of fire. Neither side was able to advance. In the centre, where Fort Williams was still in Union hands, the 8th North Carolina charged across the fields and up the bluff towards the fort. Men of the 85th and 103rd opened fire. The Confederates reached the very base of the walls, to be met by grenades and fire from every smallarm the defenders could find. Finally, the broken 8th, retired, taking more losses as they fell back across the open field.

Hoke decided not to try any more assaults, but simply to use his artillery to force the Union troops to surrender. First, however, during a lull, he sent a flag of truce to demand Wessells' surrender. Recalled Private Gibson: 'At 8 a.m., a parley. Uncon. surr. dem. No surr, come and take us.'[12] Wessells declined to surrender.

But the Union defenders were in a bad spot and they knew it. The Confederate guns opened up, including those in *Albemarle* which was now alongside the town a matter of mere yards from the river bank. As General Wessells recalled: 'I was now completely enveloped on every side ... a cannonade of shot and shell was opened upon [Fort Williams] from four different directions. The terrible fire had to be endured without reply, for no man could live at the guns. The breastwork was struck by solid shot on every side, fragments of shells sought almost every interior angle of the work, the whole extent of the parapet was swept by musketry ... this condition of affairs could not be long endured without reckless sacrifice of life ...'[13]

Still hoping for a miracle, the Union garrison waited out the night. The next morning, 20 April, there was no line of black smoke along the river that would indicate a relieving flotilla of Union gunboats and transports. There was no rattle of gunfire behind the Confederate lines that would indicate reinforcements coming overland. The numbers of wounded were increasing and it was difficult to protect them from shot raining in from four sides. Wessells felt that he had no choice; he surrendered at 10 a.m.

'General,' he said to Hoke as he handed the victorious Confederate his sword, 'this is the saddest day of my life.'

Hoke's response can be excused. 'General, this is the proudest day of mine.'[14]

The Union troops were all taken prisoner, and had suffered some 300 casualties. Gibson's last note in his diary for the battle reads: 'At 10 a.m. our flag is lowered. We are prisoners of war.'[15] Many of them would not survive captivity in places like Andersonville.

On 21 April Hoke telegraphed army headquarters at Richmond: 'I have stormed and carried this place, capturing 1 brigadier, 1,600 men, stores, 25 pieces of artillery.'[16] On 23 April Jefferson Davis himself telegraphed back: 'Accept my thanks and congratulations for the brilliant success which has attended your attack and capture of Plymouth. You are promoted to be a major-general from that date.'[17] A Confederate naval salvage crew retrieved *Southfield's* 100-pounder from the water and mounted her in a works along the river, part of the town's defences against recapture.

But the victory had been hard bought: total Confederate casualties were 1,900 officers and men, more men than the Confederates had captured or killed. And these were men that the south could not replace so easily as men in the northern forces could be replaced.

Hoke's men went on to other battles in North Carolina, but ultimately had to be recalled to Virginia where Lee's army was fighting for its life. As soon as he and his men had gone, the Union troops re-appeared and quietly recaptured everything that had been lost. On 31 October 1864, just over six months after the defeat at Plymouth, Union troops retook the town, this time for good.

In the end, defeat at Plymouth was an ultimate victory.

11
The Defence of Fort Pillow
21 April 1864

In many ways the American Civil War was unlike any other civil war before or after in that by and large the participants acted with restraint and treated their opponents honourably. Naturally there were excesses from time to time – the Confederates declared that many of their men had been bayoneted after capture in the early stages of Cedar Mountain, for example – but such incidents were rare. As time went on, and the south began to suffer, however, many southerners, especially those from the frontier where violence was a normal part of life, began to grow desperate.

The states then considered western states, such as Tennessee, were usually the scenes of harsher fighting between neighbours, who claimed to represent the north or south, than states such as Virginia or Maryland. In large areas of Tennessee, as well as North Carolina and Alabama, armed mobs roamed the rural areas, torturing and killing men, women and children, usually in the name of the Union or the Confederacy, though what they were really after was booty. It was not long before for the Civil War in those areas took on the appearance of the traditional civil war that was characterized by atrocity.

Confederate supporters shed much of their conventional honourable behaviour when confronted by African-Americans wearing the uniform of the US Army. Southerners had been brought up to believe that the blacks they thought they knew, and whom they saw as behaving sometimes foolishly happy, sometimes darkly sullen, were inferior beings. A gentlemen – which every white southerner regardless of social status considered himself – could not take part in honourable activity with black men; and in the frontier and southern code, fighting was considered one of the most honourable of all activities. The entire southern way of life was based on the belief that blacks were inferior in every way, and certainly not fit to bear arms, but always present though rarely spoken of was the great fear of them. The very thought of armed blacks was quite simply too terrifying to be borne.

Of course, the Federal government was aware of these factors and had from the beginning made it a strict policy that all its soldiers be treated equally, regardless of race. Retribution was threatened against any Confederates who mistreated US soldiers of any sort, and after three years of war, which included major defeats such as the Vicksburg campaign and Gettysburg, there were more than enough Confederate prisoners for the threat to be carried out. The Confederate government knew this, and as a matter of policy did not visit especially harsh treatment on the majority of US coloured prisoners.

All of this led to the most controversial and horrendous action of the war, the overrunning of Fort Pillow, Tennessee, and the fate of many of its defenders afterwards.

Fort Pillow sat on a bluff overlooking the point where Cold Creek flowed into the Mississippi River. It had been built by the Confederates in 1861 as part of their defences of Memphis. The fort was horseshoe shaped, about 125 yards long, and faced landwards rather than towards the river. The inner wall was of packed earth, some four feet thick and six to eight feet high, behind which was an 8-foot-deep trench. The area was deeply cut by ravines and small streams.

Because the fort was so small, the garrison had built its barracks and post buildings, such as the headquarters and supply centre, outside the walls. These wooden buildings would be a danger if the fort were attacked, because they blocked some fields of fire, while affording attackers protection from both sight and shot.

After Memphis fell in 1862, the fort was abandoned by the Confederates and Federal forces soon took it over. It became one of a string of posts to defend lines of communication and supply.

In 1864 the garrison was relatively small, consisting of Companies A, B, C and D of the 7th US Regiment of Heavy Artillery, Colored – some 290 African-American soldiers. These companies, which had been organized originally as the 1st Alabama Siege Artillery (African Descent), had only been in service since March of that year. Major Lionel J. Booth, 6th US Heavy Artillery, Colored, a regiment also drawn from the old 1st Alabama, commanded the post. There were six pieces of artillery in the fort, and the US gunboat *New Era* (also known as 'Gunboat Number 7') was nearby if needed.

The 14th Tennessee Cavalry Regiment, USA, commanded by Major William F. Bradford, actually no more than a 4-company battalion, arrived at Fort Pillow on 8 February and began to recruit men for the regiment and impress horses 'from both the loyal and the disloyal, giving vouchers only to those who might furnish unmistakable evidence of their

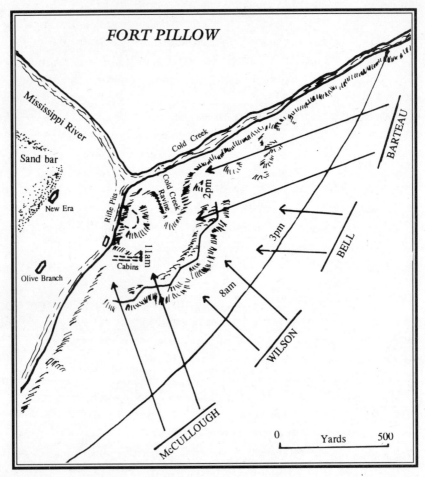

loyalty to the Government of the United States'.[1] By 10 April a fifth company had been recruited and this was ordered to Memphis, but Major Booth had heard rumours of a possible Confederate attack and made the request that they be allowed to stay until the threat had passed. His request was granted.

The 14th's strength as of 10 April was some ten officers and 258 enlisted men.

Brigadier General Nathan Bedford Forrest, a frontiersman slave trader, who had had only three months of formal schooling before the war, planned to take Fort Pillow. First he sent a brigade towards Paducah, Kentucky, to draw reinforcements away from the fort. His troops, led by Brigadier General Buford, also moved on Columbus, Kentucky. The captain commanding these troops sent a note to the garrison there, calling for their surrender to avoid bloodshed and adding: 'Should you surrender, the negroes now in arms will be returned to their masters. Should I, however, be compelled to take the place, no quarter will be shown to the negro troops whatever; the white troops will be treated as prisoners of war.'[2]

Was Forrest aware of this note? He was not there and he left no written statement, but it is unlikely that these sentiments would have been expressed by a comparatively low-ranking officer unless he had some knowledge of the thinking of his commanders. In any event, the mentality that prompted the declaration highlights the shameful blight that characterized the period.

In the early hours of 12 April, two brigades under the command of Brigadier General James R. Chalmers, a pre-war lawyer turned soldier, drove in the outer line of defenders and quickly surrounded Fort Pillow.

Union troops with flaring torches ran out, under fire, to try to burn down the barracks and other buildings around the fort. Confederate fire kept them low, and they were only able to start blazes in the row of buildings nearest the fort before being forced back behind their works. The buildings flared up and soon were smoking ruins, but the fire did not spread to the other buildings behind them. Confederate troops, protected by the ravines around the earthworks, made their way around the fort and kept the defenders' heads down with a steady fusillade. The Union troops began to suffer '... pretty severely in the loss of commissioned officers by the unerring aim of the rebel sharpshooters,' defender Lieutenant Mack J. Leaming reported.[3] Major Booth, standing at gun opening No. 2, received a mortal chest wound at about 9 o'clock, and Major Bradford assumed command.

The Confederates now launched an attack on the barracks and houses that stood near the fort. Using the ravines for cover, they soon had troops next to and inside the barracks and opened fire from this commanding position. 'From these barracks the enemy kept up a murderous fire on our men despite all our efforts to dislodge them,' Leaming wrote.[4]

Now they dashed forward and leaped down into the rifle pits which the Union troops had been forced to evacuate. They were now able to storm the fort, which was such a short distance away that their losses would be minimal.

At this point, about 3.30 p.m., Forrest raised a flag of truce and sent a message to Major Bradford claiming that he had received a fresh ammunition supply and pointing out that 'from their present position', it would be a simple matter to 'easily assault and capture the fort'. He added: 'The conduct of the officers and men garrisoning Fort Pillow has been such as to entitle them to being treated as prisoners of war. I demand the unconditional surrender of this garrison, promising that you shall be treated as prisoners of war,' and finally, 'Should my demand be refused, I cannot be responsible for the fate of your command.'[5]

Bradford requested an hour's grace so that he might confer with his fellow officers, and sent a signal to the gunboat: 'We are hard pressed and shall be overpowered.'[6] In the meantime, Forrest, worried that reinforcements might arrive by river, allowed him only twenty minutes.

During that time, a survivor later wrote: 'After our men had been fighting about four hours and were pretty well tired out, the smoke of a steamboat was seen by the river. The commander came around & said, "You have done well my boys. Hold out a little longer for there is a boat coming with reinforcements & if we can hold the place a little longer we will have plenty of help as there is a thousand soldiers on the boat."'[7]

Indeed a boat was coming up the river, so Forrest sent a couple of hundred men to each side of the river to fire on her when she came within range. The fort's defenders saw the Confederate troops moving out and realized that this meant the end of the truce, twenty minutes or not. But Bradford sent one of his officers out to talk to the Confederate parley group under protection of their white flag. Later some Confederates said that some of the Union defenders had yelled insults at their attackers during the truce.

Bradford did not believe that he and his men were facing Forrest, his emissary told the parley group. Indeed Forrest was here they replied, and there was an argument. Forrest, watching from a distance and growing impatient, saw his representative handed a note, and rode up to read it for himself: 'Negotiations will not attain the desired object.'[8]

Never one to waste time in pleasantries, Forrest asked the Union officer: 'In plain and unmistakable English. Will he fight or surrender?'[9] The officer went back to the fort and returned with a piece of paper on which was written: 'I will not surrender.'[10] The battle was on.

Forrest commanded his men to attack. He made it quite clear that he was watching them closely; that they were not to be turned loose and ignored. Indeed, he reported on 26 April: 'I dispatched staff officers to Colonels Bell and McCulloch, commanding brigades, to say to them that I should watch with interest the conduct of the troops; that Missourians, Mississippians, and Tennesseans surrounded the works, and I desired to see who would first scale the fort.'[11] Instead of leading the attack in person as was his custom, he picked a spot some 400 yards away from which to observe the conduct of the troops.

The waiting Union troops opened fire as the Confederates dashed out of their front lines around the barracks and in the ravines towards the walls. Although unsighted, the gunboat's cannon were also fired in the direction of the enemy, directed by signals from the fort, but indirect fire was at that time an extremely inexact science, and her shells had little effect on the outcome.

In the time it took for an infantryman to fire a couple of rounds, the southern troops were across the area and on top of the walls where they began firing down at the men in the fort. According to a survivor: 'During the last attack, when the rebels entered the works, I heard Major Bradford give the command, "Boys, save your lives!."'[12]

The battle was over. Confederate losses were minimal, fourteen dead and 86 wounded. Union losses until this point had not been especially great, either, but the numbers were about to increase.

Some Union men raised their arms in surrender, while others turned and ran down the banks towards the river, where a flatboat anchored in the middle offered some slight chance of survival. On 17 April one survivor wrote: 'As soon as the rebels got to the top of the bank there commenced the most horrible slaughter that could possibly be conceived. Our boys when they saw they were overpowered threw down their arms and held up, some their handkerchiefs & some their hands in token of surrender, but no sooner they were seen than they were shot down, & if one shot failed to kill them the bayonet or revolver did not.'[13]

According to Forrest the time from the attack to the last shot being fired was less than twenty minutes. He then turned his attention to a Parrott gun in the fort and organized a crew to fire at the gunboat, which promptly retired up-river.

In fact, it would appear that firing continued for longer than twenty minutes, but only from the Confederates. Many of the Union defenders, when they saw the Confederates firing into groups of surrendered soldiers, ran down the bluffs and into the water, trying to hide in the weeds along the water's edge. A large number of Confederate soldiers followed them, firing at wounded men and others who raised their arms in surrender. One Union soldier crawled into a hollow log, but was seen and killed. It looked to survivors as if the Confederates made special efforts to find those hiding in the small ravines along the water's edge, killing them as soon as found.

One soldier found a plank sticking out into the water, apparently used for a mooring. He lay face down on it, his face in the water with just enough room for air. There he lay, faking death, until it was dark enough to escape.

Corporal Jacob Wilson, one of the black artillerymen, made it down to the riverbank where he turned and saw Confederates firing into his surrendering comrades. Without a moment's hesitation, he dropped into the shallows and lay lying as still as possible in the chilly water. A Confederate soldier came up to him and asked him what was the matter. He'd been badly wounded, Wilson replied. The Confederate knelt down and began rifling his pockets. Then, after checking to see how much money he'd taken from Wilson, he walked off along the bank, apparently looking for more victims.

Wilson lay in the same position until about 3 a.m. Finally, hearing nothing more around him but the groans of the wounded, he quietly struck out for the small flatboat which had been ignored during the massacre. He lay for a while in the bottom of the boat and then as quietly as possible paddled it back to the bank where he helped three badly wounded men – as many as the boat could hold – aboard and paddled out to mid-channel where the current carried them downstream. When it finally drifted ashore the wounded men dragged themselves on to the bank, but fearing the presence of more southerners, they lay there playing dead until they were found by some Union soldiers.

Surgeon Charles Fitch, of the Union garrison, had been tending wounded below the bluff when the fort fell, and the report he produced on 30 April gives a keen insight into Forrest's thinking. As the victorious Confederates swarmed around him, their blood apparently boiling with their success, Fitch found a southern soldier in a more sober frame of mind and asked him who was in command. 'A soldier replied, "General Forrest." I asked, "Where is he?" He pointed to Forrest saying, "That is him sighting the Parrott Gun on the Gun boat." The breech of the gun was not over forty feet from me. I sprang instantly to Forrest, addressing him, "Are you Genl. Forrest?" He replied, "Yes sir, What do you want?" I told him I was the Surgeon of the Post, and asked protection from him that was due a prisoner. He said, "You are a Surgeon of a Damn Nigger Regiment." I replied, I was not. "You are a Damn Tenn. Yankee then." I told him I was from Iowa. Forrest said, "What in hell are you down here for? I have a great mind to have you killed for being down here." He then said if the North west had stayed home the war would have been over long ago, then turning to a Soldier told him to take charge of me and see that I was not harmed. For which I thanked him.'

Led away into the fort, Fitch reported seeing Confederates killing 'every negro that made his appearance dressed in a Federal uniform'. Fitch and his guard attracted the attention of every white Union prisoner around, and they flocked to the two, begging protection from their captors. In a short time, an entire detail, led by a Confederate lieutenant, had the group of prisoners surrounded, although not before '... some drunken Rebel soldiers came up and fired in among the Prisoners with their Revolvers, wounding some four or five'.[14]

D. W. Harrison, one of the loyal southerners in the 14th Tennessee, reached the bluff and turned to see a Confederate at close range aiming a revolver straight at him. Harrison shouted that he surrendered, and not to shoot. The Confederate lowered his revolver and, with a wave, told the Union soldier to go on up the bluff to the others in the fort. Harrison began to climb the bluff when yet another Confederate, his pistol raised, jumped in front of him. Again, Harrison called out not to shoot, but this time the Confederate ignored the plea and squeezed the trigger. Harrison fell, shot in the shoulder, and a moment later another Confederate shot him in the leg.

Harrison lay there, the cold shock of bad wounds taking over, when a fourth Confederate arrived, and pointed his weapon at the Union man. Harrison managed to croak that he'd been already badly wounded and begged him not to fire again. The man lowered his weapon and asked if the wounded man had any money. Harrison admitted he had a little and his watch if he wanted it. The Confederate bent over and took Harrison's watch and $90, a large sum at that time. He then walked away leaving Harrison to his fate. The end of the story is not known, but survivors believed that the Union man had probably been mortally wounded and didn't survive the shooting.

Bradford, having run into the river for safety, survived, but two days later he was shot dead at Brownsville, Tennessee. According to his captors, he had tried to escape and was killed in the process. With his death only three surviving officers, all lieutenants, of the Tennessee cavalry battalion remained, and two of them later died in a prisoner-of-war camp. Only Lieutenant Leaming was left to tell the tale.

The Confederates were venting their anger on men of both races in Union blue, but it is clear from a scrutiny of the numbers killed that the black soldiers suffered definitely greater losses than the loyal Tennessee troops. In all, 64 per cent of the black soldiers in the fort were killed or mortally wounded, as opposed to only some 31-34 per cent of white soldiers.[15]

Towards the end, some of the surviving black soldiers were made to dig mass graves for their fallen comrades. According to later testimony, many of them were then made to get into the graves and were buried alive. At least five men were so noted as having been buried while still alive. One of them, Daniel Tyler, Company B, said that he'd been shot three times and was smashed in the face, losing an eye in the process. Afterwards he was buried while alive. Amazingly, this tough soldier maintained consciousness and actually dug his way out of the shallow grave. Later he joked about being one of the best 'dug-outs' in the world.[16]

The Confederates committed these acts of senseless barbarity – for the period quite out of character – against two types of men they hated especially: African-Americans in the uniform of US Army soldiers, and citizens of their own state whom, they believed, had betrayed the state by joining the US Army.

Confederate participants in the massacre do not appear to have tried to hide what they had done from others, even civilians, although it is clear some did have misgivings. Sergeant Achilles V. Clark, one of Forrest's men, wrote to his sister on 19 April that he would leave it to her 'to judge whether or not we acted well or ill'. He went on to say: 'Our men were so exasperated by the Yankees' threats of no quarter that they gave but little. The slaughter was awful – words cannot describe the scene. The poor deluded negroes would run up to our men, fall upon their knees and with uplifted hands scream for mercy but they were ordered to their feet and then shot down. The white men fared but little better. Their fort turned out to be a great slaughter pen – blood, human blood stood about in pools and brains could have been gathered up in any quantity. I with several others tried to stop the butchery and at one time had partially succeeded but Gen. Forrest ordered them shot down like dogs and the carnage continued. Finally our men became sick of blood and the firing ceased.'[17]

Forrest himself does not appear to have realized the enormity of what he and his men had done, nor how it would play on the world stage. 'The victory was complete and the loss of the enemy will never be known from the fact that large numbers ran into the river and were shot and drowned,' he wrote on 15 April. 'The river was dyed with the blood of the slaughtered for 200 yards. There was in the fort a large number of citizens who had fled there to escape the conscript law. Most of these ran into the river and were drowned.' Then, Forrest, ended: 'It is hoped that these facts will demonstrate to the Northern people that negro soldiers cannot cope with Southerners.'[18]

In this, Forrest, who obviously failed to understand the complex relationship of war and politics and public relations and morale, was dead wrong. Black soldiers had already proven to their own satisfaction and that of the Union high command and the people back home that they could, indeed, cope with southerners in battle. The dead at Battery Wagner were mute testimony to that.

Instead, what Forrest's men demonstrated to civilians throughout the world was that they were terrorists and not soldiers of honour.

News of Fort Pillow's fall and the outcome travelled fast. The prestigious New York news magazine *Harper's Weekly* carried a report in its issue of 30 April under the headline 'THE MASSACRE AT FORT PILLOW'. The editor pulled no punches, writing: 'The annals of savage warfare nowhere record a more inhuman, fiendish butchery than this, perpetrated by the representatives of the "superior civilization" of the States in rebellion. It can not be wondered at that our officers and soldiers in the West are determined to avenge, at all opportunities, the cold-blooded murder of their comrades; and yet we can but contemplate with pain the savage practices which rebel inhumanity thus forces upon the service.'

In the US Congress, the Committee on the Conduct of the War investigated and its final report concluded that at Fort Pillow, 'The rebels commenced an indiscriminate slaughter, sparing neither age nor sex, white nor black, soldier nor civilian. The officers and men seemed to vie with each other in the devilish work. Men, women, and children, wherever found, were deliberately shot down, beaten, and hacked with sabres ... Numbers of our men were collected together in lines or groups, and deliberately shot. Some were shot while in the river; while others on the bank were shot, and their bodies kicked into the water, many of them still living, but unable to make exertions to save themselves from drowning.' The Committee's widely publicised conclusion was: 'That the atrocities committed at Fort Pillow were not the results of passion elicited by the heat of conflict, but were the results of a policy deliberately decided upon, and unhesitatingly announced.'[19]

Whether this were true or not, in the long run it did not make any difference. Southerners simply did not believe that their men would behave like this. Mary B. Chestnut, wife of a Confederate general and one of the inner circle of influential southern civilians, noted in her diary on 11 April: 'The garrison at Fort Pillow said to be put to the sword. Tell that to the marines!'[20] To the outside world, Confederate officials simply said that Fort Pillow was a normal battle, with an unfortunate number of deaths, but all within the rules of law.

But Europeans believed that a massacre had taken place, and Fort Pillow became another nail in the coffin of European support. Northern civilians believed it, and it strengthened their resolve at the same time that it gave them added compassion for the lot of the black in the south. Fictional figures in books such as *Uncle Tom's Cabin* convinced them that slaveholders were indeed able and willing to kill blacks without the slightest remorse. Northern soldiers believed it and many of them felt, as did Union Brigadier General August Chetlain, who commanded US Colored Troops, that those types of terrorist activities were games '*at which two can play*'.[21] Indeed, a USCT officer later wrote of capturing ten Confederates and immediately killing five: 'Had it not been for Ft Pillow, those 5 men might be alive now. "Remember Ft Pillow" is getting to be the feeling if not the word. It looks hard but we cannot blame these men much.'[22]

So it was that, in the long run, the action of Forrest's men — and there is no real evidence that he ordered their actions — did more to hurt the southern cause than help it. Fort Pillow, a defeat for the Union, eventually helped create its victory.

12
The Battle of the Crater
30 July 1864

The Army of the Potomac had been unable to budge the Army of Northern Virginia outside Petersburg, Virginia, for months. A fluid war of movement, which both armies had previously known, had settled down into formal siege warfare as lines of entrenchments, bristling with cannon, spread east and west of the Petersburg area.

Traditionally, there were several means by which a siege could be brought to an end. The first was to starve the besieged out. But Petersburg was not a true siege in that the Confederates still controlled the railroad lines west over which passed their supplies, so this would not work. One could break through at a weak point in the defenders' lines. Grant had tried that, at Cold Harbor for example, and had learned that entrenched, defending artillery and infantry could beat off almost any force that could be brought against it.

From early times a third method had been used, that of digging a tunnel under the fortifications through which the attacking troops could get behind the defences. With the advent of gunpowder, mines were exploded in the shaft and the besieging troops endeavoured to exploit the breach thus made. Lieutenant Colonel Henry Pleasants, 48th Pennsylvania Volunteer Infantry Regiment, an engineer with coal-mining experience in Schuylkill County, Pennsylvania, thought that he could solve the problem in this way. He had overheard some of his ex-miners discussing the possibility of running a sap beneath a Confederate artillery salient, Elliott's Salient, and blow it apart. Pleasants decided that a large enough mine would completely sever the Confederate line.

He chose a point where the opposing lines were only about a hundred yards apart, separated by a deep ravine, so that the Union diggers could begin their work behind the Union lines hidden from Confederate view. There was one drawback. The chosen point was edged by higher ground on each side and directly behind, so that if the defenders were given enough time to reorganize after the mine was blown, an attack would probably fail.

Pleasants first discussed the idea with two friends, Captain George Gowan of his own regiment and Captain Frank Farquhar, XVIII Corps chief engineer, who agreed with the concept. He then convinced his divisional commander, Brigadier General Robert Potter, that the scheme would work. These two then convinced Major General Ambrose E. Burnside, XI Corps commander, who in turn suggested to the army commander, Major General George G. Meade, and the general in chief, U. S. Grant, that it would work, and they agreed to give it a try. Grant, however, later claimed that he approved the idea only 'as a means of keeping the men occupied'.[1] How much support did Grant and the top command give the project? It seems as if the plan were received with something less than real enthusiasm. One of Grant's staff officers, Horace Porter, later said that the site selected was 'in some respects unfavorable for an assault; but it was not thought well to check the zeal of the officer who had proposed the scheme, and so an authorization was given for the undertaking to continue'.[2] Unfortunately, this exercise in supporting an officer's zeal would cost many lives.

Grant drew up detailed plans for Meade as to how the attack was to be made. The attack would be a big one indeed, with IX Corps under Burnside going in first, followed by XVIII Corps, and the corps next to IX Corps in the front line were to be concentrated near Burnside's men. Just before the mine exploded, all the parapets would have to be cleared, and the *abatis* and other defensive obstacles removed so that nothing would slow down the attackers. Grant specifically ordered Burnside to ensure that his men did not enter the mine crater, but push on until they reached the top of the crest beyond the salient, a crest known as Cemetery Hill, it being the site of the Blanford Church cemetery.

At midnight on 25 June 1864 the first group of men from the 400-strong 48th began to dig, working in groups of 210 each for a full day on, although only two men could actually work at the face of the shaft. They could not obtain mining picks so had to use ordinary army-issue picks which they had straightened by blacksmiths. Unlike the rocky soil of Schuylkill County, the soil here was sandy and a great number of props was required to prevent the shaft from collapsing. Pleasants was careful in his placement of the props, some as close as three feet apart where the soil was mostly sand, and up to 30 feet apart when the diggers reached a stratum of marl.

That the high command were not particularly impressed with the plan is further evidenced by the fact that there was a distinct lack of assistance from the several regiments of trained engineers present, or even equipment from their stores. 'I found it impossible to get any assistance from anybody,' Pleasants later testified to the US Congress's Committee on the Conduct of the War. 'I had to do all the work myself. I had to remove all the earth in old cracker-boxes; I got pieces of hickory and nailed on the boards in which we received our crackers, and then iron-clad them with hoops of iron taken from old port and beef barrels.' In all, the miners removed 18,000 cubic feet of earth in their cracker boxes. Pleasants could not even get the army engineers to lend him a theodolite for calculating distance and direction. 'General Burnside told me that General Meade and Major [James C.] Duane, chief engineer of the Army of the Potomac, said the thing could not be done that it was all clap-trap and nonsense; that such a length of mine had never been excavated in military operations, and could not be; that I would either get the men smothered, for want of air, or crushed by the falling of the earth; or the enemy would find out and it would amount to nothing.'

There could well have been a certain amount of professional jealousy on Duane's part. Not only was he the army's chief engineer, but he was also the author of the standard US Army textbook on military engineering – including a section on mining enemy fortifications – yet he had not suggested such an operation himself. Now a mere volunteer officer was proposing this very thing, and saying that his men could do the work without the professional military engineers.

Burnside had an obsolete theodolite sent from Washington.[3] Having to use it while exposed to enemy fire, Pleasants covered it with burlap, and had his men put their caps on their ramrods and raise them above the parapet to draw fire away from him. Strangely enough, no one on the Confederate side seemed to associate the Union officer surveying their works with the rumours of mining that were rife in the ranks at this time.

In the meantime Pleasants had a railroad bridge dismantled for its timbers and, when those ran out, started up an abandoned saw mill to produce more lumber for supports inside the shaft. Ventilation was a problem. He designed a vertical shaft 27 feet long and two feet wide at the mouth of the tunnel. He had an airtight canvas cover fitted over the entrance way with a square wooden box pipe as far out as the end of the shaft. Then he had a fire lit under the vertical shaft which drew foul air up the chimney, drawing fresh air in through the wooden box pipe to keep the shaft well ventilated.

Burnside chose a division of African-American soldiers under Brigadier General Edward Ferrero to lead the charge through the gap once the mine had blown, and they began to rehearse tactics for the attack. They were keen to lead the assault as much to prove themselves as anything. 'Both officers and men were eager to show the white troops what the colored division could do. We had acquired confidence in our men. They believed us infal-lible. We had drilled certain movements, to be executed in gaining and occupying the crest,' recalled Colonel Henry G. Thomas, a brigade com-mander in the division.[4]

Even with poor equipment, the miners worked on. Each evening, regi-mental pioneers covered up the face of the shaft with freshly cut brush so that Confederates could not see what they were doing. On 23 July the shaft was completed: 511.8 feet long, five feet high and 4.5 feet wide at the bot-tom and two feet at the top. The miners had also dug two lateral galleries, the left one 37 feet long and the right one, 38 feet long, under the Confed-erate entrenchments to spread the effect of the explosion.

For four days the men laboured to bring in 320 black-painted kegs con-taining a total of 8,000 pounds of gunpowder; the original plan had stipu-lated 14,000 pounds, but Meade had ordered this to be cut down. The kegs were stacked on wooden platforms to keep the powder off the damp ground, some seepage from the galleries having been detected. Pleasants had been unable to obtain a fuse of sufficient length so was obliged to splice short lengths which he obtained from unofficial sources. The fuse was to be fired by a galvanic battery. The main shaft was then sealed so that the blast would vent upwards.

The day before the mine was due to be exploded, Meade ordered Burn-side to switch the assaulting division from Ferrero's to an all-white division, having realized that Ferrero's men had not been in contact with the enemy to any extent, and fearing that it might be thought that black lives were being thrown away if the assault went awry. Burnside insisted that Ferrero's men lead the attack, however, so the question was referred to Grant.

Grant and his aide, Horace Porter, arrived at Burnside's headquarters in the afternoon of 29 July, the day before the mine was due to be exploded. Divisional commanders Potter, James H. Ledlie, and O. B. Willcox were already there and Meade arrived shortly. Again Grant told Burnside to be sure to remove obstructions from his front so that the attacking troops would be able to cross the field in front of them without breaking forma-tion.

The question was then settled as to who would lead the assault, Grant finally agreeing with Meade. Burnside did not choose a replacement division himself, but had his three divisional commanders draw straws for the honour. Brigadier General James H. Ledlie picked the short straw. For all his criticisms later, Grant did not apparently think it important to overrule this, though he declared Ledlie to be the worst possible candidate, considering him unqualified and inefficient. Potter's division was slated to follow Ledlie's troops on the right of Cemetery Hill, while Willcox's were to move on the left. These final arrangements were quite different from Burnside's original plan.

The divisional commanders returned to their own headquarters where briefings were held down to company level. By 3.30 a.m. on 30 July the troops, most of whom had spent a sleepless night preparing equipment and moving into position, were ready to go. Luckily the night was clear and moonlit. Unluckily, many of the men found themselves in a maze of unfamiliar trenches and were rather disoriented by the time they reached their destinations.

The men were unhappy because they felt – quite erroneously – that they were to be sacrificed while the black troops remained behind in safety. The truth was that the black troops were equally displeased and didn't wish to be relegated to a later wave.

The explosion of the mine was timed for 3.30 a.m. Pleasants' men lit the fuse which sputtered into the dark shaft entrance, but no detonation occurred. The waiting generals sent a courier to find out what had happened. 'The general-in-chief stood with his right hand placed against a tree,' Porter wrote, 'his lips were compressed and his features wore an expression of profound anxiety, but he uttered few words. There was little to do but wait.'[5]

After several anxious minutes, two volunteers from the 48th, Lieutenant Jacob Douty and Sergeant Henry Rees, ducked into the shaft and found that the fuse had been inadequately spliced. They put matters right, re-lit the fuse and ran as fast as they could for the entrance. The spark reached the powder at 4 a.m. and, to the troops in the area, it seemed as if the very world had come to an end.

'A dull jarring explosion shook the ground,' wrote a Massachusetts soldier, Private Warren Gross, 'and then a mass of earth, through which blazed the ignited powder, was thrown into the air two hundred feet. Like a dense cloud, through which dark objects could be discovered, it hung suspended for a moment, and then fell back, and a black cloud of smoke hung over the place and floated away.'[6]

With the generals watching from Fort Morton, the strongest point in the nearby Union lines, Porter saw rise '... two hundred feet in the air great volumes of earth in the shape of a mighty inverted cone, with forked tongues of flame darting through it like lightning playing through the clouds. The mass seemed to be suspended for an instant in the heavens; then there descended great blocks of clay, rock, sand, timber, guns, carriages, and men whose bodies exhibited every form of mutilation. It appeared as if part of the debris was going to fall upon the front line of our troops, and this created some confusion and delay often minutes in forming them for the charge.'[7]

The result was a kidney-shaped hole 170 feet long, from 60 to 80 feet wide, and 30 feet deep.

Men and equipment, tin cups and cannon, horses and flags, all went flying high into the air. 'Cannon from the fort and fragments of gun-carriages were found several hundred feet inside our lines, so terrible was the force of the concussion,' Gross wrote.[8] Afterwards it was found that 256 Confederates of the 18th and 22nd South Carolina Infantry Regiments and Pegram's Battery had been killed in the explosion, either from the blast, or by being thrown up or buried alive. Union soldiers ducked as bits of men and equipment rained among them. Some ten minutes were lost trying to get the men back into formation and ready to move out, while the Union observers watched Confederate survivors fleeing to the rear as fast as they could.

At that moment Union artillery added their barrage to the mine's explosion. From all along the line 144 cannon, including mortars, opened fire on the Confederate position. It was one of the greatest single artillery barrages of the war. Plumes of white smoke, mixed with the red sandy soil of Virginia, floated in the sky, turning the rising sun blood-red with its haze.

The attackers then climbed out of their trenches – without scaling ladders which had been forgotten by the staff officers. Men had to stick their bayonets into the walls of their own trenches to form ladders so that their comrades could climb out and form up on the crest. The bayonet owners had to be pulled up after the others. Wherever possible, men threw up sandbags to use as steps out of the trenches. Then they began moving across no man's land. Here it was that Grant made his first criticism of Burnside's preparations: 'Burnside seemed to have paid no attention whatever to the instructions, and left all the obstruction in his own front for his troops to get over in the best way they could.'[9]

Once out of the trenches, the men had to remove many of the wooden *abatis* and *chevaux de frise* that had been wired together to slow down the enemy. Although these were supposed to have been removed prior to the mine's explosion, they had not been touched.

Ledlie's division moved out without its commander who remained in a bombproof shelter drinking medicinal brandy during the attack. Of all the divisional commanders in XI Corps, only General Potter, who had initially been approached with the plan by Colonel Pleasants, actually accompanied his troops forward. Bartlett, who had been three times wounded in previous battles, assumed command of the division.

'There was some delay on the left and right in advancing,' Grant recalled, 'but some of the troops did get in and turn to the right and left, carrying the rifle-pits as I expected they would do.'[10]

The Union soldiers were untrained in the special tactics required for the assault. They should have skirted the edges of the crater itself, fanning out into and beyond Confederate trenches before the southern troops had a chance to reorganize. They did not, nor did any of their officers lead them on. Bartlett, however, led the division he was now commanding, trying to keep ahead despite his artificial leg with the help of an ivory-handled Malacca cane.

As a result, most of the men involved in the attack simply jumped into the trenches, stopping to help dig out wounded Confederates and look for souvenirs. The first troops there found several stunned Confederates and two brass Napoleons which had survived and not been buried. Major Charles Houghton, 14th New York Heavy Artillery, was in the lead brigade. He realized that there must be a magazine near the cannon and sent his men to find it. They did so quickly, and he turned his artillerymen turned infantrymen back into artillerymen again to engage in counter-battery fire against a Confederate cannon that was firing at the Union troops near the crater. His section of two guns then broke up a small attempt at a Confederate counter-attack.

One of Ledlie's staff officers was among the first into the crater and was astonished to find it:
' ... filled with dust, great blocks of clay, guns, broken carriages, projecting timbers, and men buried in various ways – some up to their necks, others to their waists, and some with only their feet and legs protruding from the

earth. One of these near me was pulled out, and proved to be a second lieutenant of the battery which had been blown up. The fresh air revived him,
and he was soon able to walk and talk. He was very grateful and said that
he was asleep when the explosion took place, and only awoke to find himself wriggling up in the air; then a few seconds afterward he felt himself
descending, and soon lost consciousness.'[11]

Union troops came across a Confederate soldier who had lost both legs
in the explosion trying to drag himself to safety, leaving two trails of blood
behind him.

While some Union soldiers milled around, helping wounded and looking for souvenirs, others found safe places from which to fight around the
crater itself. Months of trench warfare had changed the military thinking of
the infantrymen in the hole. Now instead of charging across open fields
without a second thought, as they were apt to do in the war's early years,
they looked for holes in the ground from which to fire.

They found plenty of these. The crater had broken up the elaborate system of covered ways, bombproofs, and rifle pits and turned them into separated foxholes. Finally, a second brigade officer yelled for his men, now
totally mixed with those of the first brigade, to get moving. They promptly
jumped into the hole, followed by those of the first brigade, and started
climbing out the other side. Confederates still in rifle pits behind them
began firing on the men as they tried to climb up and out of the crater. Dead
and wounded alike rolled back into the crater.

During the half-hour after the explosion there were no organized
defences in the Confederate lines. Hardly a shot was fired at the attacking
Union troops. During that time, however, Confederate Major General
William Mahone, area commander, dashed about, getting his forces reor-
ganized and into line against the stalled Union troops. Some Confederate
gun crews got their cannon in action by 7 o'clock, however, firing into the
crater and the Union line beyond that. By 8 o'clock Mahone had stitched
his line together again.

'There was now a crowded jumble of men in the crater and around it,'
wrote Private Gross. 'The heat was becoming intense. Our men were driven back every time they attempted to advance on Cemetery Ridge.'[12]

Bartlett tried to get his men to move out to take the ridge. Men from
the lead attacking force did manage to push on towards the crest, but were
unable to force their way to the top. It seems that they did not try very hard.
Colonel John Haskell, a Confederate artillery commander, managed to get

some of his guns manned in front of where the Union attack was floundering. 'Even after I got my guns in position, a couple of good companies, deployed as skirmishers, could have taken them with little trouble; the ground was rough and broken, for protection, and the distance not over three hundred yards, but they did not attempt it,' he wrote. 'Time after time, they did come part of the way, only to break as we threw a few shells into them, and the only cries we heard were appeals for quarter of a good many who saw the way shorter into our lines than back into theirs.'[13]

Back in the crater, the two brigade commanders tried to bring some order out of chaos and begin returning the Confederate fire. However, wrote Ledlie's staff officer, 'owing to the precipitous walls the men could find no footing except by facing inward, digging their heels into the earth, and throwing their backs against the side of the crater, or squatting in a half-sitting, half-standing posture, and some of the men were shot even there by the fire from the enemy in the traverses.'[14]

The Confederates managed to switch many of their cannon around to face into the crater as gray-clad infantry reformed and began firing into the crater. The Union troops inside were now trapped. Confederate artillerymen also covered the field between the crater and the Union lines so reinforcements had to dash through a field of fire to reach their objective.

Ledlie, from his post back in the bombproof, sent orders forward for the brigades to move up and out of the crater. But by now the Confederates were firmly in control. Wrote Ledlie's staff officer, 'the firing on the crater now was incessant, and it was as heavy a fire of canister as was ever poured continuously upon a single objective point. It was as utterly impracticable to re-form a brigade in that crater as it would be to marshal bees into line after upsetting the hive; and equally as impracticable to re-form outside of the crater, under the severe fire in front and rear, as it would be to hold a dress parade in front of a charging enemy.'[15]

Burnside, unaware that his attack had stalled in the crater itself instead of taking the crest beyond it, rushed two more divisions, including Ferrero's division of US Colored Troops, as reinforcements to the troops stalled in the crater. Ferrero himself, instead of accompanying his troops, reported to Ledlie in his bombproof where the two shared a bottle as the men moved out.

Grant, unable to stand watching the confusion in the area, mounted and rode through the woods towards the front until he reached a brigade of colored troops sitting about, their arms stacked. Colonel Thomas, who was so eager to prove his troops' valour, jumped to his feet and, in astonishment to see Grant there, saluted as Grant came up to his headquarters, clearly marked by its unique flag.

'Who commands this brigade?' Grant asked in a slow, calm tone of voice.

'I do,' Thomas said.

'Well, why are you not moving in?'

'My orders are to follow that brigade,' Thomas said, pointing to another body of men in front of his own. He paused, worried that opportunity was slipping away from them. 'Will you give me the order to go in now?'

'No,' Grant said, not wanting to interfere with the unit commander's plans. 'You may keep the instructions you have.'[16]

Grant then rode further towards the front, and came across the men of a Pennsylvania regiment lying on the ground, their knapsacks removed and equipment ready for the attack. The men rose silently, all noise having been previously strictly forbidden, as the unit's commander saluted the general. As Grant, Porter, and an orderly got closer to the front, Porter suggested that the area was too dangerous for mounted men and Grant handed the reins of his horse to an orderly to have taken to the rear, and continued on foot.

Finally Ferrero's men moved out of the trenches and towards the crater. 'At ten o'clock the colored troops moved to the attack obliquely from our left. I saw them when they charged towards the crater. At that time there was an artillery duel going on; the shell, grape, and canister made dismal music over their heads, and they went into this vortex of death with artillery and musketry fire from front and flank,' Gross recalled. 'The colored troops passed beyond the crater and towards the crest, where they encountered a converging, raking fire of artillery, which drove them back in confusion, with the men who had preceded them.'[17]

A white Union sergeant, one leg badly wounded, was being helped to the rear as the black troops advanced. 'Now go in with a will, boys,' he called to the passing blacks. 'There's enough of you to eat 'em all up.'

'That may be all so, boss,' replied a black sergeant, 'but the fact is we haven't got just the best kind of appetite for them this morning.'[18]

The US Colored Troops passed around the crater on the left, smashing into the mass of Confederate troops who lined the top of the crater firing at the white troops inside. One black sergeant acting as a file closer, stripped to the waist in the heat of the day, came across a straggler from his own company near the crater. 'None of your damn skulking, now,' he yelled at the man, grabbing at the waistband of his trousers. Carrying him to the crest of the crater, he tossed the man to the other side, and quickly followed him.[19]

Initially, the shock of the assault pushed the Confederates back, and the black soldiers recovered a stand of US Colours which had been captured earlier. They also captured several hundred Confederates in hand-to-hand fighting.

The Confederates near the crater fell back, and the USCT officers spent almost 20 minutes trying to reform their units, which had become disorganized in the fighting, while Confederate fire steadily increased. Finally, they all fled to the relative safety of the crater itself. Many of them didn't pause at the crater but, accompanied by white Union soldiers who saw their chance in this setback, ran all the way back to their original line of entrenchments.

A lieutenant of Colored Troops saw a colour-bearer shot down. He jumped up from the relative safety of the crater, dashed forward, and picked up the brigade guidon. As he headed back to the crater, sword in one hand and flag in the other, he called out to his men. His movements attracted Confederate attention and all fire was directed at him Bullet after bullet found their mark, and he twirled around like a top several times before his riddled body hit the ground.

Many white Union soldiers weren't at all happy to be joined by their black compatriots. It was well known that while in most areas the two sides declared unofficial truces during most days of siege warfare, Confederates would never agree to truces with black Union soldiers in trenches across the front from them. Therefore, it was much more dangerous for white Union soldiers near trenches occupied by blacks at any time. As a result, some soldiers alleged that Union white soldiers bayoneted black soldiers as they tried to reach the relative safety of the crater.[20]

Grant had meanwhile reached the front-line trenches where he saw for himself the confusion of the attacking units as wounded men streamed back to safety through the ranks of the reinforcements. 'It was one of the warmest days of the entire summer, and even at this early hour of the morning the heat was suffocating,' Porter wrote. 'The general wore his blue blouse and a pair of blue trousers – in fact, the uniform of a private soldier, except [for] the shoulder-straps. None of the men seemed to recognize him, and they were no respecters of persons as they shoved and crowded to the front. They little thought that the plainly dressed man who was elbowing his way past them so energetically, and whose face was covered with dust and streaked with perspiration, was the chief who had led them successfully from the Wilderness to Petersburg.'[21]

First Sergeant William E. Christian, 8th Michigan Infantry, was one of the wounded men making his way past Grant to safety. He had been dashing across the field when a canister ball hit his upper left arm, breaking the bones into slivers and cutting the tricep muscle to the bone.

The men still in the crater fought on. An officer of the 45th Pennsylvania was next to the crater wall when a Confederate officer stuck a rifle in his face, calling for his surrender. Quickly the Pennsylvanian knocked the rifle up, at the same time ramming his sword deep into the Confederate's body. The Confederate fell back, mortally wounded. General Bartlett, nearby, saw the act. He unbuckled his own sword belt and handed it, sword and all, to the Union captain saying, 'Captain, you are more worthy to wear it than I am.'[22]

But fighting was becoming impossible in some parts of the crater where men were crowded so closely that movement was difficult. Many of the men were wounded, and those who weren't were splattered by blood and pieces of flesh from others around them. Many wounded men were ground into the loose earth by others trampling them in an effort to get to safer places. Other areas, usually those more exposed to enemy fire, were still relatively clear and men could load and fire their weapons easily enough here.

Confederate Colonel Haskell, borrowed pistol in hand and leading some of his men, walked carefully through the trenches to where the Union troops were pinned down. He rounded a curve and suddenly ran into three soldiers, one white and two black. 'The white man called to the negroes to fire, and at the same time raised his pistol. I jumped back, firing at the white man as I did so, and called to our men to charge. They dashed around the corner and got fifteen or twenty negro soldiers, who were close behind the white man I had fired at. I found him lying on his face, shot through the head. He was, one of the negroes told me, the colonel of their regiment, but like all the officers of negro regiments, he had no insignia of rank. I never saw one of them with any in a fight; they had learned that our men did not readily give quarter to officers of negro regiments, so they preferred, when caught, to pass themselves as privates of white regiments.'[23]

Other Confederates had run out of ammunition and simply threw chunks of iron, rocks or other debris into the crater. Some even fixed their bayonets and hurled their muskets like spears into the mass of Union soldiers below.

At the Union front, Grant managed to reach Burnside and his staff who were observing the attack. 'The entire opportunity has been lost,' Grant announced to Burnside. 'There is now no chance of success. These troops must be immediately withdrawn. It is slaughter to leave them here.'

Burnside was unhappy with the order, still hoping to achieve some success with the attack. Grant then left for his headquarters. Burnside also left his place at the front, and went to argue his case with Meade, but although a heated argument ensued he was obliged to order the retreat.[24]

Calling for a retreat was easier said than done. Headquarters sent a messenger to the men in the crater ordering them to retire, but Confederate fire was sweeping the area between the crater and the Union trenches.

The generals in the crater: Potter, Bartlett, Simon G. Griffin and John F. Hartranft, had a quick discussion as to how to get out of the situation. Major Houghton who was also present said that he was going to make a run for the rear. The generals told him not to; if they could they would have a covered way dug back to Union lines or, at worst, wait until nightfall. The area between the crater and Union lines, Houghton wrote, was being 'swept by both artillery and infantry fire of the enemy from both directions and was so thickly strewn with killed and wounded, both white and black, that one disposed to be so inhuman might have reached the works without stepping on the ground.'

Houghton thought that by nightfall everyone there would be either dead or taken a prisoner, and decided to make a break for it, accompanied by his orderly, Corporal Bigelow. 'I gave the word that when the next shell came Corporal Bigelow and I would start, keeping a little apart. We did so, and, passing through showers of bullets, we reached our line in safety and I ordered my men to open fire on the enemy's line. They replied by a furious fire, and soon the smoke settled over the field, and under cover of that fire all the general officers but Bartlett escaped.'[25]

The 35th Massachusetts was assigned the task of digging a trench out to the crater through which the survivors could retreat. They had made but little progress when the trench filled up with Union soldiers trying to escape the fury of the Confederate fire. The Massachusetts men were unable to work in the confusion and overcrowded trenches. Finally, one of their officers told his men, 'Bury them if they won't move.' But the men wouldn't budge, and the trench was not completed.[26]

Men inside the crater in the fierce heat suffered from lack of water as canteens were quickly drained. 'The crater now became a terrible place,' Private Gross wrote. 'There was no order; confusion reigned supreme. The intense rays of the sun were converged like a burning glass into this airless hole; a raking fire from three different directions decimated the ranks of those huddled together there.

'If a shot of any kind stuck into the crater, it was almost certain to kill one or more. At twelve o'clock the men were ordered to withdraw, every man for himself; it was three o'clock p.m. when they fell back. There was no formal withdrawal; the men saved themselves as best they could.'[27]

The killing went on. At about 12.30 a group of Confederates, hiding just below the crater's lip, raised their caps and hats on their ramrods. A Union volley blasted the headgear, whereupon the Confederates jumped up, leaped over the lip and into the hole. The antagonists went for one another with bayonets and musket butts. The Union troops were, however, outnumbered, exhausted, hungry and thirsty. Some made the desperate attempt to cross the field back to their lines under heavy infantry fire; for some reason, the Union cannon had fallen silent.

Eventually a Confederate officer called out that he promised that everyone who surrendered would receive adequate treatment, but those who resisted would die. By this time there were almost as many wounded and dead as active men within the crater. Concerned that the wounded might die if left unattended, Union officers present urged their men to give it up. Finally, they agreed, and it was over.

General Bartlett, handicapped by his artificial leg, was among the prisoners. Earlier, worried staff officers had seen him fall and heard the sound of a bullet hitting him. They quickly picked him up.

'Put me any place where I can sit down,' the general said.

'But you are wounded, general, aren't you?' a staff officer asked.

'My leg is shattered all to pieces.'

'Then you can't sit up. You'll have to lie down.'

'Oh no,' the general said, with what must have been his only laugh of the day. 'It's only my cork leg that's shattered.'[28]

Many USCT officers were worried that they would be executed for serving with African-Americans, since, indeed, such was the stated official Confederate policy. When their captors asked them their units, therefore, they lied, giving the designations of white units. The blacks under their command understood their dilemma and did not betray a single officer who so lied.

Other white officers showed more pride in their units and themselves. After hearing a few of his fellow officers giving false information, when the

Confederates came to one lieutenant, he proudly said he was 'Lemuel D. Dobbs, Nineteenth Niggers, by God!'[29] As it turned out, Dobbs received no worse treatment than any officer who surrendered after the Crater.

The Union casualties numbered 3,798. Generally US Colored Troop units lost more in proportion than did white units, taking 40 per cent of the fatalities and 35 per cent of the casualties even though their numbers were a much smaller percentage of the total attacking force. One such infantry unit, the 29th US Colored Troops, charged with 450 officers and men and when roll was finally called that night had only 128 survivors. 'I felt like sitting down & weeping on account of our misfortune,' a white officer in one USCT unit wrote home.[30]

Many USCT men died while prisoners. While Colonel Stephen Weld was being led to captivity together with a black private, three Confederates approached the two and without saying a word shot the black soldier dead. A Confederate officer later reported that 'it was the first time that our troops had encountered the Negroes, and they could only with difficulty be restrained.'[31]

Confederate losses, including the 256 killed in the initial explosion, were some 1,500.

Ledlie, Ferrero and Burnside later faced a court of inquiry at which they were censured and relieved of their commands. Two weeks after the failed assault, Burnside was given leave and never returned to command. Ledlie resigned his commission. Ferrero was found guilty of 'being in a bomb-proof habitually, where he could not see the operation of his troops [or] the position of two brigades of his division or whether they had taken Cemetery Hill or not'. Despite this he retained his commission, being stationed in the defences of Bermuda Hundred and, in December, actually was breveted a major general for 'meritorious service in the present campaign before Richmond and Petersburg'.[32]

Pleasants also received a brevet, as a brigadier general, 'for skilful and distinguished services during the war, and particularly for the construction and explosion of the mine before Petersburg, Virginia.'[33]

13
The Raid on Centralia, Missouri, 27 September 1864

T he action during the Civil War was by no means confined to a series of epic battles, but included thousands of minor skirmishes in small towns with little result save grief and bitterness, especially in the frontier areas. Missouri, for example, had been torn by fighting between the pro- and anti-slavery factions long before war was declared between the belligerent parties, each with formal governments and armies. There were no front lines in states like Missouri. Neighbours attacked neighbours. Uniforms meant little, both sides wearing each other's as needed. The combination of Civil War and frontier ethics made for a situation where life was cheap. Yet life went on. People tried to raise families and earn a living. Many Missourians joined the regular forces, and subjected themselves to law and order. Some went north and some went south, but eventually, they returned home.

At first guerrillas were not a problem in Missouri. Although armed bands based there had raided into Kansas before the war had begun, when it started most of the men who professed a belief in one side or the other joined regular army forces. William Quantrill, a known gambler, thief and murderer before the war, was one of these. He joined a Confederate unit and fought at the Battle of Wilson's Creek. Afterwards, however, he and many like him became discouraged and returned home, with or without the formalities of discharges. They often formed bands to wage war against their own neighbours, theoretically only those who were for the Union.

In 1862 Quantrill organized such a band in Missouri. In April of that year the Confederate government officially recognized units designated partisan rangers that fought behind Union lines and their leaders received army commissions. Quantrill received a captain's commission. His band, however, behaved like bandits rather than soldiers or even true partisan rangers. In November 1862, for example, they captured a wagon train and killed its dozen teamsters. One of these, found after the event, had been shot through the head – obviously after the fighting was over.

Quantrill wanted a larger command, and one that would be officially recognized so that if he were captured he would not be hanged for his crimes under the rules of war. To this end he went to Richmond in an endeavour to get his group recognized as a full regiment. His reputation had preceded him, however, and it was not so recognized, but as a sop he was given a colonel's commission.

In early 1863, Quantrill was back in Missouri and, on the strength of this ill-advised commission, formed two 'companies' of bandits under the name of Confederate rangers. He gave command of one of these companies to 'Bloody Bill' Anderson.

Anderson, a 20-year-old, styled himself 'W. Anderson, Commanding Kansas First Guerrillas'. However, he later wrote, 'I have killed many. I am a guerrilla. I have never belonged to the Confederate Army, nor do my men.'[1] He recruited some of those who after the war were to become the west's most famous outlaws. Jesse James and Frank James, for example, joined Fletch Taylor's gang in 1864; Taylor had been a member of Anderson's 'company'.

Anderson was a colourful, if psychopathic, character. Today he would be rated as a homicidal maniac or, at least, a cold-blooded killer in the best traditions of modern terrorist organizations with loose connections to some national cause. Anderson was reported as being seen in battle crying and frothing at the mouth, unlike the calm Quantrill.[2]

His father, a killer and robber, died in a shootout with the law in 1862. Anderson, who'd ridden with his father on his raids, then went off to, in his words, fight for the South. He was said to carry eight revolvers on his person, although it is hard to imagine sticking eight revolvers in one's belt, and another four in his saddlebags. After the death of his sister on 14 August 1863 in the collapse of the Federal gaol in Kansas City, Missouri, where she was being held a prisoner, he took to carrying a silken cord, into which he worked a knot for the death of every 'Union' man he killed in revenge.

Anderson himself rationalized his behaviour: 'I have chosen guerrilla warfare to revenge myself for wrongs that I could not honorably revenge otherwise. I lived in Kansas when this war commenced. Because I would not fight the people of Missouri, my native State, the Yankees sought my life, but failed to get me. Revenged themselves by murdering my father, destroying all my property, and since that time murdered one of my sisters and kept the other two in jail twelve months. But I have fully gutted my vengeance.'[3]

On the evening of 26 September 1864 some 225 of Quantrill's men were encamped at a farm, owned by a family named Singleton, about four miles south of Centralia, Missouri. Anderson had his own 'company' there, about 80 men whom he proposed to take into Centralia for a bit of fun. One of Quantrill's captains, a Scotsman named George Todd, the overall camp commander, declined to bring more men despite Anderson's urging.

Centralia was not much of a town. It had about a dozen houses, only two of which had two storeys. Anyone looking out of an upstairs window could see for miles over the flat, featureless prairie. The town boasted a railroad depot and, to serve its passengers, two hotels. T. S. Sneed, a southern sympathizer, owned one, the Boone House, as well as a general store, one of the two stores in the town. The other hotel, the Eldorado House, was owned by Joe J. Collier. The town also boasted a doctor's office, staffed by Dr A. F. Sneed.

Early next morning Anderson's men, wearing captured Union army uniforms, mounted up and rode into the town where they broke into stores and houses, looting and terrorizing the inhabitants. They found whisky bottles both at saloons and in some of the houses, and many of them were drunk before noon. Anderson himself stopped at the Eldorado House where he talked for a while to Valentine Collier, the brother of the hotel's owner. Seeing the town's doctor pass by, Collier called to him to come over. When he joined them, Collier said, 'Doctor Sneed, this is Captain Anderson.'

Anderson, after some small talk, said, 'This is a fine location doctor – a pretty place for a fight. If those Feds over at Sturgeon will come down, I'll give them a twist. I don't want to go there, but if they will come down here I'll fight them. I don't suppose they will want to come here.'[4]

While Anderson was engaged in polite conversation his men were amusing themselves tossing looted bolts of cloth into the street, trying on new boots, and tossing china out of windows. One man found a barrel of whisky which he rolled into the street. He was joined by a number of his fellows who knocked the head in and dipped their tin cups into the whisky.

A Concord stagecoach from Columbia arrived in town at about 11 a.m., the driver as yet unaware of the guerrillas. They quickly surrounded the stage, asking if there were any Union soldiers inside. There were none, and the men contented themselves with forcing the passengers out on to the street. One of them was US Representative James S. Rollins, on his way to a Democratic Party meeting in the town of Mexico, Missouri, who did a magnificent acting job, pretending to be an ardent southern sympathizer. The men took the passengers' money, watches and jewellery, and unhitched the best horses from the team and led them off. Rollins managed to slip away and hid in the Boone House.

On the morning of the 27th a Northern Missouri Railroad express train with baggage car and three coaches left St. Charles bound for Centralia. On board were some 125 passengers including several railroad officials and about 25 Union soldiers who were going on leave, some of them recovering from wounds received while serving with Sherman's army. One of them had left a leg on an eastern battlefield and was on crutches. They were all wearing their dark-blue coats and caps and sky-blue trousers. Only two of the group were armed – two cavalrymen were carrying their issue revolvers. All were happy to be away from the danger of the battle front.

Anderson's men, having finished with the stagecoach passengers, made for the train station where they piled railroad ties on the tracks to make sure the train stopped, and then waited, passing round whisky bottles.

As the train approached, the driver, Engineer James Clark, saw armed men around the tracks. His first thought was to stop and reverse back to Mexico, the next town on the line, but he suddenly realized that a freight train loaded with gravel was coming up behind him, so he had no choice but to come into the station.

Aboard the coaches there was some confusion, the passengers wondering if these blue-coated men were Union soldiers. A 1st Iowa Cavalryman was the first to realize the truth and shouted 'Those men are guerrillas.'[5] Panic spread through the cars.

Clark opened the throttle, hoping that its speed would make the train a difficult target, but of course it ploughed into the ties and the cow-catcher stuck. The brakeman, standing on an open platform at the end of the train, had seen the obstruction and applied his brakes, which brought the train to a complete stop. The guerrillas began firing at the brakeman and at the engine. The brakeman jumped from his platform to the tracks and ran away. Clark and his fireman, who had got down on the floor of the cab, got up to shut off the steam. The fireman was shot in the chest, though not fatally, and Clark surrendered.

Anderson's men swarmed aboard the coaches, one of them, Peyton Long, telling the Union soldiers, 'Surrender, you are prisoners of war.' 'We will have to surrender, for we are unarmed,' replied one of the soldiers.[6]

Yelling and cursing, the gang went through the train, relieving the passengers of their money, watches and jewellery, and even clothing such as hats and fancy vests. Anderson and a couple of his men entered the express car where the messenger gave up immediately, surrendering the keys to the safe from which Anderson took some $3,000, while Long and Frank James found a valise containing even more. Generally, however, the guerrillas only took gold and silver pieces, having no time for US government or northern bank paper money.

The Union soldiers received special attention. Anderson's men, cursing and firing their revolvers into the coach ceiling, made them strip to the buff and forced them down on to the platform. About fifteen of the outlaws stood around, their guns held ready for use, as Anderson had the prisoners lined up and marched off down the street.

'What are you going to do with them fellows, Captain?' asked 18-year-old Archie Clements, one of the most ruthless and cold-blooded of Anderson's men. 'Parole them of course,' Anderson said. 'I thought so,' Clements said with a laugh. 'You might pick out two or three of them and exchange them for Cave, if you can.' Cave Wyatt, one of Anderson's men, had been wounded earlier and was now a Federal prisoner.

'Oh, one will be enough for that,' Anderson said, turning to the Federals. 'Boys, is there a sergeant among you?' Although there were indeed several non-commissioned officers in the group, not one of them replied, not wishing to draw attention to himself. 'I say,' Anderson demanded, rather more sharply, 'is there a sergeant in this line?'[7] After a slight pause, one of the men, Sergeant Thomas Goodman, 1st Missouri Engineers, stepped forward. He fully expected to be shot on the spot, but he was pushed aside, and Anderson told two of his men, Hiram Litton and Richard Ellington, to take care of him; they led him off to a nearby stable.

Then Anderson turned to Clements and, in a low voice, said, 'Arch, you take charge of the firing-party and when I give the word, pour hell into them.'[8] Arch walked around passing the word on to his 25 men while Anderson turned back to the line of shivering soldiers and screamed, 'You are all to be killed and sent to hell!'[9] Then he yelled to Clements' group to open fire and took the first shot himself.

Sergeant Valentine P. Peters, 1st Missouri Engineers, roared in anger and charged directly at the firing-party. Fists flailing, he knocked five down before being shot again and again through the body. Bleeding from his five wounds, he ran back to the station and tried to hide under the platform. Several guerrillas followed him and set fire to it when he wouldn't come out. When, smothered by the smoke, he emerged he was shot through the brain.

Another Union soldier ran in the opposite direction when the firing began, ducking into a building near Judge Hall's home. A guerrilla followed him on horseback, dismounted and dashed after him. As the guerrilla entered the soldier ran out by another door, jumped on the horse and fled across the prairie. The guerrilla fired but missed, and the soldier didn't stop until he'd reached a peaceful neighbourhood where he obtained some civilian clothing and rode on to the nearest army base.

Some of the soldiers pleaded for their lives, some tried to run for it, or, if badly wounded, crawled away. Clements' men finished them all off with a bullet in the head. Finally every man, save Goodman, lay dead. It is said that Anderson's men then mutilated the bodies, scalping seventeen of them. One man is said to have cut off a Union soldier's nose, while others reportedly castrated another corpse and stuffed the genitals into his mouth.

The guerrillas now set fire to the station and the train. Having cleared the track, they ordered Clark to start the burning train and then jump off, leaving it to head west and burn out elsewhere. Judging that the guerrillas would know nothing about running a locomotive, Clark opened a valve so that the water would run out of the boiler, and the train ran out of steam a couple of miles out of town where the four cars, the flames fanned by the wind as the train sped west, collapsed in cinders and ashes. Shortly afterwards the freight train arrived. The gang forced the station personnel to switch it to a siding, boarded the train and robbed the crew.

Meanwhile a shocked Goodman was tied on a mule in the stable, and taken with the rest of Anderson's men back to the Singleton farm. Goodman rode between two guerrillas, one of whom asked the other, 'I say, Bill, I wonder how in the hell Anderson has permitted that damn Yankee to live so long?' 'Don't know. Can't say, lest like 'twas a Providence; for 'taint like Old Bill, is't?'[10]

On the way to the farm several scouts joined the group, and Anderson had Goodman mounted on a horse so as to keep up. The guards were ordered to shoot him if he tried to escape. At the farm, Anderson's men, jubilant with whisky and booty, untied Goodman. They bragged about what they'd done to the men who had remained behind. Todd, however, was displeased with the affair, according to the later account of one of his men, and told Anderson that he could not condone such behaviour.[11] Goodman managed to escape three days later and eventually regained Union lines unharmed.

Meanwhile, three companies of the 39th Missouri Infantry, a mounted unit armed with infantry weapons, approached Centralia. The group, some 158 officers and men, represented the regiment's Companies A, G, and H – all men who had been in service for only about a month. In fact organization of the regiment, at Hannibal, Missouri, had begun on 18 August and had only been completed seven days previously. The regiment had been attached to the Department of Missouri, with headquarters in St. Louis, and had seen service on scouting and anti-guerrilla operations in that state. As a result, the men had never been adequately trained in many of the basics of warfare or even much beyond the loading and firing of their M1853 Enfield rifled muskets.

Major A. V. E. Johnson was in command of this group of recruits and he carried with him orders from Brigadier General Clinton B. Fisk, district commander and an avowed abolitionist, teetotaller and non-smoker, to 'exterminate the murderous thieving bushwhackers' in the area.[12]

They arrived at Centralia late in the afternoon. Residents told him that Anderson's men were nearby and that the area was dangerous. Doctor Sneed took Johnson to the roof of one of the hotels, from where he could see some fifteen men in the direction of the guerrilla camp across the prairie. Johnson, obviously furious at the death of so many unarmed men, decided to follow Anderson and capture him and his men, whom Sneed said had only revolvers as their weapons. The longer-range firepower of his men's rifled muskets, he thought, would more than compensate for any numerical superiority the guerrillas might have.

How many are there of these fellows?' he asked Sneed, who said he thought there were some 400 in all.

'But you told me a little while ago there were only eighty of them in town this morning.'

'Yes, but the remainder of them were in camp,' Sneed said.[13]

Johnson decided to go after Anderson anyway. He split his force, leaving Captain Adam Theis and 35 officers and men of Company H with his wagons and their two teamsters in Centralia to protect it if any other guerrilla bands should arrive. He led the rest of the men after Anderson, flying, according to one of Quantrill's men, a black flag that signified that no quarter would be given.

The guerrillas were hard men, but no fools. They'd sent about a dozen men to scout near the town to warn them if Federal soldiers approached their camp. In a short time, the scouts came galloping back into camp with word of Johnson's approach. The guerrillas quickly mounted up and rode out along the plains to a creek bed where they dismounted and, under Todd's command, set up a line of battle. Every fourth man held the reins of his own horse and the horses of three comrades, regular army fashion. Anderson's company formed the centre, while Todd's company and a company commanded by Silas Gordon went to the left. A fourth company, under David Pool, was posted behind and slightly overlapping Anderson's company.

Johnson and his men headed off in the direction where he'd seen the guerrilla scouts on the flat prairie.

At about 4 p.m., as the sun was beginning to set, Johnson and his men rode over the slight crest of a hill and saw the guerrilla line. Unable to charge and fight, being armed as infantry, and unable to retreat safely being so outnumbered, the Union troops halted, dismounted and formed into a ragged battle line. 'We are ready, come on,' Johnson challenged the guerrillas. His challenge was met by silence. 'Wait for us', Johnson again yelled, 'you damned cowards.'[14]

With that, he ordered his line to fix bayonets and advance. 'The fools are going to fight us on foot,' John Koger, one of Todd's men, was heard to say 'God help 'em.'[15]

The guerrillas opened fire on the advancing Union infantry, but before the Union line had got very far Todd called out, 'Remount. Charge and kill them!' According to a southern participant, 'We sprang into our saddles and started after them, each one of us trying to get there first. They fired one volley and then, becoming utterly demoralized, stampeded in all directions, some of them running for their horses and some of them starting for Centralia afoot. We followed them into the town of Centralia, which was about three miles away, dealing death at every jump.'[16]

Johnson was among the dead, killed in an exchange of revolver shots with the later outlaw Jesse James, according to his claim. His body, reported to have been stripped naked, scalped, and the nose broken, was found after the battle.

The hasty Union volley did very little damage. Two men, Hank Williams and Frank Shepherd, were the only two guerrillas killed. Shepherd was hit in the head: 'He was riding between Frank James and I when he was shot and the blood from his wound spurted on Frank's boot. Dick Kinney was shot through the knee and afterwards died from his wound.'[17] Richard Kinney died of lockjaw several days later.

Only two of Johnson's men actually reached their horses and managed to ride back to Centralia to alert the others of their disaster. One of them, Louis F. Marquette, an 18-year-old private, was wounded, however, in the fight and although he reached the town he later died of his wounds.

Then, their blood up, Todd and the guerrillas galloped all the way back to Centralia. There, when the two survivors of the main body arrived on sweating horses, guerrillas visibly behind them, Captain Theis quickly ordered two men to mount fresh horses and ride to Paris to let his superiors know of the battle. Then he formed up the little band of Union soldiers to meet the guerrillas.

Some of the guerrillas halted when they saw the line of Union soldiers. 'Hold on, boys,' one of them is supposed to have said to his comrades in Todd's company. 'We've killed enough.'[18] Most of the guerrillas galloped on. Pool, one of the first to reach the town, saw Theis' couriers starting out of town and, dashing after them, shot them from their horses at a distance of some 50 yards. Turning in the saddle, he noticed Dr Sneed watching him from the roof of his kitchen. With a curse, he snapped a shot at the doctor, splintering shingles around the doctor. Sneed quickly scrambled inside. .

Some of the Union soldiers fought from inside and beside buildings and the station. Two were killed while trying to hide in the privy of the Eldorado House. Others tried to mount up and ride to safety. 'Get out of here,' one Union officer yelled to the men. 'Every one of you will be killed if you don't run.'[19]

One guerrilla stopped at a house and yelled out for a drink of water. While waiting for the water, he noticed a Union soldier running for a nearby fence and dashed after him. Within a short distance he dropped the soldier with one shot from his pistol and then coolly returned to the house. 'I'll take that drink of water now,' he yelled.[20]

Theis and eighteen of his men managed to mount up and dash for the safety of a Federal blockhouse in nearby Sturgeon. Clements and Frank James followed them to within rifle range of the Union defenders, firing at the backs of the fleeing Union troops before returning to the streets of Centralia.

When the smoke had cleared, Todd and his men had killed most of the Federals, murdering those few who made the mistake of surrendering.

Losses to the 39th were 116 men killed, two wounded and six missing. When the regiment was mustered out of service in July 1865, it counted up all its casualties and found that in all two officers and 120 enlisted men had been killed or mortally wounded. So it was that the tragic defeat at Centralia did more damage to the regiment than all its other service combined. Moreover, news of the affair terrified the peaceful and pro-Union inhabitants and even soldiers so that it was some days before Federal troops began patrolling in the area again.

14

The Battle of Cedar Creek, Virginia, 19 October 1864

The Shenandoah Valley – also known as the Valley of Virginia – was one of the most important pieces of real estate in the entire Confederate States of America, producing as it did a large proportion of the food consumed by both civilians and soldiers in the Richmond area. It was important to the Confederates, too, because as long as it was under their control, they threatened the north's capital city of Washington.

The Valley had long been the scene of important Confederate victories. Stonewall Jackson had made his reputation there, in 1862, when he destroyed three small Union armies that tried to take it. Later, cadets from the Virginia Military Institute joined another successful Confederate army which defended the Valley once again, in the Battle of New Market.

After Lieutenant General U. S. Grant, the new commander of the Union armies, had chosen one of his subordinates from the western campaigns, Major General Philip Sheridan, to head his forces in the Shenandoah Valley, things began to change for the Union there. Sheridan won battle after battle, at Winchester, Fisher's Hill and Tom's Brook, repelling a Confederate army under Lieutenant General Jubal A. Early. Union forces began the systematic destruction of the resources of the vital Valley. Indeed Sheridan boasted that his men were so successful that crows would have to carry their own provisions if they flew over the Valley.

In early October Sheridan was feeling quite comfortable in the Valley. His forces were following the retreating Confederates, as Major General John B. Gordon put it, 'very languidly'.[1] He had no idea that Early would even dream of launching an attack on his overwhelmingly superior numbers. Therefore, he left his troops encamped near Cedar Creek while he went to Washington to meet Grant and President Lincoln to plan further strategy.

But Lee would not give up the Valley without a fight. He detached troops from his already thin lines outside Petersburg and sent them to Early with instructions to clear the Valley. Meanwhile Early's agents had brought him reports that Sheridan was going to detach troops to join the Army of the Potomac, then outside Petersburg. Early figured that he had to strike quickly both to prevent Sheridan from reinforcing Grant and to recover the Valley. He realized that his smaller force couldn't take the Union troops with a frontal assault, which left a flanking manoeuvre as the only possibility. He sent Major General John B. Gordon, Brigadier General Clement A. Evans and a civilian topographical engineer, Jedediah Hotchkiss, who had prepared maps of the valley for Stonewall Jackson almost two years before, to the rugged Massanutten Mountain to examine Union positions on the right flank and find a way round them. Arthritis prevented Early from climbing the steep mountain to see for himself.

At the same time he sent another of his generals, John Pegram, to the left, who returned with word that an attack on the left would be hard to achieve because the banks of Cedar Creek, just in front of the Union lines, were quite high while their flank there was well guarded by the bulk of the Union cavalry.

Gordon and Hotchkiss reported back that the Union flank was only lightly guarded, with only a small cavalry picket on the North Fork of the Shenandoah. Most of the Federal cavalry was posted on their right flank. Several officers objected that there was no way to move infantry between the sheer face of the Massanutten and the North Fork. Indeed, the Federals obviously felt that this route was impassable because they had left it virtually unguarded. It seemed to Gordon, however, that an infantry column could move through that area, smash into the Federal left flank and roll it up.

The attack would be a gamble, perhaps as large a gamble as when Lee split his army at Chancellorsville. The Union force outnumbered the Confederates as much as two to one. But if it succeeded, the Valley would be cleared for another year, Grant would not have more men to destroy Lee's main army, and Early's army would be the toast of the Confederacy.

Early gathered his main force on his right, sending Hotchkiss ahead to supervise the building of a temporary bridge across Cedar Creek. Meanwhile the men were ordered to leave their canteens and tin cups, usually hooked through the handle to the canteen cork or haversack strap, behind in camp so that the usual clanking noises that accompanied a marching infantry unit wouldn't alert Union pickets. The men were ordered to pack two days' rations in their haversacks. As they drew near the front, talking would be forbidden except in whispers.

Then the men set off on the route laid out by Gordon. The moon, which had been full only three days earlier, was not obscured by clouds, so visibility was quite good. Hotchkiss' bridge wasn't big enough for all the men to cross over, and many had to wade through the icy water. One soldier in the 31st Virginia said the water 'felt like cutting the legs at the top water line'.[2] Many men slipped on the muddy banks and had to be helped

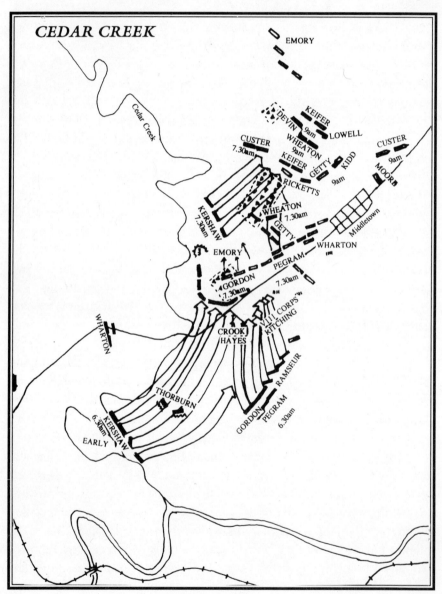

out. Once out of the water the men had to double time to catch up, which helped to dry them out and warm them up.

Well before dawn on 19 October, everything was ready. 'The whole situation was unspeakably impressive,' Gordon wrote. 'Everything conspired to make the conditions both thrilling and weird. The men were resting, lying in long lines on the thickly matted grass or reclining in groups, their hearts thumping, their ears eagerly listening for the orders: "Attention, men!" "Fall in!" "Forward!" At brief intervals members of the staff withdrew to a point where they could safely strike a match and examine watches in order to keep me advised of the time.'[3]

'Douglas, I want to win this battle,' Major General Stephen D. Ramseur told a staff officer, Henry Kyd Douglas, 'for I must see my wife and baby.' The general had been married for only a year and had just learned of the birth of his first child, a daughter.[4]

As the hours passed towards early morning, a fog rolled in and hid the moon.

Early himself, nervous as might be expected, peered through the night. Suddenly he heard the unmistakable sound of rolling wheels in the direction of the Union camp. 'It's all up with us,' he exclaimed. 'We are discovered, and that is the enemy's artillery.' Hotchkiss, nearby, said that he thought not. In a few moments the sounds were heard to recede, obviously some wagons going to the rear.[5]

At 4.30 Early sent five infantry divisions through the thick fog and against a thinly held picket line directly into the Federal camps. A Georgia brigade hit the Union forces first, easily brushing aside pickets of the 5th New York Heavy Artillery before reaching the Federal trench line. Jumping in, the Confederates began firing on either side, driving the confused Union troops back without any resistance to speak of. Then, screaming the terrifying 'Rebel yell', they charged on.

Three Union infantry corps, totally surprised, fled without much of a fight. Some soldiers, caught coming out of their tents, made a brief stand, fighting hand-to-hand. A Connecticut captain later remarked on the surprisingly large number of dead found after the battle who had been killed with bayonets or who had their skulls bashed in by musket butts – something rarely seen on Civil War battlefields.[6]

One group of selected Confederate cavalrymen dashed past the Union lines to where the Federal headquarters had been spotted, plainly marked by the headquarters flag, in an unsuccessful attempt to captured the Union commander. Many entire Union units fled without firing a shot or being fired on, being hidden in a fog one Ohio regiment soldier described as being 'so heavy you could hardly see the length of a regiment'.[7]

The dense fog hid the infantry battle in front of the supporting artillery, whose crews had been unable to fire a shot before being suddenly surrounded by victorious Confederate infantrymen. Many of them tried to defend their guns with sponge staffs, sabres and pistols, but they were no match for the Confederate infantry. A handful of cannoneers managed to get their guns hitched to their limbers and drove off, hidden from capture by the same fog that cloaked their attackers.

For the Confederate attackers, the fog not only hid them, but their objectives as well. They had to advance towards their general goal, the Valley Turnpike, which ran north and south through the Valley, and to the sound of guns. Fleeing Union troops obviously headed away from that same sound.

Regular US Army troopers of the 5th Cavalry deployed as a skirmish line behind the front line in an attempt to stem the tide of fleeing Federal troops. They failed. 'Dazed by the surprise in their camps, they acted like men who had forfeited their self-respect,' wrote a member of Brigadier General George A. Custer's Michigan cavalry brigade. 'They were chagrined, mortified, mad at their officers and themselves – demoralized; but, after all, more to be pitied than blamed.'[8]

A reporter for the *New York Herald*, who had been using a small stone house on the field as his quarters, was caught outside the building when the attack began. Running back, he found the door barred by its civilian occupants. He banged his fists on the door, crying that he wanted his blanket roll. The door opened a crack, the blanket roll was thrust out, and, as he took it, the door slammed shut again.

'The surprise was complete,' Gordon wrote. 'The victory was won in a space of time inconceivably short, and with a loss to the Confederates incredibly small.'[9] The sun was just beginning to rise, the Confederates had captured nearly all the Union artillery and scattered most of the Union troops. Few Union units offered any resistance. 'There was panic in the air,' wrote a Union captain. 'It seemed to me that the whole army was scared.'[10] One Southern infantryman's unit came across a number of Federal soldiers hiding in a tree-covered ravine and later recalled that 'it looked like murder to kill them huddled up there where they could not defend themselves, while we had nothing to do but load and shoot'.[11]

Many Union soldiers did not even try to hide near the front line, but fled as fast as possible. A VI Corps surgeon was surprised to see 'stragglers filling the fields, taking rapid strides toward the rear, scarce any two of them going together, some without hats, others destitute of coats or boots, a few guns, many wearing the shoulder straps of officers, all bent on getting a good way to the rear, never stopping to answer a question or explain what was going on at the front,' he wrote.[12]

Other Union soldiers did not try to hide or run away as fast as they could. These were not raw recruits who did not know how battles went, but seasoned veterans who grudgingly walked away from a front line they knew could not be held. Even officers realized that they were unable to stop their men from retreating and joined them, looking for a superior officer to stem the tide. Captain John De Forest, a staff officer from Connecticut, saw many of the fleeing Union soldiers but initially thought they were just camp-followers and non-combatants going to the rear. When he came closer to the front, however, 'the number of fugitives increased to a wide-spread swarm of twenty or twenty-five hundred, utterly without organization and many of them without arms. They were not running, not breathless and looking over their shoulders, but just trudging tranquilly rearward like a crowd hastening home from a circus.'[13]

Many retreating Union soldiers seem to have been shocked out of any sense of reason by the experience, typical of those suffering from mental shock. Captain Ezra Farnsworth, 26th Massachusetts Infantry, was walking along a narrow footpath leading to the bank of the Meadow Brook when he found the way blocked by a private standing at the edge of the creek, not moving, staring into the water.

'Move on,' Farnsworth ordered.

'I am afraid I shall wet my feet,' came the reply.

'I'm dead sure you will,' Farnsworth said as he unceremoniously pushed the man forward into the water and got the line behind them going again.[14]

'Random bullets tossed up whiffets of dust from the hard-trodden earth,' Captain De Forest noticed, 'and their quick, spiteful *whit-whit* sang through an air acid with the smoke of gunpowder. Here and there were splashes of blood, and zigzag trails of blood, and bodies of men and horses. I never on any other battlefield saw so much blood as on this of Cedar Creek. The firm limestone soil would not receive it, and there was no pitying summer grass to hide it.'[15]

Only the VI Corps and the Union cavalry units, on the Union right flank, managed to retain their organization, and stood long enough to let the other Union troops escape. Major General James B. Ricketts, the VI Corps commander, came across the 116th and 123rd Ohio Infantry Regiments and led them in a minor counter-attack that was quickly driven back. Ricketts himself was soon carried from the field, hit by a bullet that caught him in the chest and would cripple him for life. Brigadier General Daniel D. Bidwell led his brigade of the VI Corps forward in another desperate counter-attack which was stopped by Confederate artillerymen, mostly using captured Union guns. Bidwell himself was struck by a shell fragment and was taken to a hospital in the rear.

'Doctor, I suppose there is no hope of recovery,' he asked Surgeon George Stevens.

The doctor said that there was none. 'Oh, my poor wife,' the general said, adding a few minutes later, 'Doctor, see that my record is right at home. Tell them I died at my post doing my duty.' A few hours later he died.[16]

Towards the rear, after about a 3-mile retreat, by about ten in the morning the Union officers had managed to get many of the remainder of their units under control and reformed. Stragglers were stopped along the line and pressed into impromptu units. Their new line, which was fairly well drawn up by about 7.30, rested its left flank on the small town of Middletown.

'There was now a heavy fog, and that, with the smoke from the artillery and smallarms, so obscured objects that the enemy's position could not be seen,' Early later wrote, 'but I soon came to Generals Ramseur and Pegram, who informed me that Pegram's division had encountered a division of the [Union] 6th corps on the left of the Valley Pike, and, after a sharp engagement, had driven it back on the main body of that corps, which was in their front in a strong position. They further informed me that their divisions were in line confronting the 6th corps, but that there was a vacancy in the line on their right which ought to be filled.'[17] Early ordered a division up to reinforce these troops and the attack went on.

The Federals continued to fall back, although their resistance stiffened as many officers managed to get some semblance of control over their troops. As the fog lifted, by 9.30 they had managed to halt along a new defensive line, some two miles north of Middletown. Here they dug in, using tin cups, spoons and bayonets, as they had learned to do whenever they halted in a line of battle.

In the meantime, many Confederates, who were away from Richmond's supply depots and therefore often poorly clad and even worse fed, stopped in the overrun Union camps to eat superior Union rations and put on warm Union clothing. A Confederate private later recalled: 'Hundreds of men who were in the charge and who captured the enemy's works were barefooted. Every one of them was ragged. Many had on everything they had, and *none* [his emphasis] had eaten a square meal for weeks. As they passed through Sheridan's camp, a great temptation was thrown in their way. Many of the tents were open, and in plain sight were rations, shoes, overcoats, and blankets. The fighting continued farther and farther, yet some of the men stopped. They secured well-filled haversacks and, as they investigated the contents, the temptation to stop and eat was too great. Since most of them had nothing to eat since the evening before, they yielded. While some tried on shoes, others put on warm pants in place of the tattered ones. Still others got overcoats and blankets – articles so much needed for the coming cold. They had already experienced several biting frosts to remind them of the winter near at hand.'[18]

These Confederates were not really robbers. For example, Private E. Ruffin Harris, 14th North Carolina, stopped three northern soldiers who promptly threw up their hands and offered him anything that he wanted. He declined their money or watches or even food from their haversacks. Instead, he ended up taking their rifled muskets and ammunition; the rest he let them take to the rear to where provost marshal troops were gathering Union prisoners for the trip south.

Also, even in well-disciplined units, the charge through the camp areas combined with the heavy fog broke up formations, so that the Confederates had to halt and attempt to reform. The fog caused many Confederate soldiers to become separated from their units; indeed many units did not even know where they were in relation to their superior unit, or where they were supposed to be. 'Our ranks soon became almost as much disorganized as those of the enemy,' complained Captain D. Augustus Dickert, 3rd South Carolina.[19]

The fog also hid the disarray of the retreating Union forces. Had observing Confederate generals been able to see the relative capabilities of the two sides, they surely would have pressed harder, farther and sooner and completed their victory. As it was, they could not.

'It was now apparent that it would not do to press my troops further,' Early decided. 'They had been up all night and were much jaded. In passing over rough ground to attack the enemy in the early morning, their own ranks had been much disordered, and the men scattered, and it had required time to re-form them. Their ranks, moreover, were much thinned by the advance of the men engaged in plundering the enemy's camps.'

Early, therefore, decided to stop where he was, carry back all the captured weapons and equipment, and dig in to fight off any counter-attacks. 'Well, Gordon,' he said as he rode up to where that general was directing his troops' advance, 'this is glory enough for one day. This is the 19th. Precisely one month ago to-day we were going in the opposite direction.'

'It is very well so far, general,' Gordon replied, pointing to where the VI Corps had dug in, 'but we have one more blow to strike, and then there will not be left an organized company of infantry in Sheridan's army.'

'No use in that,' Early replied, 'they will all go directly.'

'That is the Sixth Corps, general. It will not go unless we drive it from the field.'

But Early had been badly shaken by the spectacle of his units' disintegration, the men running everywhere through the Union camps looking for food and clothes. The fog had blocked much of his view of the enemy lines before he left his post and advanced to the front. 'Yes,' he insisted to Gordon, 'it will go too, directly.' And he would not allow a further advance.[20]

Gordon's heart sank. All he could think of was the first day at Gettysburg where Lieutenant General Richard Ewell, new to Stonewall Jackson's command, did not advance past the town of Gettysburg to take Cemetery and Culp's Hills and destroy the last vestiges of the Union XI and I Corps while he had a good chance of so doing. Many in the Confederate army thereafter blamed Ewell for the defeat at Gettysburg. And, now all Gordon could see was Early doing the same thing.

'Why we did not attack at once, before they got over the confusion and demoralization caused by the surprise and stampede, I do not know,' Confederate staff officer Douglas later wrote. 'We had much to gain by taking the offensive, everything to lose by delay. True our infantry had been scattered and demoralized in stopping to plunder the camps they went through, and the temptation of food and the smell of cooking were too great for their famished stomachs to resist. At any rate *our* victory was over by ten o'clock.'[21]

Before daybreak of that same morning, Sheridan, at Winchester, twenty miles away, heard the rattle of smallarms and boom of artillery. At about 8.45 he mounted his horse and dashed back towards the sound of the guns, reaching his retiring men at about 10.30. Recalled Sheridan: 'Just as we made the crest at the rise beyond the stream, there burst upon a view the appalling spectacle of a panic-stricken army – hundreds of slightly wounded men, throngs of others unhurt but utterly demoralized, and baggage-wagons by the score, all pressing to the rear in hopeless confusion, telling only too plainly that a disaster had occurred at the front. On accosting some of the fugitives, they assured me that the army was broken up, in full retreat, and that all was lost; all this with a manner true to that peculiar indifference that takes possession of panic-stricken men.'[22]

Sheridan was soon joined by one of his staff officers who largely confirmed the soldiers' stories, adding that the Union headquarters had been overrun and the battle totally lost. Sheridan continued forward to see the extent of the disaster at the front for himself. As he rode across the fields, the roads being blocked with men and wagons, he passed dozens, then hundreds of men who had fled the front until they felt safe, then, as Union soldiers were so wont to do, stopped to build small fires and boil coffee. When they caught sight of short, stocky Sheridan with his easily distinguished black broadbrimmed hat, they stood up, cheering. Many of them shouldered their muskets and headed back to the front in his wake.

From time to time Sheridan stopped at larger groups, telling them, 'If I had been with you this morning this disaster would not have happened. We must face the other way; we will go back and recover our camp.'[23]

As he drew closer to the last Union defensive line he passed ever larger groups of soldiers. Indeed, the streets of Newtown, the next town north of Middletown, were so packed with soldiers of all ranks that he was forced to ride around it. There he ran into Major William McKinley, an officer on the staff of Major General George Crook, who went into Newtown to spread word of Sheridan's return as the commander rode on towards Middletown.

Eventually he came to the front line, held by a division of the VI Corps, along a breastworks made of fence rails. Only a thin Confederate skirmish line was in their front, and firing was sporadic between the Union defenders and the halted Confederate attackers. 'What troops are those?' Sheridan shouted to the nearest officer.

'The Sixth Corps,' came the reply of dozens of voices.

'We are all right,' Sheridan yelled back.[24] 'Jumping my horse over the line of rails,' he wrote, 'I rode to the crest of the elevation, and there taking off my hat, the men rose up from behind their barricade with cheers of recognition.'[25]

As Sheridan rode along the demoralized but robust line, he saw dozens of regimental and national Colours rise as from the earth. The standard-bearers of many units, now disorganized, had fallen in behind the VI Corps troops for a final stand.

Sheridan picked a point right behind the line as his new headquarters and rapidly gave orders for a counter-attack. Then he remounted and rode off to survey the rest of the line. Everywhere he rode, he ran into troops who cheered him, hurrying back to battle, their rifled muskets at shoulder shift. Then he decided to ride all along the front to view the enemy's positions. He started riding behind the lines but soon 'I crossed to the front and, hat in hand, passed along the entire length of the infantry line,' bringing more cheering Union soldiers to their feet.[26]

In every Union unit, the word was passed along: 'Sheridan has come, Sheridan has come; and there is to be an advance all along the line.'[27]

Confederate Signal Corpsmen on top of Massanutten Mountain, who had a magnificent view of the entire field once the fog had lifted and gunsmoke began to be blown off as firing diminished, saw the Union troops rally. 'The Yankees are halting and reforming,' they signalled to the generals on the field. Within minutes they sent another message: 'They are moving back, some on the main pike and some on other roads.' Finally, they notified the generals that the Federal cavalry had stopped the Confederate cavalry and was moving forward, too.[28]

Some Union officers, chagrined by the morning's performance, felt that Sheridan should be content with a stabilized line. 'They are not going to fight well,' one of them said of his men to Captain De Forest. 'They haven't recovered their spirits. They look scared.'[29] He was wrong; Sheridan had turned things around.

At 4 p.m. Sheridan hurled his re-inspired troops forward in an oblique attack on the Confederate left with the idea of cutting around the Confederates and taking the Valley Pike. This would cut off a large number of Confederates from their rear, forcing their surrender.

The cavalry led the advance, dashing too far ahead at first. Confederate infantrymen caught the cavalry advance in a crossfire, stopping it and driving it back. The Union cavalrymen fell back to a ravine where, out of range, they reformed. In the meantime, the Union infantry crashed into the Confederate infantry line.

The Confederate left flank rolled up, and the whole line fell apart. 'Every effort was made to stop and rally Kershaw and Ramseur's men, but the mass of them resisted all appeals, and continued to go to the rear without waiting for any effort to retrieve the partial disorder,' Early wrote. 'Every effort to rally the men in the rear having failed, I now had nothing to do but to order these troops to retire also. When they commenced to move, the disorder soon extended to them, but General Pegram succeeded in bringing back a portion of his command across Cedar Creek in an organized condition, holding the enemy in check, but this small force soon dissolved. A part of Evans' brigade had been rallied in the rear, and held a ford above the bridge for a short time, but it followed the example of the rest. I tried to rally the men immediately after crossing Cedar Creek, and at Hupp's Hill, but without success.'[30]

Gordon, on his sector of the front, had a similar experience. 'Regiment after regiment, brigade after brigade, in rapid succession was crushed, and, like hard clods of clay under a pelting rain, the superb commands crumbled to pieces. The sun was sinking, but the spasmodic battle still raged. Wrapped in clouds of smoke and gathering darkness, the overpowered Confederates stubbornly yielded before the advancing Federals.'[31]

Ramseur, riding along the front in a desperate attempt to stop his men, was hit. Falling from his horse, he was quickly surrounded by Union soldiers and borne to the rear where he lived for only a couple of hours, never to see his infant daughter.

Sheridan had a happier view. 'My whole line as far as the eye could see was now driving everything before it, from behind trees, stone walls, and all such sheltering obstacles,' he wrote.[32] As the Confederates fell back, Sheridan's cavalry dashed forward, used exactly as cavalry should be used, to sabre down retreating men before they could reform defensive lines. With this the ability of Confederate officers to maintain formations ceased. It was every man for himself, as they threw away equipment and weapons in an attempt to stay alive. Even Gordon, mounted, had to plunge into a deep ravine to escape the hard-riding Federal troopers.

Staff officer Douglas was overrun while on horse back, 'but as it was now dark I was not noticed. I had on a black overcoat, buttoned up to my neck, and top boots. I mingled with the [Union] cavalry and rode along with them, as with much noise and many oaths they captured wagons and guns and ambulances. It was a novel sensation, but didn't last long. Coming to a rocky and steep descent which led down to a ravine I had discovered a few days before, I determined to try it. My horse did not hesitate at the dark descent and was out of reach before my captors could stop me.'[33]

The Confederates ran in every direction with escape their only goal. The road to Strasburg was littered with abandoned Confederate guns, wagons and ambulances, with dead or exhausted horses still hitched to them. They had lost 2,900 men they could ill afford, including 1,200 as prisoners, and 23 cannon together with ordnance wagons and ambulances, going from a morning success to an evening disaster. One of the cannon, a southern-made iron gun, had an inscription painted by a down-hearted southern worker back in Richmond: 'Respectfully consigned to General Sheridan through General Early.'[34] Early would go on to issue Sheridan more arms and equipment, but Cedar Creek would be the last Confederate offensive in the Valley.

'Thus ended the day which had witnessed a most brilliant victory converted into one of the most complete and ruinous routs of the entire war,' concluded Gordon.[35] 'One thing is certain,' Douglas added, 'it was to us an irreparable disaster, the beginning of the end.'[36]

15
The Battle for Fort Stedman
25 March 1865

W hile Lee's Army outside Petersburg could stand Grant's army off for the time being, prospects for the long term looked bleak. The Confederacy was running out of everything needed to fight a war – men, equipment and food. Lee's Army couldn't hang on indefinitely, and everyone knew it. All the Union Army of the Potomac had to do was play the waiting game. As early as 22 August 1864 Lee had written to President Davis, 'I think it is his [Grant's] purpose to compel the evacuation of our present position by cutting off our supplies, and that he will not renew the attempt to drive us away by force.'[1]

Meanwhile, Lee's army continued to shrink, his battle losses exacerbated by malnutrition and desertion. Soldiers were bombarded by letters from home, often by now behind enemy lines, begging them to return as their families were in danger of starvation. These were hard to resist, especially for a cause that was beginning to look so doomed. Lee wrote to his Secretary of War on 26 December 1864: 'I do not know where I am to get troops to resist him [Grant], as ours seem rather to diminish than to increase.'[2] And on 27 January 1865 he wrote again: I have the honor to call your attention to the alarming frequency of desertion from this army. You will perceive, from the accompanying papers, that fifty-six deserted from Hill's corps in three days. I have endeavored to ascertain the cause, and think that the insufficiency of food and non-payment of the troops have more to do with the dissatisfaction among the troops than anything else.'[3]

Those Confederates who remained loyal to the colours became less and less physically able to withstand the rigours of campaigning. On 8 February 1865 Lee reported that a number of his men had not eaten any meat for three days, 'and all were suffering from reduced rations and scant clothing, exposed to battle, cold, hail, and sleet.'[4]

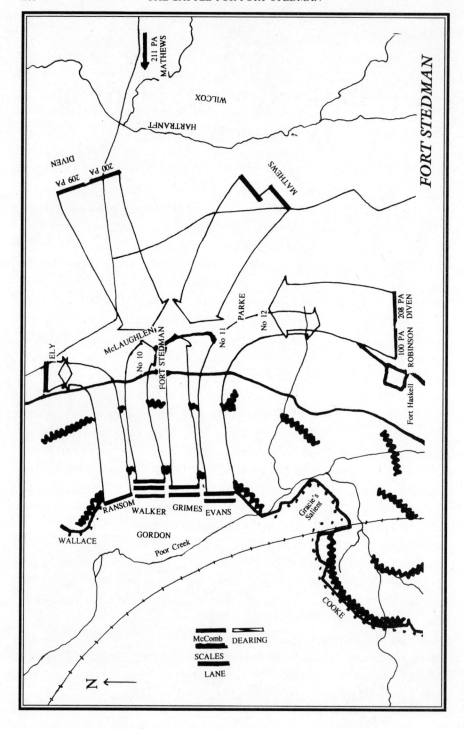

FORT STEDMAN

Grant, however, was not the type of general to let his forces stay totally static. He constantly extended his lines to the Confederate right, where their vital rail link west and south was vulnerable. Lee had to stretch his already attenuated lines, but he knew there was a limit.

Indeed, wrote Confederate staff officer John Esten Cooke, 'General Lee became aware, as the end of March [1865] drew near, that preparations were being made in the Federal army for some important movement. What that movement would be, there was little reason to doubt. The Federal lines had been extended gradually toward the Southside Railroad; and it was obvious now that General Grant had in view a last and decisive advance in that quarter, which should place him on his opponent's communications and completely intercept his retreat southward.'[5]

By early 1865 it was obvious to most that the Army of Northern Virginia had no chance against the Army of the Potomac which was vastly superior in terms of numbers and equipment and, by then, at the very least the equal in terms of fighting abilities. In the Valley of Virginia Union forces under Major General Philip Sheridan had virtually wiped out the small Confederate army under Lieutenant General Jubal Early on 2 March. Sheridan's forces were now free for the most part to join Grant's already overwhelmingly strong army. The only chance to maintain the fight would be to withdraw the army defending Petersburg to link up with Joseph Johnston's army down in the Carolinas in front of the advancing forces led by Major General William Sherman.

The best way to achieve this would be by breaking out east of the city. Major General John B. Gordon came up with a plan. He would take three divisions of the Second Corps (in effect practically 50 per cent of Lee's total forces) and capture a salient point in the Union lines named Fort Stedman. This post was defended by a division of Union infantry supported by a regiment of heavy artillery.

The opposing lines at Fort Stedman were particularly close to one another. One Confederate officer later recalled that, 'A boy with a strong arm could have thrown a stone from the works of one into the works of the other. To expose one's head an inch above the works was at the risk of a hole in it. In the salient the rifle pits were made into apartments and the approaches to them were covered for protection against mortar shells, etc.'[6]

When Gordon had worked out the details of the attack, he submitted it to Lee. 'I can take Fort Stedman, sir,' he declared confidently.

'How, and from what point?'

'By a night assault from Colquitt's Salient, and a sudden, quick rush across ditches, while the enemy's pickets are on watch, running over the pickets and capturing them, or, if they resist, using the bayonet.'

'But the *chevaux de frise* protecting your front is, I believe, fastened together at Colquitt's Salient with chains and spikes. This obstruction will have to be removed before your column of attack can pass out of our works. Do you think you can remove these obstructions without attracting the attention of Union pickets which are only a few rods away? You are aware that they are especially vigilant at night, and that any unusual noise on your lines would cause them to give the alarm, arousing their men in the fort, who would quickly turn loose upon you their heavy guns loaded with grape and canister.'

'This is a serious difficulty; but I feel confident that it can be overcome. I propose to entrust the delicate task of getting our obstructions removed to a few select men, who will begin the work after dark, and, with the least possible noise, make a passageway for my troops by 4 a.m., at which hour the sally is to be made.'

'But suppose you succeed in removing the obstructions in front of your own lines without attracting the attention of General Grant's pickets and get your column under full headway and succeed in capturing or killing the pickets before they can give the alarm; you will have a still more serious difficulty to overcome when you reach the strong and closely built obstructions in front of Fort Stedman and along the enemy's works. Have you ascertained how these obstructions are made and thought of any way to get over them or through them? You know that a delay of even a few minutes would ensure a consuming fire upon your men, who, while halting, would be immediately in front of the heavy guns in the fort.'

'I recognize fully, General, the force of all you say; but let me explain. Through prisoners and deserters I have learned during the past week all about the obstructions in front of General Grant's line. They are exceedingly formidable. They are made of rails, with the lower ends deeply buried in the ground. The upper ends are sharpened and rest upon poles, to which they are fastened by strong wires. These sharp points are about breast-high, and my men could not possibly get over them. They are about six or eight inches apart; and we could not get through them. They are so securely fastened together and to the horizontal poles by the telegraph wires that we could not possible shove them apart so as to pass them. There is but one thing to do. They must be chopped to pieces by heavy, quick blows with sharp axes. I propose to select fifty brave and especially robust and active men, who will be armed only with axes. These axeman will rush across, closely followed by my troops, and will slash down a passage for my men almost at a single blow. This stalwart force will rush into the fort with the head of my column, and, if necessary, use their axes instead of bayonets in any hand-to-hand conflict inside the fort. I think I can promise you, General, that we will go into that fort; but what we are going to do when we get in is the most serious problem of all.'

This was indeed a problem. Confederate intelligence reported that three small forts commanding Fort Stedman were located behind the front lines. In fact the reports were in error; the Confederates, from their vantage points across the lines, appear to have seen old fortifications built by southern troops several years earlier. Lee and Gordon did not know this, and believed that these forts would also have to be carried for the assault on Stedman to be anything more than a sortie to spike guns and tear up trenches. Lee wondered how this could be done.

Gordon went on: 'Those forts, General, cannot be taken by direct assault when fully manned, except at great sacrifice to our troops. In front of them is a network of *abatis* which makes a direct advance upon them extremely difficult. There is, however, an open space in the rear of them, and if I can reach that space in the darkness with a sufficient number of men to overpower the guards, I can take those three forts also, without heavy loss. I suggest that we attempt their capture by a legitimate stratagem; if that fails, then at dawn to rush with all the troops available towards Grant's left, meeting emergencies as best we can.'[7]

Once in the fort, Gordon explained, three groups of 100 men, each commanded by a Confederate officer using the name of a Union officer actually on duty near Fort Stedman, would dash towards the small forts. Since the character of the terrain had been so much changed by the cutting down of all the trees and brush and the digging of bombproofs and trenches, the picked leaders would have to be men who had grown up in the area and could quickly locate the forts. Under cover of darkness, these officers and their men were to shout as they ran: 'The Rebels have carried Fort Stedman and our front lines!' They were not to move in anything like parade ground formations, but as a loose bunch, keeping close to their leader. If challenged on their way to the rear, they were not to fight, but to halt and the phoney 'Union officer' would declare: 'The rebels have captured our works, and I am ordered by General McLaughlin to rush back to the fort in the rear and hold it at all hazards.' Once the small forts had been occupied, the remainder of Gordon's force would drive on, enfilading the Union lines and attacking the route to Grant's supply base at City Point. A cavalry unit behind the infantry would dash forward, through the gap in the Union lines, to destroy the Union railroads and telegraph lines and cut away Union pontoon bridges.

Lee agreed to the attempt, which offered his only chance for victory, and had three officers selected to lead the 100-man parties. He also called for Pickett's Division to be ready to follow up, together with two other nearby brigades. General Gordon's wife herself contributed by making strips of white cloth to be worn around the chests of the axemen and the 300 men of what a century before would have been called the 'forlorn hope'. Many of the men were drawn from élite units of sharpshooters, marked by their red sleeve patches, one battalion of which was assigned to each division in Lee's Army. Gordon briefed his picked men, promising each man a silver medal and a month-long furlough if the attack succeeded.

These men had been briefed and trained on what they would do; the rest of the infantry was kept in the dark so that the plans could not be given away by a deserter. 'On the night before the battle we were in camp,' wrote a member of the 21st Virginia later, 'and quietly sleeping, when about midnight we were awakened and told to "fall in" as soon as possible. As soon as the line was formed we were marched off hurriedly through the woods and fields, over ditches and fences and finally formed a line of battle facing east.'[8]

'I pray that a merciful God may grant us success and deliver us from our enemies,' Lee wrote to Gordon on the afternoon before the assault.[9]

Zero hour would be 4 a.m. on 25 March. As the hours ticked by, Gordon stood on top of the blackened breastworks, watching out over the dark night. He could make out the tops of a few stalks of corn, sad relics of what had been a farmer's corn field in happier days. An infantryman stood near him, ready to fire a single shot from his rifled musket as a signal for the attack to begin. Through the darkness the general saw some debris of Confederate obstructions that the pioneers had missed. He quietly ordered a couple of men over the top to get this stuff out of the way.

'What are you doing over there, Johnny?' a Federal picket, aroused by the noise, shouted across the darkness. 'What is that noise? Answer quick or I'll shoot.'

'Never mind,' the private standing near Gordon quickly replied. 'Lie down and go to sleep. We are just gathering a little corn. You know rations are mighty short over here.'

'All right, Johnny; go ahead and get your corn. I'll not shoot at you while you're drawing your rations.'[10]

Finally, the last obstructions were cleared. Gordon gave the command to fire to the private, who hesitated, obviously loath to fire on a Union soldier who would let his enemy gather corn safely. 'Fire your gun, sir,' Gordon ordered sharply.

The private looked over into the darkness and yelled, 'Hello, Yank! Wake up; we are going to shell the woods. Look out; we are coming.' Then, his conscience cleared, he raised his musket towards the Union lines and fired.[11]

The Confederates climbed out of their trenches and dashed between the lines. Gordon, back in his trench, could see nothing, but within minutes heard the thud of axes. The complicated Federal obstructions were soon dealt with, and the infantry dashed through and over the forts' walls. The totally surprised Union gunners in the main fort had no time to get off a single round. The Union section commander, Lieutenant E. B. Nye, was shot down as he tried to get the guns into action. In the dark, many of the fort's defenders couldn't distinguish Confederate from Federal. Some Union soldiers jumped over the fort's walls, firing into the fort from outside at the attacking Confederates inside.

Other Union forces, in the earthworks to the left of the fort, aroused by the noise when the attack began, had better luck, capturing a number of the Confederates attacking their position together with the colour of the 26th South Carolina.

'There was a rush in the dark across 200 yards,' wrote the commander of Gordon's leading brigade, 'capture of the pickets, tearing away of the *abatis*, a few sentinel shots, and we were over the fortifications and had Fort Stedman. Turning the captured guns to right and left, they swept the redoubt and drove the enemy from it. Other troops of the same command crossed the works and an advance was made inland.'[12]

'The streaks of day were just beginning to show themselves when we were turned loose,' a 21st Virginia private wrote, 'and we ran over two lines of the enemy's breastworks almost before I can tell about it, the troops on our right capturing at the same time the fort. We halted a short time after passing the second line of breastworks, reformed lines, and then were ordered forward again.'[13]

Gordon's men had captured Fort Stedman and three supporting batteries nearby, quickly and easily. Within minutes they'd taken nearly 1,000 prisoners, including Colonel A. B. McLaughlin, the Union brigade commander, nine heavy cannon and eleven mortars. Gordon saw his men on the fort's walls as the first rays of the sun began to light the field, and then ran over and into the fort. There he proclaimed himself the fort's new commander.

Men of Stribling's Artillery Battalion, who had been assigned to accompany the attacking infantrymen, quickly got Fort Stedman's four guns into action against Union troops to their flanks and rear. Other gunners manned the guns in the adjoining Battery No. 10 against the surprised Union troops.

Gordon had been lucky in that at this time both Grant and the Army of the Potomac's commander, Major General George G. Meade, were away from their headquarters on a steamer off City Point during a presidential visit. When a telegraph message of the attack arrived, in the early morning hours, a staff officer woke Grant up and read it to him.

At the same time another officer alerted Meade. 'Meade was greatly nettled by the fact that he was absent from his command at such a time,' wrote one of Grant's staff officers, 'and was pacing up and down with great strides, and dictating orders to his chief of staff, General Webb, who was with him, in tones which showed very forcibly the intensity of his feelings. The President, who was aboard his boat anchored out in the river, soon heard of the attack, and he was kept informed of the events which were taking place by his son Robert [an officer on Grant's staff], who carried the news to him.'[14]

The reaction from the Union high command was slow, but in the event this mattered little because the Union commander on the field, Brigadier General John F. Hartranft, was quick to recover. He began to gather a counter-attacking force almost immediately. As he wrote later, 'It was better to attack than be attacked.'[15]

Gordon sent a courier back to Lee, who was on a nearby hill behind the lines, to report that the fort was in Confederate hands.

The Confederates fanned out to take the three smaller forts as the false dawn began to lighten the sky. The deception they needed to get behind the forts without firing a shot depended in large part on darkness, and sunrise would be at about 5.50.

One group advanced towards Fort Haskell, to the right of Fort Stedman. One Confederate sharpshooter officer later indicated that this group was less than dedicated to the attack. 'The troops sent off to attack Fort Haskell did so in a hesitating, half-hearted manner,' he later wrote.[16]

Unfortunately for them, a picket just outside Fort Haskell had been alerted by the sounds of the Confederate axeman tearing down the *abatis* between Haskell and Stedman. He carefully made his way towards Fort Stedman in the dark, only to see a column of men in two ranks moving his way. The picket turned and ran back to Fort Haskell, telling the artillery-men there to get ready to fire. In the meantime, Haskell's garrison, hearing firing around Fort Stedman, quickly got ready for action.

Crouching behind the earthen walls, the defenders could see the flash of smallarms fire around Stedman and soon could hear the tread of advancing troops. A voice was clearly audible: 'Steady! We'll have their works. Steady, my men!'[17]

With that, the Union defenders opened up with artillery and smallarms, and drove the Confederates to ground. The head of the attacking column was stopped cold, but others behind them charged on. Wrote a Union defender of Haskell: 'But this repulse did not end it; the survivors closed up and tried it again. Then they divided into squads and moved on the flanks, keeping up the by-play until there were none left. Daylight soon gave us perfect aim, and their game was useless.'[18]

Other Confederates tried to move past Battery No. 10 to take neighbouring Battery No. 9. Gunners there were also alert, however, and swept the field with canister. Every attempt to take the battery failed.

Now things began to fall apart around Fort Stedman. There were no supporting forts; Confederate intelligence had been faulty. The guides could not find forts that did not exist, and the three bands of men wandered about aimlessly behind Fort Stedman as the sky grew brighter. Meanwhile, formations fell apart in the maze of trenches and rifle pits which the Union forces had built around Fort Stedman itself.

A courier reported back to Gordon that the group of men he was with had lost their guide and not found any fort behind Stedman. Reports from the other two columns were almost the same. Gordon, facing the fact that his attack had stalled, sent word back to Lee that the rear forts had not been found. The attack, he wrote, had been halted. As the Confederates began to mill around, the Union troops, now rallied, began their counter-attack.

Gordon realized that he could not expect reinforcements. Pickett's Division had not been ordered to move until late the previous afternoon for fear of the plan being blown by deserters. The division had got under way promptly, but the railroad had suffered from years of neglect and disrepair, and the going was too slow to get them to the scene in time. Gordon's men were alone. At about 8 a.m. Lee ordered Gordon to call off the attack and retire to the original Confederate lines.

Taken by enemy fire from three sides, the Confederates fought back, being unable to advance or retire. Some men braved the fire to dash back to the safety of their own trenches, but most declined to take the chance: 'Officers ordered, threatened, and begged their men to fall back to their old lines in vain,' wrote a Federal officer who'd been captured in the initial attack and watched the Confederates from the safety of a bombproof in which he was being held.[19]

Gordon himself was slightly wounded in his dash across no man's land through what he called 'a literal furnace of fire',[20] and Brigadier General Philip Cook, one of Gordon's brigade commanders, was wounded in the arm.

Clouds of heavy grey smoke filled the fort, making breathing and vision difficult. Some Confederates inside the fort's walls fought with a fury born of desperation. They met the Union troops at the parapets and sally port with bayonets and musket butts. The colour sergeant of the 57th North Carolina went down, and a Union sergeant major fought his way to his body and claimed the regimental colour as a Union souvenir. As it turned out, the 57th had captured the colour of the sergeant major's regiment, the 57th Massachusetts, at the Battle of the Crater.[21]

At Fort Stedman, however, other troops already discouraged by a war that was so clearly not going their way, that seemed as if it would end fairly soon with their surrender anyway, gave up. And, eventually, all the gray-clad survivors of the attack bowed to the inevitable and raised their muskets in the air as a sign of surrender.

After the last shots died down, the Confederates raised a white flag of truce and asked the Union commander for permission to carry their wounded and dead off the ground between the lines. The Union commander readily agreed. Wrote the Confederate officer who arranged the truce: 'Men ran over the field from each side and gathered up their comrades, taking time, when they could, to exchange pipes, tobacco, penknives, hardtack, and anything that was tradable.'[22] After battle, men on the two sides, at least in the eastern theatre, obviously harboured, after four years of war, little animosity against one another.

But for the Confederate troops who had survived, the battle was not yet over. The Union sent in a successful counter-attack that afternoon and took some 834 prisoners.

By 8 p.m. the fighting had ended. More than 4,400 Confederate troops had been listed as killed, wounded or taken prisoner. It had been the heaviest Confederate loss in a single day since the Bloody Angle. The Union army had lost only 1,500 officers and men. The Army of Northern Virginia had made their last attack of the war. The way to Appomattox was clear.

Notes

1. THE SURRENDER OF FORT SUMTER

1 Scott, Robert N. *The War of the Rebellion, A Compilation of the Official Records of the Union and Confederate Armies.* Washington, DC, 1880 (hereinafter *ORs*), Series I, vol. 1, p. 90

2 Swanberg, W. A. *First Blood: The Story of Fort Sumter*, p. 91, New York, 1957.

3 Swanberg, p. 93.

4 *ORs*, op. cit., p. 89.

5 Johnson, Robert U. and Buel, Clarence C. (eds.). *Battles and Leaders of the Civil War*, New York, 1956 (hereinafter B&L), vol. I, p. 44.

6 *B&L*, p. 45.

7 *B&L*, p. 2.

8 *B&L*, p. 45.

9 Woodward, C. Vann., *Mary Chestnut's Civil War*, New Haven, Connecticut, 1981, p. 45.

10 Richardson, James D. *A Compilation of the Messages and Papers of the Confederacy*, Nashville, Tennessee, 1906, p. 56.

11 Executive Document No. 1, *Message of the President of the United States*, vol. I, Washington, DC, 1861, p. 584.

12 Williams, T. Harry. *Beauregard, Napoleon in Gray*, New York, 1962, p. 80.

13 *B&L*, p. 76.

14 *B&L*, p. 47.

15 Woodward, op. cit., p. 47.

16 Swanberg, op. cit., p.53.

17 Woodward, op. cit., p. 53.

18 Executive Document No. 1, op. cit., p. 588.

19 *Philadelphia Weekly Times, The Annals of the War*, Dayton, Ohio, 1988, pp. 328–9.

20 *B&L*, op. cit., p. 73.

21 Executive Document No. 1, op. cit., p. 589.

22 Executive Document No. 1, ibid., pp. 589–90.

23 *B&L*, op. cit., p. 73.

24 Executive Document No. 1., op. cit., pp. 590–1.

25 *Philadelphia Weekly Times*, op. cit., p. 329.

26 Wainwright, Nicholas B. (ed.). *A Philadelphia Persepctive: The Diary of Sidney George Fisher*, Philadelphia, 1976, p. 385.

27 Woodward, op. cit., p. 50.

---

2. THE BATTLE OF BALL'S BLUFF

1 Holien, Kim Bernard. *Battle At Ball's Bluff*, Orange, Virginia, 1989, pp. 22–3.

2 *The War of The Rebellion, a Compilation of the Official Records of the Union and Confederate Armies* (hereinafter *ORs*), Washington, 1981, Series I, vol. V, p. 290.

3 Ibid., pp. 295–6.

4 Farwell, Byron. *Ball's Bluff*, McLean, Virginia, 1990, p. 74.

5 Ibid., p. 79.

6 Ibid., p 82.

7 Ibid., p. 85

8 Ibid., p. 91.

9 *ORs*, p. 321.

10 Farwell, p. 94.

11 Ibid., p. 95.

12 Holmes, Oliver Wendell, Jnr. *Touched With Fire*, Cambridge, Massachusetts, 1946, pp 23–4.

13 Banes, Charles H. *History of the Philadelphia Brigade*, Philadelphia, 1876, p. 26.

14 Holien, p. 66.

15 Farwell, p. 109.

16 Holmes, pp 24-6.

17 Harris, William C. Prison-Life in the Tobacco Warehouse in *Richmond*, Philadelphia, 1862, p. 14.

---

3. THE DEFENCE OF FORT HENRY, TENNESSEE

1 Nichols, James L. *Confederate Engineers*, Tuscaloosa, Alabama, 1957, p. 42.

2 Taylor, Jesse. 'The Defense of Fort Henry,' *B&L*, vol. I, p. 369.

3 *ORs*, Series I, vol. VII, p. 817.

4 Nichols, p. 45.

5 *ORs*, p. 838.

6 *B&L*, p. 370.

7 *ORs*, p. 148.

8 Ibid., p. 794.

9 *B&L*, p. 369.

10 *B&L*, p. 370.

11 *B&L*, p. 370.

12 *ORs*, p. 151.

13 *B&L*, p. 371.

14 *ORs*, p. 152.

15 *ORs*, p. 141.

16 *B&L*, p. 371.

---

4. THE LOSS OF FORT DONELSON

1 *ORs*, Series I, vol. VI, p. 817.

2 *B&L*, vol. I, p. 401.

3 Grant, U.S. *Personal Memoirs*, New York, 1952, p. 158

4 Ibid., p. 157.
5 *B&L*, vol. I, p. 401.
6 Wills, Brian Steel. *A Battle from the Start*, New York, 1992, p. 60.
7 *ORs*, Series I, vol. VII, p. 255.
8 Ibid., p. 262.
9 Ibid., p. 260.
10 Ibid., p. 395.
11 Wills, p. 60.
12 Ibid., p. 60.
13 Ibid., p. 61.
14 *ORs*, p. 293.
15 Ibid., pp. 299-300.
16 Ibid., p. 386.
17 *ORs*, ibid., p. 299.
18 Wills, p. 63.
19 *ORs*, p. 297.
20 Wills, p. 63.
21 *ORs*, p. 298.
22 Wills, p. 64.
23 Ibid., p. 64.
24 Ibid., p. 65.
25 *ORs*, Series I, vol. VII, p. 386
26 Denney, Robert E. *Civil War Prisons and Escapes*, New York, 1993, p. 48.
27 Grant, p. 159.
28 Jones, John B. *A Rebel War Clerk's Diary*, New York, 1958, p. 68.
29 Younger, Edward. *Inside The Confederate Government*, New York, 1957, pp. 25-6.

5. THE CAMPAIGN IN NEW MEXICO
1 *B&L*, vol. II, p. 700.
2 Ibid.
3 Gardiner, Charles, letter dated 3 May 1862, collection of Donald Gaither, Terre Haute, Indiana.
4 Hall, Martin H. *Sibley's New Mexico Campaign*, p. 37, Austin, Texas, 1960.
5 Alberts, Don E. (ed.). *Rebels on the Rio Grande*, p. 43, Albuquerque, New

Mexico, 1993.
6 Ibid., p. 43.
7 Ibid., p. 44.
8 Ibid., p. 48.
9 Ibid., p. 76.
10 Ibid., pp. 77-8.
11 Ibid., p 86.
12 Scurry, W.R. Report dated 31 March 1862, in *Confederate Veteran*, October 1927, p. 371.
13 Ibid, p. 372.
14 Gardiner.
15 Ibid.
16 Ibid.
17 Thompson, Jerry D. *Westward The Texans*, p. 7, El Paso, Texas, 1990.
18 Alberts, p. 91.
19 Ibid., pp. 107-9.
20 Thompson, p. 100.
21 Alberts, p. 110.
22 Thompson, p. 101.
23 *B&L*, p. 111.
24 Ibid., p. 700.

6. THE ASSAULT ON FREDERICKSBURG
1 *ORs*, Series I, Vol. XXI, p. 87.
2 *B&L*, Vol. III, p. 107.
3 U.S. Congress, Joint Committee on the Conduct of the War, *Report*, Washington, 1863, Part 1, pp. 652-3.
4 *B&L*, p. 126.
5 *ORs*, p. 171.
6 Cogdon, Don, *Combat: The Civil War; The Climatic Years*, New York, 1967, p. 8.
7 Ibid., pp. 5-6.
8 Stevens, George T. *Three Years In The Sixth Corps*, Albany, New York, 1866, p. 170.
9 Rice, Thomas E., 'Desperate Courage', in *Civil War Times Illustrated*, November/December 1990, p.63

10 Gross, Warren L. *Recollections of a Private*, New York, 1890.
11 Cogdon, p. 15.
12 Rice, p. 64.
13 *B&L*, p. 113.
14 Donald, David H. (ed.). *Gone For A Soldier*, Boston, 1975, p. 182.
15 Gross, p. 129.
16 Ibid., pp. 132-3.
17 Longacre, Edward G. (ed.) *From Antietam to Fort Fisher*, Rutherford, Long Island, 1985, p. 90.
18 Sypher, J. R., *History of the Pennsylvania Reserve Corps*, Lancaster, Pennsylvania, 1865, pp. 412-13.
19 Ibid., pp. 420-1.
20 *ORs*, pp. 228-9.
21 *B&L*, p. 138.
22 Sypher, pp. 418-19.
23 Cogdon, p. 19.
24 James Pratt Papers, U.S. Army Military History Institute, Carlisle Barracks, Pennsylvania, letter dated 16-19 December 1862.

7. PICKETT'S CHARGE
1 Longstreet, James. 'Lee in Pennsylvania', in *The Annals of the War*, Dayton, Ohio, 1988, p. 416.
2 Davis, Jefferson. *The Rise and Fall of the Confederate Government*, vol. II, pp. 437-8, New York, 1881.
3 Taylor, Walter H. *Four Years with General Lee*, p. 93, New York, 1962.
4 Longstreet, James. *From Manassas To Appomattox*, p. 334, New York, 1991.
5 Jomini, Baron A. H.

de. *The Art of War*, pp. 184-5, New York, 1862.
6 Longstreet, James. 'Lee in Pennsylvania', p. 421.
7 Ibid., p. 421.
8 Longstreet, *From Manassas To Appomattox*, pp. 385-6.
9 *B&L*, vol. 3, pp. 342-3.
10 Taylor, pp 103-4.
11 Stewart, George R. *Pickett's Charge*, p. 90, New York, 1963.
12 Ibid., p. 106.
13 Lord, Walter (ed.). *The Fremantle Diary*, p. 208, New York, 1954.
14 Gallagher, Gary W. (ed.). *Fighting for the Confederacy*, pp. 254-5, Chapel Hill, North Carolina, 1989.
15 Stewart, pp. 110-11.
16 Longstreet, *From Manassas To Appomattox*, p. 390.
17 Gallagher, p. 257.
18 Lord, p. 208.
19 Lewis, John H. *Recollections From 1860 to 1865*, p. 81, Washington, DC, 1895.
20 Stewart, p. 133.
21 Moore, Edward A. *The Story of a Cannoneer Under Stonewall Jackson*, pp. 192-3, New York, 1907.
22 McCarthy, Carlton. *Detailed Minutiae of Soldier Life in the Army of Northern Virginia*, pp. 106-7, Richmond, 1882.
23 Gallagher, pp. 258-9.
24 Longstreet, *From Manassas To Appomattox*, p. 392.
25 Pickett, George. *The Heart of a Soldier*,

pp. 98–9, New York, 1913.
26 Stewart, p. 157.
27 Lewis, p. 82.
28 Gallaher, p. 261.
29 Stewart, p. 171.
30 Haskell, John. *The Haskell Memoirs*, p. 51, New York, 1960.
31 Ibid., p. 51.
32 Lewis, p. 84.
33 Lord, p. 212.
34 Ibid.
35 Stewart, p 177.
36 Ibid., p. 184.
37 Ibid., pp. 40, 185.
38 Lewis, p. 85.
39 Stewart, p. 203.
40 *B&L*, vol. III, p. 366.
41 Stewart, p. 213.
42 Stewart, p. 225.
43 Stewart, p. 227.

8. THE ASSAULTS ON BATTERY WAGNER
1 *B&L*, vol. IV, p. 59.
2 Ibid., p. 58.
3 Niven, John. *Connecticut For The Union, New Haven*, p. 175, Connecticut, 1965.
4 Chisman, James A. (ed.). *76th Pennsylvania Volunteer Infantry*, pp. 33–4, Wilmington, North Carolina, 1988.
5 Niven, p. 177.
6 *B&L*.
7 Burchard, Peter. *One Gallant Rush*, p. 133, New York, 1965.
8 Ibid., p. 133.
9 Ibid., p. 135.
10 *B&L*, p. 59.
11 Burchard, p. 136.
12 Emilio, Luis F. *A Brave Black Regiment*, p. 85, New York, 1992.
13 Niven, pp. 177-8.
14 *B&L*, p. 59.
15 Emilio, p. 87.
16 Burchard, p. 138.
17 Emilio, p. 89.
18 Long, Richard A. (ed.). *Black Writers and the American Civil War*, pp. 61–2, Secaucus, New Jersey, 1988.
19 *B&L*, p. 59.
20 Price, Isaiah. *History of the Ninety-Seventh Regiment, Pennsylvania Volunteer Infantry*, p. 171, Philadelphia, 1875.

9. THE CAPTURE OF USS SATELLITE AND USS RELIANCE
1 All quoted material, including conversations, is taken directly from reports appearing in the *Official Records of the Union and Confederate Navies in the War of the Rebellion*, Series I, vol. 5, Washington, 1897.
2 Official US Navy reports say that the Confederates began their attack at 12.20, while Confederate reports have it that they waited until 1 a.m. Time zones were not at all standard during this period, varying by as much as an hour from city to city in what would today be the same time zone.

10. THE SIEGE OF PLYMOUTH, NORTH CAROLINA
1 Warner, Ezra, J. *Generals In Gray*, p. 31, Baton Rouge, Louisiana, 1959.
2 Trotter, William R. *Ironclads And Columbiads*, p. 241, Winston-Salem, North Carolina, 1989.
3 Trotter, p. 241.

4 Denney, Robert E. *The Civil War Years*, p. 394, New York, 1992.
5 Trotter, p. 244.
6 Blakeslee, Bernard F. *History of the Sixteenth Connecticut Volunteers*, p. 55, Hartford, Connecticut, 1875.
7 Nichols, Roy F. 'Fighting in North Carolina Waters' in *North Carolina Historical Review*, p. 79, January 1963.
8 Denney, p. 394.
9 Ibid., p. 394.
10 Ibid., p. 394.
11 Ibid., p. 394.
12 Ibid., p. 394.
13 Trotter, p. 248.
14 Ibid., p. 248.
15 Denney, p. 394.
16 *ORs*, Series I, vol. LI, Part II, p. 870.
17 Ibid., p. 874.

11. THE DEFENCE OF FORT PILLOW
1 Civil War Centennial Commission, *Tennesseans in the Civil War*, Part I, pp. 253–4, Nashville, Tennessee, 1964.
2 *ORs*, Series I, vol. XXXII, Part 1, p. 553.
3 Ibid., p. 559.
4 Ibid., p. 559-60.
5 Ibid., p. 596.
6 Long, Richard A. (ed) *Black Writers and the American Civil War*, p. 38, Secaucus, New Jersey, 1988.
7 Bodnia, George (ed.). 'Fort Pillow "Massacre" Observations of a Minnesotan' in *Minnesota History*, p. 188, spring, 1973.
8 *B&L*, vol. IV, p. 419.

9 Wills, Brian Steel. *A Battle from the Start*, p. 183, New York, 1992.
10 Ibid., p. 183.
11 *ORs*, p. 615.
12 *ORs*, pp. 566-7.
13 Wills, pp. 186-7.
14 Camprich, John and Mainfort, Robert C., Jnr., 'Dr. Fitch's Report on the Fort Pillow Massacre', in *Tennessee Historical Quarterly*, pp. 36-7, spring, 1985.
15 Cimprich, John and Mainfort, John C., Jnr., 'The Fort Pillow Massacre: A Statistical Note', in *Journal of American History*, pp. 835-7, December 1989.
16 Long, p. 40.
17 Wills, p. 193.
18 *ORs*, p. 610.
19 Long, pp. 42–3.
20 Woodward, C. Vann. *Mary Chestnut's Civil War*, p. 596, New Haven, Connecticut, 1981.
21 Glatthaar, Joseph T. *Forged In Battle*, p. 157, New York, 1990.
22 Ibid., p. 157.

12. THE BATTLE OF THE CRATER
1 Grant, U.S., *Personal Memoirs of*, New York, 1952, p. 462.
2 Porter, Horace. *Campaigning With Grant*, p. 259, Bloomington, Indiana, 1961.
3 *B&L*, vol. IV, p. 545.
4 Ibid., p. 563.
5 Porter, p. 263.
6 Gross, Warren Lee. *Recollections of a Private*, p. 334, New York, 1890.
7 Porter, pp. 263–4.
8 Gross, p. 334.

9 Grant, p. 466.
10 Ibid., p. 467.
11 *B&L*, p. 551.
12 Gross, p. 335.
13 Haskell, John. *The Haskell Memoirs*, p. 73, New York, 1960.
14 *B&L*, pp. 552–3.
15 Ibid., p. 553.
16 Porter, pp. 264–5.
17 Gross, p. 335.
18 Porter, op. cit., p. 268.
19 *B&L*, pp. 556–7.
20 Wilkinson, Warren. *Mother, May You Never See The Sights I Have Seen*, p. 254, New York, 1990.
21 Porter, p. 266.
22 Gross, p. 336.
23 Haskell, pp. 76–7.
24 Porter, pp. 267–8.
25 *B&L*, p. 562.
26 Wilkinson, p. 259.
27 Gross, p. 335.
28 *B&L*, pp. 558–9.
29 Glatthaar, Joseph T. *Forged In Battle*, p. 159, New York, 1990.
30 Ibid., p. 154.
31 Pleasants, Henry Jnr., and Straley, George H. *Inferno At Petersburg*, p. 145, Philadelphia, 1961.
32 Warner, Ezra, J., *Generals In Blue*, p. 151, Baton Rouge, Louisiana, 1964.
33 Pleasants, p. 166.

13. THE RAID ON CENTRALIA, MISSOURI
1 Fellman, Michael, *Inside War,* New York, p. 136, 1989.
2 Brownlee, Richard S., *Gray Ghosts of the Confederacy*, p. 137, Baton Rouge, Louisiana, 1958.
3 *ORs*, Series I, Vol. XLI, Part 2, p. 75.
4 Hale, Donald R., *They Called Him Bloody Bill,* p. 43 Clinton Missouri, 1992.
5 Ibid., p. 45.
6 Ibid., pp. 45–46.
7 Ibid, p. 46.
8 Ibid., p. 47.
9 Smith, Robert B., 'The James Boys Go To War,' *Civil War Times Illustrated,* January/February 1994, p. 58.
10 Hale, p. 62, taken from Thomas Goodman, *A Thrilling Record,* Des Moines, Iowa, 1868.
11 Barton, O.S., *Three Years With Quantrill,* p. 163, Norman, Oklahoma, 1992.
12 Hale, p. 50.
13 Ibid., p. 50.
14 Ibid., p. 51.
15 Brownlee, p. 219.
16 Barton, p. 165.
17 Ibid., p. 166.
18 Ibid., p. 165.
19 Hale, p 59.
20 Ibid., p. 60.

14. THE BATTLE OF CEDAR CREEK, VIRGINIA
1 Gordon, John B. *Reminiscences of the Civil War,* p. 327, New York, 1903.
2 Lewis, Thomas A. *The Guns of Cedar Creek,* p. 206, New York, 1988.
3 Gordon, op. cit., p. 337.
4 Douglas, Henry Kyd. *I Rode With Stonewall,* p. 317, Chapel Hill, North Carolina, 1940.
5 Lewis, p. 204.
6 De Forest, John W. *A Volunteer's Adventures,* p. 212, New Haven, Connecticut, 1946.
7 Wert, Jeffry, D. *From Winchester To Cedar Creek*, p. 180, New York, 1987.
8 Kidd, J. H. *Personal Recollections of a Cavalryman,* p. 414, Ionia, Michigan, 1908.
9 Gordon, p. 339.
10 De Forest, p. 216.
11 Wert, p. 186.
12 Stevens, George T. *Three Years In The Sixth Corps*, p. 416, Albany, New York, 1866.
13 De Forest, pp. 210–11.
14 Wert, p. 195.
15 De Forest, pp. 214–15.
16 Stevens, op. cit., p. 420.
17 Early, Jubal A. *Narrative of the War Between the States,* p. 444, New York, 1989.
18 Worsham, John H. *One of Jackson's Foot Cavalry,* p. 177, Jackson, Tennessee, 1964.
19 Wert, p. 184.
20 Gordon, p. 341.
21 Douglas, op. cit., pp. 316–17.
22 Sheridan, Philip. *Civil War Memoirs,* p. 274, New York, 1991.
23 Ibid., p. 276.
24 Stevens, p. 423.
25 Sheridan, pp. 276–7.
26 Ibid., p. 278.
27 Kidd, p. 420.
28 Gordon, p. 346.
29 De Forest, p. 223.
30 Early, pp. 448–9.
31 Gordon, p. 348.
32 Sheridan, p. 280.
33 Douglas, p. 318.
34 Gordon, p. 331.
35 Ibid., p. 351.
36 Douglas, p. 319.

15. THE BATTLE FOR FORT STEDMAN
1 Dowdey, Clifford and Manarin, Louis H. (eds.). *The Wartime Papers of R. E. Lee*, p. 843, New York, 1961.
2 Ibid., p. 879.
3 Ibid., p. 879.
4 Ibid., p. 890.
5 Wheeler, Richard, *Witness to Appomattox,* p. 41, New York, 1989.
6 Douglas, Henry Kyd, *I Rode With Stonewall*, p. 328, Chapel Hill, North Carolina, 1940.
7 Gordon, John B. *Reminiscences of the Civil War,* pp. 401–4, New York, 1903.
8 Worsham, John H. *One of Jackson's Foot Cavalry,* p. 181, Jackson, Tennessee, 1964.
9 Gordon, p. 407.
10 Ibid., p. 408.
11 Ibid., pp. 409–10.
12 Douglas, p. 328.
13 Horsham, p. 181.
14 Porter, Horace, *Campaigning With Grant,* p. 404, Bloomington, Indiana, 1961.
15 *B&L*, Vol. IV., p. 587.
16 Dunlop, W.S. *Lee's Sharpshooters*, p. 247, Dayton, Ohio, 1988.
17 *B&L*, p. 580.
18 Ibid., p. 581.
19 *ORs*, Series I, vol. 46, Part 1, p. 359.
20 Gordon, p. 412.
21 Wilkinson, Warren, *Mother May You Never See The Sights I Have Seen,* p. 333, New York, 1990.
22 Douglas, p. 329.

Index